# Business Graphics
# for the
# Macintosh™

## Gregory R. Glau

Dow Jones–Irwin
Homewood, Illinois 60430

For Tracy—
I Love You

ISBN 0-87094-693-5
Library of Congress Catalog Card No. 85-70891
*Printed in the United States of America*

1 2 3 4 5 6 7 8 9 0 ML 2 1 0 9 8 7 6 5

# Contents

# Acknowledgments

In any project like this, people close to the author necessarily hear about it in considerably more detail than they might like. For the author's family this isn't a problem; after all, they have a vested interest in the book (hopefully it'll pay part of the food bill next year). For friends and fellow workers, though, it can get old awfully fast.

For *not* complaining during the whole process, for listening graciously as I explained this chapter or that graphic concept, for simply being there to let me think out loud, the following deserve special thanks: Ken Kuhnke, Tony Malizio, Bob Porter, Carol and Walt Webb, and Ed Wood. Frank Sobek always has good questions and helpful advice.

Barbara Brubaker at Microsoft arranged to provide a pre-release version of their *Chart* program so we could create our graphic images. Thanks, Barb.

I also owe a special debt of thanks to Don Beil, a professor and author who also reviewed the manuscript from start to finish. Don always has words of encouragement and can—more often than I—see the forest for the trees. You're a good friend, Don.

My Mom reads everything I publish and seems to have more fun with all this than I do.

As in all my work, I get continuous help from my wife, Courtney Ann. She deserves my special thanks for doing the drudge work on these book projects: typing and proofing the index through at least six drafts of the thing. I couldn't do it without you, Babe.

**Gregory Glau**

# Preface

If there's one certain thing in business, it's that nothing remains static. *Everything changes*. Oh, we might not recognize it, as we may see the same faces every day and perform many similar tasks much of the time, but inside, every business owner knows that nothing stays the same.

Some changes are minor, of course, while others are more obvious, but the fact is that everything in your business is in constant motion. Cash flows both in and out every day (often more seems to go *out* than *in*). Employees change jobs or leave; new people are added. Some new customers pay like clockwork while others only promise that your check is in the mail. Work is quoted and sold, bids are typed, advertising ordered, problems solved, payroll (somehow) made.

## The Influence of Movement

Because much of our work is done in the midst of this state of flux, successful businesspeople must have some way to see where they've been, where they stand right now, and estimate where their business might be headed. Because graphics gives you a snapshot of one moment in time, successive pictures can give you something of a moving record of your data, a visual history of where all your sales came from, a look at where all those dollars were spent.

In addition, certain types of graphs—the line graph in particular—help the business owner *feel* this movement. In any graph, what's important is not to be able to extract the exact data from the graph (you get that from the numerical information itself) but what the chart shows. People relate differently to an image than they do to rows of numbers; *they understand the picture*. Also, while graphs give us more of a look at the overall situation, rather than at the details, they're an ideal way to help us absorb large amounts of information.

# The Problem with Graphs

The problem with business graphics is twofold. First, they're something few businesspeople received any training in. If you want to plot sales and advertising, what kind of graph should you use? What scale should it be in? What do you do about the fact that last month's sales were $27,500 while advertising only amounted to $157? How do you label it? What data should you examine? Over how long a period? For some reason, once you open a business you're automatically expected to *understand* graphs and ratios and the *acid test* and *Flow of Funds statement*. Many of us don't, but only because we've never been trained for it.

Second, making graphs can be a plain chore. Besides having to figure out what to plot and how to chart it, the act of creating a graph is often difficult and time-consuming. It's something we're just not used to doing.

# The Solution

The purpose of this book is to give the businessperson a guide by which he or she can examine various areas of his or her business using graphics. You'll learn what's important about cash flow, what to look for, where to extract the pertinent information, and how to plot it. You'll discover how to examine sales and their components, the best way to focus on your costs, how to dig out the details inside of your payroll that you might think are minor but can cost major dollars. Through all this we'll suggest the type of graph best suited to help you understand the specific information you're working with. This book is, we hope, the solution to the first problem with business graphics.

Your Macintosh computer is the answer to the second difficulty. With an easy-to-use program or two, your microcomputer can take all those figures from inside your books and create intelligent, helpful charts, images that will not only tell you where you've been and where you are now, but give you a peek into the future, at where your business will be if current trends are accurate guides to the months ahead.

That's important, because one of the primary differences between businesses that are successful and those that fail is the ability of their managers to analyze trouble areas *in time* to do something about them. There are all sorts of hidden threats to your business, surprises that spring up that you shouldn't have to cope with. Graphs can provide an early warning system to signal that something might be wrong inside one area or another, often soon enough to allow the business owner to act to solve it.

Many businesspeople know they should look at pictures of their information, to make charts for sales and expenses and costs, but it's next to impossible to keep up with them all, every month. So we don't do it, and the information we could ascertain from this visual data is lost. Our Macintosh is a tool that does all the hard work for us—it truly gives us the power to *understand* our own numbers.

# Cause and Effect

Most business conditions occur because one thing causes another. Someone's washing machine stops working, so the customer must get it repaired or replaced. A rise in business prompts the need for a more powerful copying machine, and thus creates a sale. Clothing wears out (causing a purchase of new clothes), automobiles break down (causing parts to be purchased, or a new car ordered), people get fed up with an uncomfortable home (and so buy air conditioning). A lot of business analysis and data examination concerns itself with this relationship. After all, if we can find the *cause,* perhaps we can vary the effect. If we can determine the optimal media to advertise in for our business, perhaps we can figure out if more advertising will create more sales. If we can find out *why* people use our products or services, perhaps we can extend this knowledge to other prospects, so they, too, will become customers.

# How to Use This Book

Each chapter focuses on a specific business area. We did things in this manner because this is the way most businesspeople see their figures. They know (or can quickly find out) how much they spent last month for payroll, they know what their current accounts receivable are, they know what they owe.

The questions for each section vary with its focus. How can we best compare sales last year to sales this year? Is a pie chart good to compare data sets? When should we use a bar chart? A column graph? Are there business uses for a scatter graph? Can we show a trend? We want to focus on each chart from the viewpoint of what happens inside the business itself; in other words, we want to start with the business function (payroll, general accounting, inventory, etc.), see how it's handled now and then move to how we can convert all that numerical data into helpful business graphics.

While the fancy overlays and color charts and 3-D images we see in some publications are impressive, the business owner needs and looks more for *clarity* and *comprehension.* We want to show you how business graphics can be a tool to help you understand things, not necessarily a showpiece. Like a budget forecast in a column and row format, the graph or chart is simply a *tool.* The advantage a graph has over all those pages with numbers on them is that you can understand a graph easier and faster. You also get a *feeling* for the movement of the data, a feel for how things happen inside your business.

# Accounting

Since almost any financial data you want to examine relates to accounting, we have to touch on it. Our focus, though, will be on the specific ratios that are helpful for various areas of a business, along with some guidelines as to what accounting data to examine. We'll explain the type of accounting information we'll look at, in easy-to-understand terms. For example, our chapter on cutting costs covers not just total payroll, but other associated payroll costs that sometimes we don't consider, like payroll taxes and fringe benefits. Is a particular payroll item *direct* payroll that's related to sales, or *overhead* payroll, that we have to pay whether we sell anything or not?

# Business Graphics

Since your Macintosh will do most of the work for you, there's not a lot you need to know in order to create helpful graphs. However, even some of the best programs don't scale things to meet our needs, or put all the labels and information that we need to really understand them automatically onto the charts. Since graphics lets us understand our financial information better than any other method, we need to have a basic understanding of what makes up a good graph. Chapter 1 gives you this.

Chapters 2 through 10 cover specific business areas and examine in detail the financial information associated with each. There are some obvious comparisons we all know we should make—things like sales this year versus last, tracking our utility usage and truck repair costs, comparing sales to payroll, and so on. But there are other, helpful ideas that often aren't widely known, and we touch on many of them. We also chart things over different time periods, as that's what you'll do.

When you examine one area or another in any business, the sort of information you have to work with lends itself to a specific type of graph. While all parts of a business are interrelated, some are closely connected to others, while others *directly* depend on another.

The advertising dollar you spend this month won't affect sales until some date in the future. When is it for your business? A graphic look at things will tell you exactly. Every month you collect $x$ number of dollars from your customers. For most businesses, this figure varies directly by the sales volume and/or the month-end total of your accounts receivable. If you sell $50,000 worth of goods and services this month, how much can you expect to collect next month? Once a customer lets their account go for, say, 120 days, what's the probability that you'll collect it? What percentage of your accounts are over 90 days old? Is that what it normally is? Is the percentage growing?

What will happen to your cash position if your sales make a sudden spurt? Will you have enough cash available—are you *liquid* enough—to pay the bills until your customers pay you? With the right selection of business graphic images, you can visually *see* how each item relates to the others.

Chapter 11 gives you some ideas on how to use graphs as a sales tool, and focuses on specific techniques on how to incorporate graphics into your sales presentation.

The last section of each chapter will make additional suggestions that might apply to your own business. Obviously, we can't cover every possible thing you may want to examine; our purpose here is to suggest some ideas for you to explore, to help you learn what's important to your own business. You also don't want to go overboard and try to chart all the areas that we cover—there are simply too many. Since we don't know what's vital to you and your operation, we've tried to make enough valid suggestions and explain enough example graphs so you'll know what comparisons make sense and how to make them—once you find what's valuable to you.

Chapter 12 is a tutorial that takes you step-by-step from initial data entry to printing a graph. It starts with putting your information into a Multiplan worksheet, runs through a brief manipulation of the data, saves it on disk, sends it along to the graphics program Chart, and creates a graph from it. Appendix A and Appendix B are a magazine and book bibliography, respectively.

# A Positive Look

Even though there are all kinds of things we could use as bad examples, we've tried to stay away from them and stress the positive side. The example charts you'll cover are not only clear and simple, but *correct*. Rather than trying to tell you to *not* do this or that, we've left the incorrect thoughts out and tried to show you how your charts and graphs should appear. We want you to know what to look for, instead of what to avoid.

The data for all the charts is fictitious. Because there are relationships between data sets for some businesses but not for others, no one enterprise could illustrate all that we have here. The figures are consistent with one another, of course, but are not from a single financial statement.

As you read through each chapter, jot down or mark in the book particular comparisons you feel might be helpful to your own business. Pick out a dozen or so to focus on and chart them monthly. As the year progresses, you'll have a continuing picture of the data that's valid for you. Other ideas will suggest themselves to you, of course, as time goes along, so add these new ideas as you find them. Once you start to create these moving pictures of your work, you'll be astonished at the information you'll glean from the images.

**Gregory R. Glau**

# Graphic Basics

1

For anyone who struggled back in high school geometry with X and Y plots, a computer program that creates graphs is more than a useful tool, it's a blessing. Once you start working with such a program (and there are many, running from the simple and basic to the complex and powerful), you'll find that you don't need to know which axis is the X axis or which quadrant to put things in. Instead, you can concentrate on exactly what you should be zeroing in on: a study of your own financial information.

Not every graphics program will create perfect graphs for you. That isn't to say they won't be accurate, but rather that there are some design limitations inside of every system, both for the software, which will make your graphs, and in the hardware, which will display and print them for you. For example, not all programs will create bar charts, where the bars run on a horizontal plane. Most have the capability to make column charts (where columns of information run up and down, like the columns in front of old buildings), and these often can tell the same story as bar charts. The printed charts you get from your system are also hardware-dependent. If you have an Imagewriter dot-matrix printer, you won't be able to have colored graphs (although you can *shade* your data), and in fact, unless color becomes a Macintosh option, you're pretty well stuck with printers that work only in black and white.

## Business Graphics

There are generally considered to be three basic areas involved with business graphics. One is the collection and display (and printing) of historical financial information. The second area is analytical graphics and involves what you'd expect—using graphs to help analyze and understand information. The third area is the use of graphs to persuade people to a particular point of view and can run from explaining to your employees why your labor costs must be cut to using charts to show prospects how they can save money, if they'll buy what you're selling.

## A Historical Look

The first area of business graphics—gathering and summarizing financial information—gives the business owner a picture of his or her past history: where the business has been, what it's done, and so on. This approach can embody a wide-range look at things (total sales on a yearly basis) or focus in very tightly on a specific area (freight costs for just the service department). The main purpose of this examination is the tracking of data, often over a long time frame, with the main thrust to summarize the financial information, to gather it together and make it easier to understand. In many (but obviously not all) cases, this is an ideal use for business graphics, as pictures are often easier to understand than rows and columns of figures.

## An Analytical Look

The second area of business graphics is an analytical look at things. Now, rather than just plotting the historical data, we want to use the charts to try to find out *why* things happened. This is a more difficult area to get involved with, but graphs can be particularly useful to help you spot any variations in your data, aberrations caused either by an incorrect entry in a file or more importantly, a change in the way your business is doing business.

For instance, your overhead, as a percentage of your total sales, would be calculated each time you receive a financial statement from your accountant. It might run, on a historical basis, in the 25 to 30 percent range. You can plot this, and it's easy to spot the average range. Once this is done, any aberration in either direction will immediately show up on the chart and serves as a signal to the business owner that something has changed. It might be for the better, of course—if you're charting your overhead as a percentage of your sales, perhaps you've made changes to cause the plotting line to go down. In that case, the graph would show you that whatever steps you took are working. Or, you might see a jump in your overhead percentage, which (hopefully) will motivate you to find out why your overhead is running at a higher percentage of your sales and to do something to correct the situation before it gets worse.

You might want to add a trend line to your information, to translate its data as it relates to the time period on your graph. A trend line indicates the overall direction of the information.

One of the nicest things about doing graphs on your Macintosh is that you simply have to ask your plotting program to create and graph a trend line for you (much business software has this capability); you don't have to know or understand the mathematics involved. The basic concept of a trend line is to create a straight line through a group of plotted points to indicate their average direction. You do need to realize the limitations of trend-line forecasting. For example, any trend line you create and plot is based on your past historical data. Current business conditions, however, might be completely different than what happened to you over the last few years. More or better competition, a costly employee contract, a change in your basic market—all contribute to a shift in the state of your business, a change in direction that cannot be foretold with a trend line. The trend line, let's remember, is based *only* on past information, things that have already happened. As such, it can serve as a guide to what *may* take place in the future, and should be regarded as only that—an indication of the direction of future performance, if things stay as they were in the past.

Associated with this is the fact that the more data you have on which to base your trend line, the more accurate it will be in terms of the overall direction your information is heading. However, if you were to plot your monthly sales totals for the last 20 years, a trend line would be useful to show their average heading, but would be of little value as an indicator of future performance. Much of the information is too old to help you make a projection into the next year. Also, the more information focused on the same subject, the more your trend line will smooth out, and the greater its tendency to be flat. So while the past few years (or accounting periods) won't give you a long base on which to create a trend line, they will serve as a more accurate guide to what you might expect for your sales during the next few months.

Even with all that, however, a trend line is an important piece of statistical data that you need to work with and use. Just as you often can't understand a large array of figures, it's sometimes impossible to examine a graph and learn the general direction the data is moving. There may be so many ups and downs that while you can see the variations, you can't tell if the overall trend is going the way you want it to. A trend line will show you. Also, if you somehow could predict the future of one part or another of your business, it would be a tremendous help, and a trend line at least gives you an indication of where one part of your work may be a few months from now.

# COMMUNICATION

The third major area of business graphics is called persuasive graphics and focuses on the use of images to persuade others that a specific course of action should be taken. At first glance it might seem that in most small businesses the only person who needs convincing is the boss—he or she makes all the decisions, so any use of graphs should be directed there. However, any business with employees needs some way to communicate things to those people, to present ideas and concepts over and above what they understand from their paycheck.

For example, if you have more than one location or department, it's worthwhile to spend the time to create graphs to show how one area is performing in relation to the other(s). Who's making money for the business, and who isn't? Although you probably wouldn't want to publish profit data on an individual basis, you can do it for each store or department, and your people won't be upset. You might want to put out graphs for your salespeople, to show who's selling the most, both to congratulate your best performer and to encourage your worst. So inside your business are ways you can use graphs to communicate with your people. You can take things a step further and use them to tell your sales story to your sales prospects: an individual graph, designed specifically for a prospect, is a powerful selling tool.

## What Do You Need?

Each business is different in what it wants to do with business graphics, and that determines how complex (and expensive) your system needs to be. However, you'll find that in most instances, the simpler (and less costly) you can keep things, the more use you'll get out of them.

For internal use, the Imagewriter you bought with your Macintosh is more than acceptable. While it might be nice to have a better quality graph to present to your sales prospects or employees, they more likely than not haven't seen any fancy computer graphs, and so they won't think anything else is even available. If you do them on nice paper, the graphs will serve their purpose. All the graphs in this book were made with an Apple Imagewriter, the standard printer for your Macintosh.

The bottom line is simply that you must determine your needs in terms of software and hardware, and start there. In almost every case, simplicity and speed are a hard combination to beat. If you buy software that's too complex for you and your people to use without constant referral to its manual, or hardware that creates beautiful images but takes a half-hour to do just one, you may find you simply won't use the system.

# Basic Concepts

A graph is simply a picture of information. For most business applications, we look at *time series* data, where we record, say, sales over a period of time. The whole idea of using a graph is to communicate, to present the information in a more understandable manner than you might with a page filled with figures. Unless the graph does that—communicates with the user in an easy, understandable way—there's no reason even to create it. A graph isn't an end in itself, but rather an aid to our understanding.

The first goal, then, is simplicity. A user should be able to look at a graph and understand it quickly, with little reference to associated data.

One limitation in almost any chart is that a graphed image cannot portray the data to its complete degree of accuracy. No graph allows a reader to look at it and say, "Yes, our sales in May were $56,302.20" (unless the figure is entered on the chart itself). If you must find the exact information, you'll need to go to the data from which the graph was created. A chart gives you a representation of the numerical information, a *feeling* for its quantity, a comparison in relation to other quantities, an indication of how the information is moving.

# Getting Started

Let's begin with a simple line graph, based on this set of data from the records of a fictional business:

### SERVICE DEPARTMENT LABOR SALES VOLUME

| MONTH | LAST YEAR | THIS YEAR |
|-------|-----------|-----------|
| 1 | $39,503 | $38,361 |
| 2 | 38,202 | 34,687 |
| 3 | 42,981 | 46,602 |
| 4 | 39,027 | 42,850 |
| 5 | 42,981 | 49,707 |
| 6 | 48,202 | 50,981 |

So you can see the various stages a graph goes through on your video screen, we'll enter this information into the Microsoft® Chart software program and see how it handles things.* This particular program was chosen not just because it was the first graphics system available for the Macintosh,

---

* Microsoft® is a registered trademark of Microsoft Corporation.

FIGURE 1-1

but also because it's representative of what a good graphics package can do. We'll start by plotting the data from last year's labor sales.

Figure 1-1 is a simple line graph, using Chart's ability to add in horizontal grid lines when it creates your pictures. The name of the data series (LABOR LAST YEAR) is shown at the top as a title (this particular program uses the name of the first data set it graphs as a title). The X-axis has an X to mark its location along the bottom of the graph, and the Y-axis has a Y on the left side of the picture. The program automatically scales the graph starting at zero and runs slightly higher than the highest data point in this series.

The periods under study run from 1–6 along the X-axis, the bottom part of the graph. In this case the periods are designated by numbers (1–6), as that's what we asked the program to do. You also may want to use other labels for this information, depending on the data you're working with.

There are any number of ways you can choose to mark your graphs so they'll properly indicate the frequency of your data. Some software automatically does this for you, although often in a way you didn't intend when you created the chart. If your information has been saved on a yearly basis, for example, some programs may list the year and indicate the first letter of each month along the bottom of your picture—J  F  M  A (or Jan, Feb, Mar, Apr) and so on. This is what people expect to see, after all, and is perhaps the best way to increment time if your charts are on a calendar-year basis—if they start in January and end the following December.

However, if the information is valuable enough for you to track on a monthly (or quarterly) basis, it's important enough to examine it on a *latest period* basis. That is, you don't want to look at your data only as a calendar-year image, but you also need to plot the last 12 months (or whatever you find helpful) of information. Now, though, some graphics software can't grasp this concept. For this picture, of the latest *period* of data, it's better to use numbers along the bottom of your graphs, to represent months. The advantage of working with just the numbers is that you can create graphs in the same format, whether the data is for months, quarters, or years. We'll generally use the numerical format for the sake of consistency.

## The Zero Line

We usually don't want to create a graph without a zero line unless it serves a useful purpose. Often it can (as we'll see), because a narrow focus will help us understand the information on a chart. A graph without a zero line means our data will move differently, as the scale is much tighter. The rise and fall of the lines will be more severe. The one rule is to simply indicate on the graph that it doesn't have a zero line, so the reader knows the rise and fall of the information will be different than it would be with that zero line in place.

Let's add in our second data set, for LABOR THIS YEAR, and overlay it on our picture.

As we see in Figure 1-2, we've plotted both last year's information and the data for the current year. Chart automatically rescales the graph, to adjust for the new data's higher amounts. The first data set we saw (LABOR LAST YEAR) is marked with solid dots for each plotting point, and the new

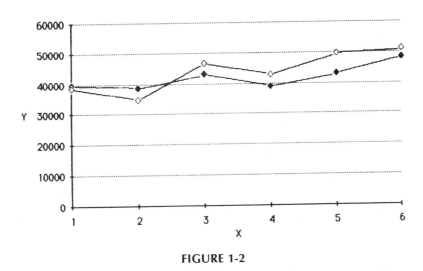

FIGURE 1-2

data (LABOR THIS YEAR) is marked with hollow dots for each plotting point. We can further differentiate these data by using Chart's legend function, which will place a small box on the graph to tell the user what each plotting point means.

Figure 1-3 shows the same image we just saw, but with the addition of a bottom legend to mark what the lines are for (this legend can be positioned in other spots, and can have different type styles and sizes). While some users like to use legend boxes, we prefer to put legend information right in the body of the chart itself—it makes it easier to understand the information. Let's do that now, and also clean up the X- and Y- axis titles. We'll make the X-axis ← MONTHS → to tell someone looking at this graph that the periods are monthly, and mark the Y-axis with a dollar sign, so the user will know the values represented are in dollars. The dollar sign is used instead of the word DOLLARS, simply because it's easier and faster to understand.

Figure 1-4 eliminates the legend box and instead puts the legend information in the body of the chart, right next to the line the data represents.

The title, though, still shows LABOR LAST YEAR—the original name of the first data set we plotted. There are a couple of ways (using this particular program) to change the title to reflect the comparison we're making between sales this year and sales last year. One is to CUT the old title and replace it with a new one. The other is to replace the name of the first graphed data set with the title you'd like to use, and the program will position it as a title for you. Whichever method used, it's important to have a title that reflects what your graph conveys to its readers. It's also a good idea to

FIGURE 1-3

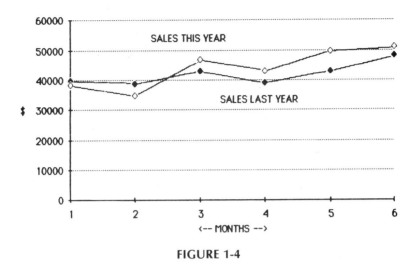

FIGURE 1-4

have a border around your picture. A border on a graph connects it and shows the user where the information starts and stops. You almost always should have a border, and most programs will add one for you automatically. Let's add a border and a new title to our sample graph.

Figure 1-5 shows a complete image to someone looking at this data. Each data set is marked on the graph, so it's easy to see what's what. The title reflects the comparison between labor sales this year and last year. The scale is clear and readable, and starts with a zero line so we get an accurate feel for the value of the information. Both the X-axis and Y-axis are marked so the reader will know what the data represents. Finally, horizontal grid lines help us see the range in which our data moves.

One disadvantage of using a microcomputer to create graphic images is that the programs often add too many grid lines to a picture. In this case, with only six months of information, grid lines that run both directions (horizontally and vertically) probably wouldn't detract from the graph. In many cases, though, particularly when you have years and years of data plotted, it doesn't help to have lines running up and down on the graph to indicate each month. A good rule of thumb is to almost always use horizontal grid lines (like these graphs do) as they relate to the numerical data on the chart but rarely use vertical lines, because we can usually see, when we need to, where each month or quarter or yearly plot is.

Grid lines make a big difference in our understanding of the information. In this case, it's easy to see that the data represented by these two lines runs in about the 30,000 to 50,000 range. One of the lines crept a bit above the 50,000 mark on its last plot, but overall, the data stayed within the range

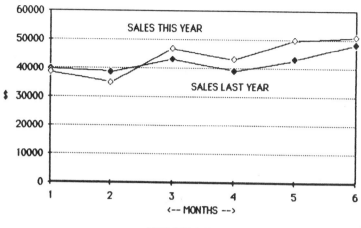

FIGURE 1-5

noted. Horizontal grid lines like these allow the user to spot any real deviation from the average; if one of these plots had dropped to, say, 25,000, it would be more than obvious.

We don't really miss vertical grid lines here; if we want to pick out one month or another, it's easy enough to do so without the additional lines.

We'll use this same basic format throughout the book; in your own work, you can use whatever you find helpful, and mark things where they're the most value to you and your work. As noted previously, you may find it more helpful to list the periods you graph by the first letter of their month. If you do charts with varying time frames, though, you're probably better off to use the numerical format to mark all periods. All of your images should be constant in terms of what the user sees; the data must be responsible for the changes in what he or she perceives from the picture.

The steps you go through to create a graph for your own information won't follow this exact sequence (unless you use the same software), but will contain the same basic elements. The important thing—the whole idea, really—is to end up with a chart people can quickly understand, that explains what you want it to cover, and that is clear. A user should be able to look at it and grasp the information without having to ask all sorts of questions like, "What does this line mean?" or "What's that mark, there?"

# A Closer Look

A logical extension of this thinking is to eliminate the zero line and plot the data on a much tighter scale. This gives the user the additional advantage of

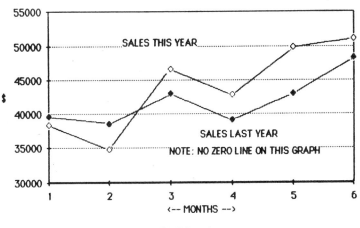

LABOR SALES THIS YEAR COMPARED TO
LABOR SALES LAST YEAR

**FIGURE 1-6**

a closeup look at things and can make the information more understandable. For instance, while we can see where current labor sales and last year's labor sales crossed each other in Figure 1-5, we might be able to understand things better if we examine it with a tighter focus.

Figure 1-6 tightens the scale we've been using to one that runs from $30,000 to $55,000. As such, the information rises and falls much more rapidly. It's also easier to spot where this year's data overtook and passed last year's information. Besides the change in scale, we added a small note in the lower right-hand corner, to indicate there's no zero line.

## A Historical Look with a Line Chart

We used a line chart for this first example because that's what most of anyone's pictures are made of—a line graph shows movement so well that it's often the best way to examine your data. One other advantage a line chart gives you is the capability of examining your financial information over a long period of time. Once you have the data in your microcomputer system, you can decide what sections of it to chart, how long a range of data you'd like to examine.

This kind of study lends itself to all kinds of analysis; probably the most obvious and easiest to see are those variations that occur on a seasonal basis. Since the data is plotted over a long period of time, if your business does have seasonal ups and downs, they should come at about the same time each year. Once a general trend has been established, it's easy to spot any variations in the data (caused either by an error in the data entry process or an aberration in the way your business is doing business). A long-range look at your data is always helpful, just to get an overall feel for how things are going now, compared to a historical look at your work.

Figure 1-7 charts the monthly sales volume for our fictional business, over the last 36 months. As we know, we could do much the same thing for a 36-month period on a calendar-year basis, if we find that's helpful. While sales appear to stay around the $40,000 per month level, there are three distinct bumps in the information—roughly during months 6–8, months 18–21, and months 30–32. If this chart was done on a yearly basis, with the first plot for January and the last for December (three years later, of course), these correspond to the summer months. As the business owner who created this chart, you'd know what these last 36 months represent, so you'd not only see your sales take those nice jumps, you'd also know *when* the increases took place.

The information is presented here to show how you can create graphs that cover different time periods yet use the same basic format. If this were the information from your business, you'd obviously know when the graph was printed, so you'd know what this 36-month period represented, whether it's done on a calendar-year basis or if it started in March (or whenever). The important thing is the basic concept: a historical examination of your business (in this case, its sales) gives you a feel for your own business cycle. In this particular example, too, recent data is heading upward, sales are improving—a good sign.

FIGURE 1-7

# A Trend Line

You can ask your plotting program to add a trend line to your time series charts to give you an idea of the overall direction the graphed data has been taking.

Figure 1-8 plots a trend line (as noted on the graph) based on the 36 months of recent information. The data we've been examining is also plotted on the graph. While you really couldn't tell from the information itself (as shown in Figure 1-7) what the overall direction of the data was, the trend line gives you the picture you'd want to see, if this were your business. The general trend of monthly sales is rising, which means your sales department (even if that department is just *you*) is doing something right.

You could carry things further and add in an inflation rate to your sales information. Are your sales rising faster than inflation? Or are your sales not keeping pace with the rate of inflation?

# Line Charts

From these examples, we can see that a line chart is particularly suited to show the *movement* of changes in the data over a period of time. It's also useful (perhaps the best way of all) to show a comparison between two sets of data and for looking at our information when it has a trend line calculated

FIGURE 1-8

and charted. There is a major disadvantage to a line chart, in that you can only work with, at best, perhaps three sets of information. More than three lines (and often, more than just two), and the graph cannot be understood, so you're limited in the number of things you can examine at any one time. As with most restrictions, though, you can turn this around and make something good out of it. It gives you the chance to examine the same data in relation to other things, on an *individual* basis—two lines on each chart. This, instead of limiting you, makes things clearer and easier to understand.

Since most business information is done with a comparison of the data to the time that's gone by, a line chart is probably the most useful tool you have in your graphics arsenal.

## Pie Charts

After that detailed discussion of line graphs, here's an easy one: pie charts. Almost everyone can relate to this kind of graph, as they have such a familiar concept. The ideal use for a pie chart is to compare a number of data items to their combined sum, to show how each relates to the total of whatever you're charting. For sales, you might want to know where your sales come from in terms of departments or locations or salespeople. For overhead, you may want to see where your dollars are spent. You can look at a large area (total sales) or an individual item (monthly advertising for March).

Figure 1-9 is a pie chart that covers the sales by the different product lines our fictional business handles, over a one-year period. Since a pie chart

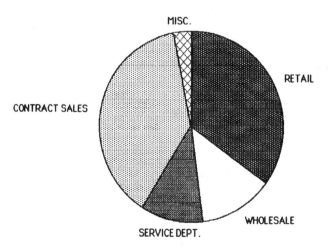

FIGURE 1-9

is ideal to see how each individual item relates to the whole (in this case, our total sales), it lends itself to a percentage breakdown. While we don't know if these percentages are what they should be or not (we'd need more information), this graph shows us the situation for a particular period of time.

With a pie chart, it's easy to see how each individual area related to our total sales for the year. In this case, since retail and contracts are the major areas, we want to highlight them, so we've made retail dark and contracts with a slight shading so they'll both stand out.

One major limitation of a pie chart is the number of slices you can effectively display. Any more than about six and the pie starts to look like a wagon wheel; it's simply cut into too many pieces. If your graphics software system can create pie charts that have a piece detached, you can use this function to highlight a specific slice of your information, to draw attention to it. Like other things you can do with business graphics (shading in areas of a picture, putting text where you want it to be, focusing on just a certain range of information), this lets you present your material in the manner you'd like, to make the point you want the chart to illustrate.

## Editorials

Since you can do things like shade a pie chart to your liking, or make one line on a line graph thicker or darker than another, this is a good place to mention that graphs, since they're a form of communication, are also a way to get your own views across. Both the selection of the type of graph you use and the information you chart (including the periods graphed) in a sense, *editorialize*. There's nothing particularly wrong with this, and it has its most useful application when you use graphs as a tool to persuade others that a specific course of action is the right thing to do.

For example, if you have one store that's consistently more profitable than your other locations, you might give some thought to the best way to illustrate this fact to your employees. In Chapter 11, where we look at ways to use business graphics as a sales tool, we'll see how to use charts and their information in an effort to get our sales message across. When you examine graphs that someone else creates, always look at them with an eye to determining if the information is being presented in the most honest manner, or if there's a particular point the person is trying to make.

## Bar and Column Charts

We like to think of column charts as the columns of old buildings—the columns go up and down. There's a similar chart that's called a horizontal bar chart that some graphics programs can provide, where the bars go across your screen or page, instead of up and down. In many cases, one can substitute for the other.

Bar and column charts are ideal for showing the relationships between items over a brief period of time, and for indicating the total quantity of each item in a data set. While line charts are more effective to show how data moves over time, particularly a long period, bar and column charts are uniquely qualified to give you a feeling for the actual quantity of the information you graph. They don't compare each individual item to the whole (as a pie chart will) but rather concentrate on the numerical value of the data itself.

Figure 1-10 is a column chart that details the truck repair costs for our fictitious business, over the last four months. We get a much better feeling for the quantities under study with this graph than we would with, say, a line chart. We can *feel* the dollars we've spent to keep our trucks on the road.

Obviously, there's an unusual rise in month 2. When the business owner spots something like this, he or she will want to dig into the details of his or her business, to find out why costs rose so much during this period. An easy way to do this might be to plot, on this same chart, the number of service calls those trucks handled during each period, to see if there's a relationship between the number of calls our people make and the repair costs for their trucks. The same thing could be done, if you had the data, on a per mile basis.

Figure 1-11 gives us more information, as there's an obvious correla-

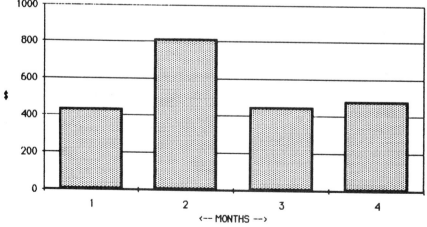

TRUCK REPAIR COSTS – LAST FOUR MONTHS

<-- MONTHS -->

**FIGURE 1-10**

TRUCK REPAIR COSTS - LAST FOUR MONTHS

FIGURE 1-11

tion between the number of service calls our business took care of during a month and the total it cost our company for truck repairs.

These two charts start an interesting line of thought. First, we may not have paid much attention to our truck repair costs unless we had graphed them, as we did in Figure 1-10. Once that was done, the jump in the second month's costs indicated a possible problem. After some thought, we broke down our service calls on a monthly basis and plotted them as a line on the same chart; the more calls, the more repair costs we had.

If we take our thinking a bit further, it looks like there's a relationship in terms of the *number* of service calls and the *dollar total* for repair costs. They appear to be about the same. This leads to another idea: let's track both data sets for a period of time to determine if this holds true. If it does, we can predict our truck repair costs each month by the number of service calls we handle during that time. We can track the service calls daily, too, on a cumulative basis, so we'll have a good idea of what our repair bills will be at the end of the month.

All this is noted to illustrate another aspect of graph basics: one idea almost always leads to another. One graph tells you its story, and that gives you an idea about something else, and so on. In this particular example, you might want to study your business even more closely to see how your truck repair costs compare to the service calls you do (for instance) within a 30-mile radius of your office. Do your trucks start to cost more to repair when you do a lot of long-range service work? Carry the idea even further: are there some preventive maintenance things you could be doing to lower your truck repair costs? How would you chart them so you'd know you were on the right track?

## Everything's Not Roses

In any business environment, no one makes money all the time, on every product they sell. A column chart can illustrate the rise and fall of our fortunes.

Figure 1-12 is the first graph we've seen with data *below* the zero line. As such, it makes it easy to pick out those months where our business made money and where it operated in the red. The column chart gives us a good grasp for the numerical information itself, too; we can *feel* those good early profits.

## Stacked Columns

A stacked column chart (also called a stacked bar chart) takes the information from more than one data set and adds it together. Then, it plots each total as a combination of the two, with each separated with different colors or shadings.

Figure 1-13 is a stacked column chart where each column plots two data sets—labor and parts sales for the repair department of our fictional business.

NET PROFIT FOR THE SERVICE
DEPARTMENT. LAST NINE MONTHS

**FIGURE 1-12**

REPAIR DEPARTMENT LABOR + PARTS

**FIGURE 1-13**

In effect, each bar indicates the combined labor and repair parts sales for each of the nine months plotted. What's obviously different about this chart (as compared to a standard column graph) is that the two individual items can each be seen, as well as their combined total.

This approach works particularly well when you have only two items to graph and when one of those remains pretty stable. In this example, the lower data set (labor costs) runs about $10,000 per month—there's very little variation in the repair department labor our fictional business recorded. Thus, when it's combined with the parts costs for the business, the real rise and fall we see at the top of the graph is derived from the *parts costs* area of things, and in fact, we learn that our total each month varies because of the difference in parts costs.

A stacked graph is almost useless when more than one of the data sets has wide fluctuations. While the top of the graph—the total of all the items for each month—will vary in a way you'll be able to see and understand, the individual demarcations of the data will be impossible to grasp. Generally, you should use this kind of chart when only *one* of your data sets has significant variations, and put it on top.

Figure 1-14 is called a *horizontal bar chart* and uses horizontal bars to illustrate its data. Not all software programs can create such a chart, although if you find you can use its unique view of things, you can put your information into a column chart format, print your graph, and simply turn your paper sideways.

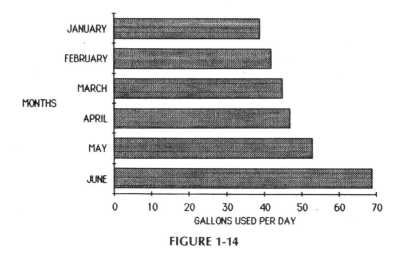

FIGURE 1-14

This approach is particularly helpful for data that's growing or shrinking on a regular basis. Figure 1-14 is a good example of this—each figure gets larger as the months run down the page. This format, like its close cousin the column chart, is ideal to use to help you grasp the quantities involved. It's less useful over a long period of time (a line chart would be more effective) and also isn't much help in comparing one data set to another.

It's almost always necessary to have a zero line on a bar or column chart. While a line graph can be used without a zero line to take a closer look at the movement of the information, bar and column charts provide their meaning through the length of their lines. As such, they're close to useless without a zero line.

## Poor Examples

Our feeling is that people generally get what they think about, and not necessarily what they want. Have you ever picked up something valuable and thought to yourself, "I'd better not drop this," or "My wife will kill me if I break this," and then—inexplicably—drop the darn thing? Part of the reason for our clumsiness is what we had going through our mind at the time—instead of thinking about how we should hold the item to protect it, we were thinking about *dropping it*. So, we did.

There are all kinds of stories about major league baseball pitchers who were told, in a critical game situation, "Don't pitch this batter high and inside," and they went right out and gave the batter that exact pitch. Why?

Because they were thinking about it. Lou Tice, a remarkable man who provides all kinds of motivational ideas from his Pacific Institute in Seattle, Washington, tells the story about when he coached high school football. He was telling his young quarterback that he'd better not hold his hands like this, or he wouldn't get a good grip on the ball, and he'd better not hold them like that, or when the center snaps the ball it might sprain a finger, and he shouldn't hold them this way, and he ought not to hold them that way . . . until the quarterback finally turned around and asked, "Well, how the heck *do* you hold them?"

The point is, all the graphs we've used as illustrations in this book are what we feel are examples of what graphs should look like. This isn't to say that the *data* will always be the way a business owner would like it to be; on the contrary, many of the examples use data that tell the businessperson he or she has a problem with their company and that something needs to be done to change the situation. But the charts themselves are done as they should be. We didn't use poor examples of charts, because then you might think about the negative side of things and create poor graphs for your own information. We feel it's more helpful to give you positive information, with examples of how to do things right.

If you'd like to see some good examples of poor charts there's an excellent book that both shows and tells you what *not* to do for graphs. It's called *Statistical Graphics,* by Calvin F. Schmid, and it's published by John Wiley & Sons, 605 Third Avenue, New York, NY 10158. Mr. Schmid also has a lot of good information on the overall design of graphics—how wide, for example, each column should be in a column graph, the overall size a line graph should be based on the relationship between its height and its width, and so on. Thankfully, your microcomputer software already takes this sort of thing into account and will almost always create a nice-looking and properly designed graph for you automatically.

## Area Charts

One useful graph for showing cumulative data is an area chart. This is basically a line chart with the area below the line filled in with color or shading. It gives you more of a feeling for the total quantity of the information than a line graph does, and since it's connected, it gives you a better understanding of the data as a whole than a column chart can.

Figure 1-15 illustrates the cumulative savings you might expect if you implement either Proposal A or Proposal B. The title tells you you're looking at the product your local utility company sells you in the form of electricity: kilowatt-hours of use. The chart is plotted on a yearly basis, with the information projected for five years.

Since the two proposals are charted in different shades, one is easy to

CUMULATIVE SAVINGS IN KILOWATT-HOURS

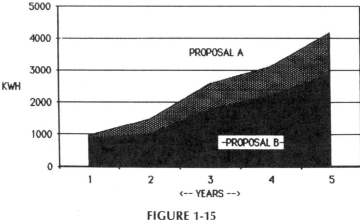

FIGURE 1-15

compare to the other. If the user has some idea of the cost per kilowatt-hour of electricity they have to pay, it's a simple process to translate this data into dollar amounts.

You could do exactly the same thing with a line chart, although you wouldn't get the same feeling for the quantities involved; the area chart helps because its areas are painted in.

As such, an area chart is ideal for plotting large quantities of information. It's not as useful as a line chart for charting the movement of that data over a period of time, nor as helpful as a column/bar chart to indicate separate periods of information. For cumulative data, however, it's ideal.

## One Other Aid

One of the best things about at least some of the new generation of graphics packages that work on your Macintosh is their capability to create semilogarithmic charts. These are designed specifically to show proportional changes in your data. A purely arithmetic chart compares absolute differences in the data. If the dollars on a graph rise $10 from one plotting point to the next, they're shown as a $10 increase. That same $10 change would be plotted as a 100 percent increase on a semilog chart.

The semilogarithmic chart concentrates on the relative change of the data; each "cycle" represents a change to the power of ten. A cycle starting with 10, then, will end with 10 squared ($10^2$), or 100. A chart that starts with 10 and has three cycles will end with $10^3$, or 10,000 ($10 \times 10 = 100$ for the first cycle; 100 × 10 = 1000 for the second cycle; 1000 × 10 = 10,000 for the third cycle).

In actual use, you don't need to be too concerned with all these mathematics, because the graphics software will create semilogarithmic charts for you automatically. If you want to use them—and they're great when you need to portray widely varying data sets—you need at least a basic understanding. A good treatment of the subject can be found in the book called *Statistical Graphics* mentioned earlier.

Our coverage here will give you just an overview of this kind of graph, and since it's available at least in the Microsoft Chart program, if you use that system on your Macintosh then experiment with it a little. Put some of your own numbers into a data file and see how they look graphed on a semilog chart.

In terms of statistical analysis, the semilog chart has some distinct advantages over those that are purely arithmetical. The semilogarithmic chart is ideal to show the percentage change of your data and generally works best for data sets that are far apart in their raw numbers and that vary by at least 100 percent. They're also terrific for displaying data sets that don't relate to one another. Whatever the scale shows in terms of numbers, the slopes representing the data will correctly display the rate of change of each item.

For example, your service department may handle about 150 service calls per week. Since your business sells equipment and supplies unrelated to your service people, you really can't divide your total sales by the number of service calls and end up with a number that means anything. But perhaps you'd like to get a feel if one *does* relate to the other, if the number of service calls vary at the same general rate that your sales do. You can plot these widely varying and (at least partly) unrelated data sets on a semilog scale, to get an idea of how one moves in relation to how the other moves.

Figure 1-16 is a standard line graph showing the number of service calls made, compared to the monthly labor cost for our business, over a 12-month period. While the raw amounts for both these items are far apart in terms of numbers, the semilog chart lets us see how each changes over time—we can see if one rises or falls at the same time the other does.

Where there is a significant rise in the data (in both sets, at months 4 and 8), we can see the jump in the lines. Figure 1-16—at least for this period of time—tells us that the number of service calls and our labor cost do vary at roughly the same rate. With the two amounts so far apart it would be almost impossible to see this relationship without using the semilog scale.

Another thing we all want to know is if our advertising is working. Most of the time, the only figure we have to go on is advertising as a percentage of our total sales, which doesn't measure the effectiveness of our ads. If you plot your advertising dollars and your sales figures on a semilogarithmic chart, you can visually see the *rate* of change of each data set, see how one

FIGURE 1-16

moves in relationship to the other, even though their raw amounts may be wide apart.

Everything's not roses with semilog charts. Most people are unfamiliar with them, and since they look so complex (because of all their lines) don't want to learn how to read one. The real key is in knowing that each grid line on the chart represents the same percentage increase. On a standard chart, each mark on the axis that runs up and down is a measure of value. If your data runs from 1 to 100, you'd have 100 possible plotting points, and a change in the data from 10 to 20 would move 10 points.

On a semilogarithmic chart, each mark designates a 100 percent increase over the one below. That is, the measurement between 1 and 2 (a 100 percent increase) is the same distance as between 50 and 100 (also a 100 percent increase). The distance in the scale betwen 10 and 20 (a 100 percent increase) is the same as between 50 and 100 (again, a 100 percent increase). That same move in the data—from 10 to 20—would only take *one* grid line (called a cycle), as it represents a 100 percent increase in the data.

Also, you don't have a zero line on a semilogarithmic chart, and it cannot plot negative amounts, so you're limited in the applications you might want to use it for. Since most people are unfamiliar with a semilogarithmic chart, they usually require more explanatory text in the body of the chart.

Since the data lines are moving on a percentage basis (instead of numerically), they won't look the same as they do on a standard chart. The important thing in how you react to a semilogarithmic chart is in the relative steepness of the plotted lines; you want to see how one line relates to others.

Since you can work with such wide scales, you can plot almost any number of data sets on this kind of chart; with a standard line chart, any more than about three lines and it's unreadable.

## The Monthly Process

Without going into exact detail (since your business is different than anyone else's), it's important to note that graphs are just another tool for businesses to use, but if they're going to help you, they need to be used regularly. It won't do you any good to read this book, pick out six graphs to make, find the information for them from your records, plot and print the graphs, and think about them. You must continue; just as your business is an ongoing thing, your use of business graphics must also be constant. Yes, one thing will lead to another, and one idea will make you pause for a moment and then plot something else another way, so your basic library of graphs might grow for some time. But the main thrust of business graphics is to find those that you find helpful and then plot their information every month (or quarter, or year—whenever you calculate it). In fact, most software programs are simple enough now that once you know which graphs you want and where the information can be drawn from, you can probably find someone in your office to create them for you, every month. You need to keep a running library of your charts, too, so you can compare one thing to another.

All this isn't to say that working with graphs and their associated calculations and printed copies is an altogether easy process. While it's a long way from what you may be doing now—plotting on blue-lined grid paper by hand—it's still work, and still takes time. There's an effort involved, as you need to think about what you want to examine, look at it from various directions until you discover what's important to you, create the graphs and play with their scales and titles until they're the most help to you, and so on.

However, once the basic work is done—much like the initial data entry into a file-handling system—the rest is downhill. Now, when you know the charts you want every month, you list them and their data, and once the information's been gathered and calculated, you (or your office people) create and print the graphs. More thought and effort will be required when you hit upon a new idea, of course, and pursue it, but for the most part, the hard work will be over. And never forget that even while you're doing the drudge part of the process—finding the information and playing with it on your video screen until you get the results you need—it's still almost *magic* as you watch your data transformed from rows and columns of figures into a simple, understandable graph.

# Other Graphs

There are other graph forms that you should be aware of, but ones we're not going to go into detail about. One is a scatter graph, that does basically what a line graph does but without the lines connecting each plotting point. One possible use in business would be to look at warranty claims or the failure rate for a particular item over a period of time. We feel the examples we'll work with in Chapter 11 for this kind of application are more effective than a scatter graph. It might be useful for you if you'd like to see where your customers are coming from, and create a graph with the areas marked to show where your business does its business, then *scatter* the dots that show the concentration of your customers.

A high/low graph is designed to show the movement of prices (particularly those from the stock market). This might be useful to you if you track such things, especially as they relate to your business. For statistical purposes, the high/low chart also can be used to indicate the mean or the average of each plotted point. If you'd find it helpful to chart, for example, the contract sales your business made that showed your highest contract sale, your lowest, and the average amount, you'll find the high/low chart to be a good way to do so.

A pictorial chart uses little images of people (or cans of food, or animals) to portray the same data as a bar or column chart. In terms of financial data for your stockholders, a pictorial chart might be useful. Unfortunately, there's little microcomputer software that can handle such things.

There are one or two programs available that will create map charts, and while they have some specialized uses, we don't cover them here.

One increasing trend in graphics software is the capability to create charts with a three-dimensional appearance—to give the lines or columns a sense of depth. In many cases, if this is done properly, it's a useful tool and adds to our understanding of the information.

# Summing Up

Since your Macintosh can handle immense amounts of data and quickly convert it into charts and graphs according to your specifications, it serves as an ideal tool for business graphics. Your financial information is constantly being updated and analyzed, checked and projected, all in an effort to become more profitable. Business graphics go hand in hand with this. You generally want to look at your financial records from a descriptive standpoint (to summarize its information), which leads to an analytical examination of the data, to search for *why* things happen as they do, and sometimes, to a persuasive approach, where you want to get your ideas across to someone else. Business graphs are an ideal way to help with all three areas.

Making a graph starts with the information itself, and rather than presenting a list of rules to follow, we've included them in the text as ideas to use. You simply start with one plotted line, make sure the scale is one that you want, and build from there. We found it's often helpful to chart things with numbers along the bottom to indicate the passage of time (months, quarters, years), rather than letters of the alphabet, so all the graphs can be done in a consistent format.

Things like grid lines and a border all add to the readability and understanding of a graph. Grid lines in particular can be used to highlight an area; if your overhead averages 23 percent of your sales, why not scale a graph that shows overhead with that 23 percent mark running across the picture? That way, it's easy to spot any variation. You can widen this approach, too, and scale your graphs (and their resulting grid lines) to mark a *range* of information. If your advertising generally runs between 3 and 4 percent of your sales, ask your plotting program to mark these figures on any graph that uses advertising as a percentage of sales. You'll instantly spot any aberration.

Titles and legends are also vital to understanding a graph—after all, if the user doesn't know what the lines or plot marks or bars mean, he or she won't have any idea what the graph says. Since some of the file names our plotting program collects its information from might not mean anything to the end user, it's worthwhile to spend the extra time to put the information on the chart, where someone can quickly spot it. Likewise, we want to shade or color the areas we want to highlight to make things clearer. The whole idea is that the difference in graphic images should come from the changes in the data itself, rather than any changes in the format or design of the chart and its titles.

A line chart lends itself to a study of information as that data moves over time—the most common use of business graphics. Whenever you think about a graph you'd like to create, the first stop is to consider if a line graph is the best way to portray the information; most of the time, it will be. You want to have no more than two or three lines on each graph. You can adjust the scale of a line graph (be sure to note it on the new picture) to get a closer look at things. Line graphs are also useful for a long-range historical examination of your business data; with grid lines to indicate the range something normally travels in, you can quickly pick out anything that's heading out of line.

Line charts also lend themselves to the use of a trend line, which will show you the overall direction your data's been heading.

Pie charts are the proper tool to use when you want to examine how a number of items relate to the total of their particular category. Since the pie represents the sum of all its slices, you get an indication of how each individual item relates to the whole.

Bar and column charts are basically the same thing, with the direction of their information changed. Column charts are especially helpful to indicate quantities—the thick columns drive the point home. It's helpful at times to add a line chart as an overlay on a column chart—this can either be a graph that details other information, or a trend line based on the data the column chart plots.

Column charts are less useful than line charts for comparing lots of data over time, as you have a tendency to get too many columns and the chart becomes confusing. Column charts can also show data that represents numbers below the zero line (as line charts can). You can also ask for stacked column charts, or one column chart in front of another. The stacked chart shows the total of two or more individual items, while one column chart in front of another is an aid to comparing the two.

If your software program can create a bar chart where the columns run horizontally (↔), you have an ideal method of looking at things that have an overall progression, that naturally lead from the smallest to the largest.

An area chart is useful to plot cumulative data, as it not only shows the upper range of the information (as a line chart would), but since the area below the line is filled in, you get a good indication of the quantity of the information itself.

If your graphics software can create a semilogarithmic chart, use it when you want to compare data sets that are far apart in terms of their raw dollar figures, and/or where they don't seem to be related. At least—once you have your data entered into the system—examine it with a semilog chart to see if this format helps you understand your information.

# A Look at Sales

# 2

There can't be much argument about it: all business starts and ends with *sales*. We're all selling something, and unless we do a good job at it, we won't be in business very long. Sales as a subject to examine is a vital area of anyone's business, and it lends itself to a close look, as most businesspeople already track its progress and make comparisons between total sales last year and this year, between the first quarter last year and the same period this year, and so on.

In fact, sales may be the single area most businesses graph on a regular basis, with the "this year–last year" comparison the most prevalent. "How are your sales?" is a common question at any local coffee shop or chamber of commerce meeting, and woe to the business owner who doesn't have the answer at his or her fingertips.

Since you probably already have a good idea of how you like to follow your sales, we're not going to spend much time on the big picture of things—a simple line graph that compares monthly sales this year with monthly sales last year, or over the latest 12 months—at least lets you know how you're doing in comparison with the earlier period. It's a worthwhile graph to create, and you should, but we're going to get *inside* your sales a bit and suggest some ways to examine this all-important part of your business that perhaps you aren't currently using.

## Your Sales Trend

One immediate advantage you have when you put your sales information into microcomputer files is that most graphics programs can perform statistical functions on that data.

FIGURE 2-1

Figure 2-1 is a column chart that plots the most recent six month's sales figures for our fictional business. It also had the graphics system create a trend line for the data. In effect, this tells business owners that their sales are rising at an almost constant rate. In all, the business is showing strong sales, and the owner should be generally happy with this picture.

Of course, there are ancillary things connected to an increase of this sort in your sales, including the need for more cash to finance their costs. In effect, the business owner should be pleased and warned at the same time by a graph like Figure 2-1: pleased that sales are on the rise (almost always a good sign) but warned that more cash will be required to support those sales.

# A Long-Range Look

Although it's worthwhile to look at sales from as tight a viewpoint as Figure 2-1 gives us, it's equally beneficial to examine sales over a period of time.

Figure 2-2 gives us a long-range look at the sales for our fictional business over a three-year period. A trend line was created based on the 36 months worth of information.

Obviously, this business has a seasonal jump in sales during the summer, followed by an equally severe plunge to a low shortly after the end of the year. The final transition period might be different than past perfor-

HISTORICAL SALES WITH TREND LINE

FIGURE 2-2

mances would predict, but the business owner who has this graph would be examining it at the end of Year 3 and probably could assume—since his or her sales are dropping again—that they'd bottom out in two or three months and (hopefully) start to rise a bit later on.

This graph gives us all kinds of information, not the least of which is that we could make a good bet that this business has terrific cash flow problems. Whenever you get such a wide variance in sales from period to period, you find yourself either without any cash (as a result of your poor sales performance) or with plenty of cash (which encourages purchases that really should not be made).

Often, too, the person who owns this type of business finds that he or she is constantly paying for a "dead horse"—current revenue must be used to pay for advertising or merchandise or services ordered and used long ago. Since there wasn't enough income to support those purchases when they were made, the business owner probably had no choice but to defer payment; however, they *hurt* the current position, where sales are good and incoming revenue is sufficient to pay all costs and leave a bit in the profit column. The sum of today's profits (and often, cash that should pay current bills) ends up paying on the old obligations. It becomes a vicious cycle, and one that is often impossible to escape.

## What About Inflation?

Figure 2-2 also indicates that the general *trend* of our sales is downward. To take a closer look at the trend line (since it appears flat when charted in Fig-

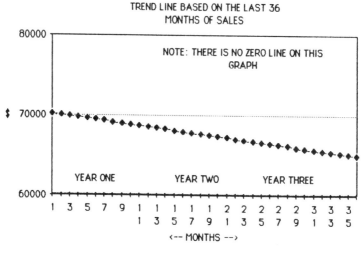

FIGURE 2-3

ure 2-2), Figure 2-3 plots just the trend line, on a much narrower scale. The zero line for this next example has been eliminated; the scale runs from $60,000 in sales to $80,000 in sales.

Once we expand just this one section of the graph in Figure 2-3 and look at the trend line by itself, we see a disturbing image. Since the trend line is based on three years worth of monthly information, it should be pretty reliable as a forecasting tool. Even if there were no inflation during this period, the general flow of our sales is downward—exactly where we don't want it to go. Of course some inflation is always present, and so the picture we see in Figure 2-3 is really worse than it appears. Our sales are decreasing while the value of the dollars we receive for what we sell is also going down. Our gross sales—which this information is based on—should increase at least at the rate of inflation.

## Sales and Costs

Whatever we sell, we incur costs, often a number of them, to bring the sale to fruition. Costs include the labor and materials directly involved with each particular sale as well as the overhead costs required to handle the paperwork and so on. Most often, what are called "direct costs" contribute the largest share to anyone's total costs, so they deserve a look here within the context of total sales. Although it's useful to plot direct costs as a percentage of sales (which we will, in the chapter on cutting costs), it's equally helpful to use their data to create a trend line, to see which way those costs are heading.

Before we look at an example graph, what should we expect? As sales rise, so will our direct costs—that's inevitable. Should they increase at the same rate?

It might seem like they must, but in fact, while we can expect them to grow, they should rise more slowly than sales do, if we work with just the raw figures (rather than percentages). This is because sales are recorded on a *retail* basis, while costs are expenses on a wholesale level.

Figure 2-4 examines the rise and fall of direct costs as a percentage of total sales for our fictional business, over a 12-month span. While this figure generally stayed in the 60 to 80 percent range, the disturbing thing to the business owner is the *variation* in his or her cost percentage. This kind of wide fluctuation is unusual and a cause for alarm. Whereas costs will vary with the work you do and the time of the year it happens to be, a 20 percent swing is out of line for almost any business. You can examine this closer with a look at the trend lines created from the raw (rather than the percentage) sales and cost data.

Figure 2-5 plots the trend line for our monthly sales along with another for direct costs, over a 12-month period. The *actual* sales took place (and costs were realized) during the 12 months these lines are based on.

Our sales and costs both rise, as they should, and it's also obvious that our sales are rising slightly faster than costs are. That is also as it should be. If this graph tells us anything negative, it's that perhaps our costs could be

DIRECT COSTS AS A PERCENT OF TOTAL SALES

**FIGURE 2-4**

FIGURE 2-5

growing slower than they actually are; anything we can do to save on costs helps on the profit end of things. You'll never find that these two lines intersect—let's not forget that *overhead* is also a cost that adds to our total cost picture. That's another data set you might want to chart and follow in terms of trends—sales on one line and the *sum* of overhead and direct costs on the other. A truly negative picture would find the two lines coming together— total costs starting to meet and exceed sales revenue. All of a sudden, you find your business deep in red ink. A trend-line projection may warn you in time.

     Though we don't want to dwell on costs in this chapter, they need to be examined in relation to your sales, on a percentage of sales basis. Figure 2-6 plots total costs (including overhead) as a percentage of sales over a seven-month time frame. As we know, this can either represent the first seven months of a year or the latest seven month period—whatever's the most help to you.

     This example is presented to show you a danger signal. For the first five months represented, direct costs as a percentage of sales remained under the 90 percent level, leaving 10 percent for net profit. The next two months, however, saw our direct costs as a percentage of sales jump above that 90 percent figure. Even without a trend line, our direct costs as a percentage of sales are rising—an unhealthy sign.

     Now, we don't know if that 90 percent figure has any particular meaning for this business, but if this graph was created along the same line as our

TOTAL COSTS AS A PERCENT OF TOTAL SALES

FIGURE 2-6

others, we should try to indicate important data as part of the chart itself. If our overhead breakeven line is 24 percent, then we should *scale* the graph to show a grid line at 24 percent. It makes the information much easier to understand. In this case, perhaps the key is that this business makes money if total costs come to less than 90 percent of its sales volume, and it loses money when the percentage grows higher. In any case, this kind of rise deserves a closer look.

Figure 2-7 eliminates the zero line and puts a tight focus on the information we just examined. Now our scale runs from 80 percent to 100 percent, and since the data is plotted on the narrower scale, its rise is much sharper. With this close look at our direct costs as a percentage of our sales, it's obvious we really have a problem. Again, even without the benefit of a trend line, we can see that our direct cost total as a percentage of our sales is taking a tremendous jump. If we plotted this same data on a *percent of change* basis, it would be even more obvious and disturbing.

The approach, as always, is once we find some problem with our data, as we noted in Figure 2-6, it's almost always worthwhile to take a closer look at things, to put the data into a tighter, narrower focus, as we did with Figure 2-7. The information is the same, of course, and the graph without a zero line changes the picture of the data, but it serves its purpose: to show the business owner he or she has a problem and (hopefully) motivate him or her to some action(s) to solve it.

TOTAL COSTS AS A PERCENT OF TOTAL SALES

FIGURE 2-7

# Sales and Salespeople

Businesses vary by how they handle the cost of sales. You might do all the estimating yourself (and you get paid whether you sell anything or not), while the business on the corner might have two outside salespeople (who only get paid on a commission basis), while Walt across the street might have one salesperson who works on a salary plus an override if they have so much in volume each month.

Associated with the *personal* cost of sales in terms of someone actually spending time out in front of a prospect are any number of contributing expenses. Do you have someone in your office who does all the estimating? Who types up the contracts and proposals and sales letters?

However you handle your sales, there are some costs that are associated with each individual sale, expenses that are well worthwhile to track and graph. You may find that one salesperson creates a lot of volume with little profit because of poor estimating or too many undeliverable promises made to each customer. You might discover that the contractor you thought was your best customer really isn't, because of all kinds of on-the-job changes, or slow payment (that cost you interest expenses), or just because your bids to that contractor are less than they should be because you don't want to lose the work. Perhaps one area of your business consumes an abnormal share of sales costs. You might sell a washer/dryer combination with one simple contract proposal and one visit to the customer, while a complete storm window installation might require five hours of estimating time, plus jobsite visits by your engineering and installation people as well as the sales-person.

The point of all this is to suggest that you examine your sales costs and track them, just as you do now with the other costs your business has. Like direct costs and overhead (and pieces of each), sales expenses can be graphed and examined and thought about either as raw data, on a percentage basis, and with or without a trend line to project where the data is headed.

Figure 2-8 plots eight months of sales cost data as a percentage of our total sales. The first month, for example, indicates that we spent 5 percent of our sales dollar to produce the sales we made. This particular set of information shows our figures running under 6 percent until the latest month, where we had a sharp jump. As always, this is a warning sign that something's not as it should be. Did someone get a larger than usual commission? Another way to examine this set of information would be to plot it on a *percent of change* basis—how much did our sales costs, as a percentage of our total sales, rise or fall last month?

The sales figure we use to compare the cost of sales can be refined, too, because rather than simply to lump all of our sales together, we need to total just those sales for which we can attribute some of the cost of our sales department. For example, if we have a retail location with someone on the counter all the time, their labor expense is more of an overhead figure, because they'll likely be paid whether anything is sold or not. So, we wouldn't want to count those sales when we compare our sales total to our sales cost amount.

SALES COSTS AS A PERCENTAGE OF SALES
VOLUME

FIGURE 2-8

FIGURE 2-9

Figure 2-8 is especially disturbing since it's based on percentages, so it simply means we're spending more of each sales dollar to create our sales. During the first month plotted here, it cost us about a nickel to produce a dollar of sales. During the last month plotted, it cost us almost a dime to create a dollar's worth of sales. Something's obviously wrong. It could be in the sales commissions we're paying or in the sales themselves—are our people selling low-volume/high-commission products? Is one of our people estimating so that jobs lose money, yet he or she still collects a full commission on each job?

To carry things to their logical conclusion, Figure 2-9 shows what our sales cost as a percent-of-sales graph should look like, after a few more months have gone by. After the sharp jump to month 8, this business owner made the right decisions to reduce sales expenses. By the end of this particular period, it cost our business only about five cents for each dollar of sales we recorded, and best of all, the recent trend of the data is downward. Whatever skewed our figures for those few months has been eliminated. This is the graph you should see if your business finds itself as shown in Figure 2-8, with such a rapid rise in the cost of your sales force.

## Our Sales Pie

If we have more than one location, it's always a good idea to break down total sales based on that and create a pie chart. It's often useful to distribute this graph to our people at each store, so they can see how they're doing in relation to their peers.

SALES BY LOCATION FOR JUNE

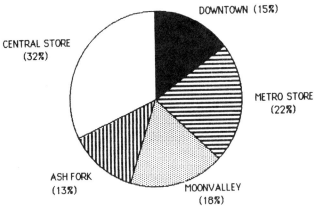

**FIGURE 2-10**

It's pretty easy to see from Figure 2-10 that our central store produces the greatest volume of sales, while Ash Fork is the worst in terms of raw sales volume. With five locations, each should provide 20 percent of the total, yet that would be a rare situation for any business.

We want to examine the sales each of our locations produces with a much tighter focus, but it's important to note that even if you only have one store, you probably have more than one *area* of your business, more than one department. You can examine sales per department on the same basis as you can sales by location (so the closer look we'll take will apply to either focus).

Figure 2-11 breaks down our sales for June into five departments; since there are five areas, we could expect each to produce about 20 percent of our total sales. As with locations, though, it would be an unusual situation (and might even be cause for more worry than the breakdown we actually have). It's obvious from Figure 2-11 that the wholesale end of things creates the greatest sales dollar, while warranty work accounts for the least. Without other figures from other periods, this doesn't tell us a lot but simply serves as a place to start our closer examination of where our sales come from. As noted, we can use the same techniques to look at both our sales by location and by department—the focus is the same.

# A Closer Look

One way to narrow our examination of sales data either by location or department is to break it down based on some common focus. For a service-

SALES BY DEPARTMENT FOR JUNE

**FIGURE 2-11**

oriented business, that might take the form of looking at each service technician individually—how many calls did he or she perform today? Last month? What was the callback rate for mistakes the technician made? And the bottom line: how many dollars in sales and/or profits did this person contribute to our total?

When we look at our sales based on the individual store locations we have, it's useful to move things along this same direction and compare the sales for each store on a *square foot* basis. After all, if one store has 2,000 square feet of display area and another only half that, we'd expect the sales of the former to be twice that of the smaller location.

Figure 2-12 is a bar chart that plots the monthly sales our fictitious business produced during June. This is the best type of graph to use to illustrate this information, as we can see at a glance who's best, who's worst, and how the rest happened to do during this particular period. Clearly the Metro store had a poor record, while our Moonvalley location topped sales for June. Naturally, we'd want to have more than one month's worth of data before we made any major decisions, but Figure 2-12 gives us a picture of a point in time, a chance to see each location in relation to the others in a way where they're all on an equal footing.

This is perhaps a more accurate look at things than what we saw in the pie chart of Figure 2-10. While that told its own story—how each store contributed to our *total* sales—Figure 2-12 gives us a better feel for how one location compares to all others, based on a common denominator. It takes into account the size of each store and quite probably the store's staff and its associated costs; the larger the location, the more people you probably have working there, the higher its overhead is (in raw figures), and so on.

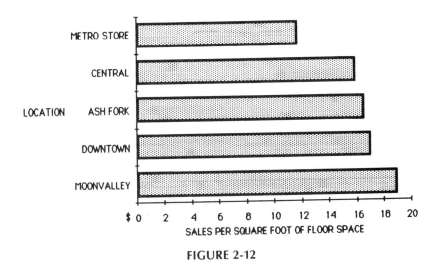

**FIGURE 2-12**

It seems obvious, too, from Figure 2-12 that the Metro store is lagging far behind not only the best location, but trails all of our other stores by a wide margin. Why? One month's worth of information on a single chart isn't going to tell you the whole story, but if you create this display every month and find that over a period of time Metro is consistently at the bottom of your sales barrel, you have a definite problem that needs to be corrected. Is it with the people? Merchandise? Location? Displays? Advertising? Can Metro make a go of things with monthly sales of less than $12 a square foot?

If you happen to find that, yes, Metro is *always* much the worse of any of your locations, then you have to decide whether to change your staff, and/or change the inventory mix, perhaps even eliminate the location completely. The important thing is that you can see, with a graph like Figure 2-12, exactly how one store compares to each of your others. It's a useful tool to hand out to your people at the end of each month, and quarter, too, so they can see how they're performing.

You can examine any individual area inside your sales with this same approach. As Figure 2-11 illustrated the sales per department, you can take that same information and break it down to some common feature, to create an accurate comparison between divisions inside your business. You can't do it (obviously) for each data set on a per square foot basis, but there's always a way to see how they compare. Perhaps you can divide sales by the number of people in each department, or the number of hours worked, or sales calls made or estimates presented. The idea is to get things down to their lowest common denominator.

## Another Look at Poor Metro

Since our Metro store is getting the worst of things here, let's take its sales data further and see how it looks on a historical basis. This is a logical next step, once we've examined the other charts, particularly when we found that Metro had a problem when we looked at sales on a per square foot basis.

Figure 2-13 gives us a long-range look at what the Metro store has contributed to our overall sales, on a percent-of-sales basis. This particular graph covers two full years plus eight months of the current year. Like other similar graphs, the scale for this example was designed to add information to the picture and make it easier to understand. It's obvious that the Metro store's been producing between 20 and 25 percent of our total sales, for some time now. Lately, as we move into the fall season, its sales are slowing. The sales line we plot has moved out of its *normal* range—that historical area between 20 and 25 percent—and worse, it appears to be heading downward. Why? Are our total sales much higher, while Metro's remained the same in raw dollar figures, which would cause it to have a *lower* percent-of-sales figure? Or is there a problem at the store?

Figure 2-14 plots Metro's sales as a percentage of our total sales as a trend line, based on 32 months of information. While we could see the recent drop in sales for this location in Figure 2-13, this illustration shows us its sales have been falling for some time. On a percentage basis, our trend

FIGURE 2-13

TREND LINE FOR THE PERCENTAGE OF SALES THAT
OUR METRO STORE CONTRIBUTES TO OUR TOTAL
SALES VOLUME

FIGURE 2-14

line projects they're heading down to around 20 percent of our total volume. They were up around 24 percent back at the start of Year 1, so the Metro store's dropped nearly four full percentage points in terms of our overall sales. If we looked at the data for this store alone, the drop as a percentage of *its* sales would be even more severe, as both of these last two illustrations are based on its percentage of *total* sales, an obviously much larger figure than the sales produced by this one store itself.

## More of Metro's Problems

Whatever the cause, there's clearly a problem with Metro. Just as we looked at a historical picture of its relationship to total sales, it's helpful to create a chart for this one store (our problem child) based on a long-range look at its sales on a square foot basis. We want to see if they average within a certain range, get a feeling for any seasonality that might cause wide fluctuations, and so on. While this doesn't make a comparison with our other stores, we could take this data a step further and create a line graph for two or three locations over a long period of time, based on their sales per square foot.

Figure 2-15 plots Metro's sales on a square foot basis over a 30-month period. The June amount we examined earlier in Figure 2-12 is the last item on this graph—if this were your business, you'd be examining this data at

**FIGURE 2-15**

the end of June. As always, our scale is plotted to help us understand the information; in this case, sales have been running within the $12–$14 range for some time now, and suddenly we see them dip and fall below the $12 mark. This might be just a passing problem, of course, but still serves as a warning that we need to investigate further.

The easiest way to do this is to narrow our focus, to create a graph without a zero line. This gives us something of a false picture of the data, as we know, but at the same time serves a purpose: in this case, it should scare the business owner into doing something about the Metro store.

Figure 2-16 eliminates the zero line from the data we just examined; the $11.72 monthly figure we've been following all this time is our latest plot. Since our scale is only between $11 and $14, the monthly gyrations in sales per square foot are much steeper. But as we see, they remained within the $12 to $14 range for more than two years, only to fall recently below that $12 figure.

When we couple this information with a trend line, we confirm the problems at our Metro store. Not only are our recent sales down, but the overall trend line heads lower, and at a pretty severe rate. Another way to examine (and get upset about) this data would be to plot it on a percent-of-change basis, where the graph would indicate how much—from a percentage standpoint—the store's sales rose or fell each month, compared to the prior month.

There's obviously a serious problem with the Metro store—all graphs confirm it—and it's up to the business owner to find out what the difficulty is and take steps to correct things. This same kind of examination can be

MONTHLY SALES PER SQUARE FOOT,
METRO STORE

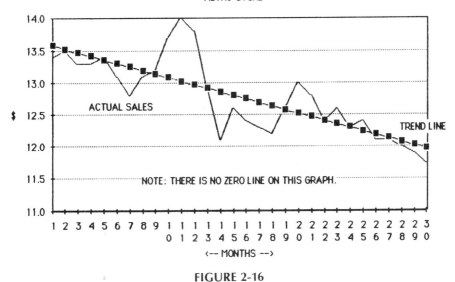

FIGURE 2-16

used for any major part of your sales; we just chose to pick on the Metro location for these examples.

## Summing Up

It's important to understand that it's vital to plot your total sales this year
compared to the same period last year, and just because we didn't provide an
illustration here does not mean you shouldn't track that data. On the contrary, that information is vital, and something that should be done every
month. But that's obvious (you probably already do it, even by hand), and so
we didn't spend time on it here. Another helpful way to look at sales last year
versus sales this year is to compare them on a percent-of-change basis—how
they compare, up or down, on a percentage basis from last year to this. Just
as you should plot monthly sales this year compared to last, it's worthwhile
to chart things on a "latest 12 month" basis. Knowing what your sales are
for the most recent 12 months is often just as valuable as plotting them on a
calendar basis.

   One thing to apply to any sales information is a trend line, to let your
Macintosh calculate and plot the direction things are heading. Too often,
monthly sales fluctuations disguise where your sales are really going, and
the trend line helps you to know. The more data you can base your forecast

on, the more accurate its picture will be, so you want to examine sales on a long-term historical basis, and plot a trend line based on that long line of sales volume.

If your trend line appears flat—which it often will, particularly if it's based on a lot of similar figures—you can squeeze the graph down a bit and plot it on a narrower scale. This, as you know, distorts the real figures, but often is the only way to discover if a seemingly flat line has any real trend, any real movement to it. Most often an examination of this type will show a rise or fall in the line—valuable information.

If you see the general trend of your sales, based on a historical picture, is downward, you have a definite problem, as they ought to at least keep up with inflation. Although it's a bit of work, you can factor in the inflation rates for whatever periods your data covers and get a picture of your sales data based on a dollar value that doesn't fluctuate.

Another way to examine sales is to plot their monthly change on a percentage basis. Although it's sometimes difficult to relate to the raw dollar totals, when you see that sales were down 22 percent from last month to this, you instantly know the meaning of the information.

You should examine sales in relation to the costs involved to produce those sales. These involve direct costs (which you can look at on a percent-of-sales basis) as well as sales costs, what it costs for the presentation and/or engineering to sell a particular job.

The business owner should also know where his or her sales come from, both in terms of location and department, if you have more than one of either. Is one store or division better than another, sales-wise? Why? You need to take a closer look at the sales information you gather from your locations and/or departments, and you can often get a good idea of what the data means by putting it all on some common ground. We chose to examine sales on a per square foot basis, as it puts those sales figures into a form where each store is graded equally.

It's also helpful to examine, on a long-range basis, how each division or location contributes to your total sales, on a percentage basis. Once calculated and charted over a period of time, this percentage should remain stable, and it's a warning sign when one store starts to produce more or less than it has been (if one location starts to provide a larger percentage of your sales, then another must be contributing less).

## Other Ideas

One useful comparison to chart is between the sales you make and your outstanding accounts receivable. Generally, you'd expect the two to rise at about the same rate and would worry if they didn't. You might find it useful to use your spreadsheet program to calculate your month-end accounts receivable total as a percentage of your monthly sales, and plot it.

The whole idea of any sale is to create a profit, so it's worthwhile when you get your monthly or quarterly profit/loss statement to plot sales along with profits. Again, one should rise and fall with the other—the more sales, the more profit we'd expect—and it would be cause for alarm if one line on the graph didn't match the other. You may have to do some numerical manipulation to get both figures on the same scale, perhaps by multiplying your profit figures by 10 or 100.

Sales are always directly tied to the salespeople who work for you; without them, there are no sales. Obviously, some businesses are more dependent on sales personnel than others, so this comparison might not be valid for your line of work. If you do have a sales staff, try plotting the sales they produce by salesperson or sales office. You might also want to examine the sales by product and/or product line—perhaps the goods you buy from one wholesaler far outsell those of another. If so, it's important that you're aware of it.

# Sales in Sections

3

The average businessperson might know that his or her total sales were $55,000 last month, probably can elaborate in terms of any profit that was recorded, and might even be able to describe why the work turned a profit. But more astute business owners spend the time required to find out where their sales (and thus profits) are generated.

Unless you handle only one product and/or service, there are subdivisions of your business that you'll find profitable to examine. A bookstore, for example, which handles only books, still will find obvious value in knowing what type of books sell the best. Your bookstore will have racks of westerns, fiction, cookbooks, computer books, romance titles, and so on. Wouldn't it be beneficial to understand which area(s) produced the most sales? The largest gross profit? The fastest inventory turnover?

If you do nothing but service repair work, wouldn't it be interesting to discover which *types* of [whatever you work on] are the easiest to service, have the least number of warranty callbacks, have the best record for parts availability, are the brand(s) your customers seem the most satisfied with?

If your work requires you to do installations for [whatever you sell] for general building contractors, would you find it helpful to know who you're doing the most work for? The least? Who has the best payment record? The worst? Who has the fewest/greatest number of on-the-job change orders? Which builder calls for the most "minor" adjustments after the sale that seem to take trip after trip before he's finally satisfied?

Within the wide context of *sales* are any number of helpful combinations business owners can track in an effort not only to learn more about how their business functions, but also—especially since the subject is sales—to examine and think about one area or another in an effort to increase their sales total. What's important to you and your work might be altogether different than it is for other businesses in your town. They might sell a lot of service and repair labor, while you handle parts on a retail basis only. Or you may handle warranty repair claims and have a small wholesale setup for some parts, while the business down the block might sell appliances and farm out any required repair service. Inside of anyone's sales, though, are areas that can be broken down on an individual basis to help the business owner know not just what's going on inside the enterprise but can also point the way to more sales and profits.

Much of the focus inside your sales concerns itself with where they come from. Who are your customers? Even if you work for a wide variety of people over the period of a year, some, and perhaps much, of your business will be for people you worked for before, and since you did a good job, they're repeat customers. Who are they? Is there something else you can sell them?

## Breaking Things Down

Inside your inventory are products that move better than others, sections that produce more profits than others. You might discover that you've got a substantial investment in the appliance parts section of your inventory, but the darned stuff just doesn't sell. Armed with this information (obviously, gathered and studied over a sufficient time period), you'd be ready to decide to eliminate the slow moving stock and put that cash into the products that consistently contribute the most to sales and profits.

In your service department are technicians who seem always to make money for your business, and others who are marginal. Graphics provides an ideal way to see how your people are performing, with a simple ongoing line graph of the dollar volume service technicians produce, along with a line graph for the same period for their *total costs*. That cost line should include the direct labor expenses, any fringe benefits, any associated taxes you must pay, along with the total cost for any callbacks that must be made because the service technician made a mistake.

Coupled with service are the sales your service people make, simply because they're out there on the job. Prospects (rightly or wrongly) have a tendency to believe a repair person, to put more credence into what he says, compared to what a salesperson might tell them. Since your service people are already on the job, have already spoken to the customer and explained their problem (and, naturally, your solution to it), the customer is more likely to buy from you instead of a competitor (and in many cases, might not even look around for another estimate). So your service department makes sales and profits *over and above* what it produces in simple service work, because of the sales it creates.

# A Close Look at Contracts

As with your total sales volume, the first and most obvious approach is to track whatever area(s) you find important on a this year versus last year basis. In fact, a basic "this period compared to that" for the most obvious parts of your business is a helpful starting point. As with sales, we're not going to illustrate that approach with a graph here, but that doesn't mean you shouldn't chart this data if you find it useful. Instead, we're going to suggest some graphs that might help you understand an area inside your sales; the *parts* of your business that you want to study (and there might be a number of them) depend on your own interests and needs.

Since a lot of our work depends on what we call contracts, that'll be our focus for much of this section. Contracts, in this context, describe those sales our fictional business makes to contractors, people who build new homes. What's important to you can be examined in exactly the same way, of course; keep that in mind as you look at the examples.

Rather than starting with an obvious look at things, Figure 3-1 illustrates an unusual idea: to analyze and graph the average sales volume for every contract the business records, in this case, over a period of 18 months.

In effect, while this example doesn't tell you the total volume that contracts contribute to your sales total, it instead indicates how they, as a group, are performing, whether the jobs you sell are larger or smaller from month to month. Do you find that you're more successful if you handle a number of smaller sales, or if the same sales total is made up of fewer, but larger items?

FIGURE 3-1

Each business is different, and while many companies strive to sell larger jobs, too many big installations can tie up a lot of cash, might force you to hire additional employees (who may or may not be qualified), and if there are problems, they're *big* ones. Most businesses prefer a mix between their large jobs and those with a smaller sales volume. It's the old question of what you'd rather have: one person who owes you a thousand dollars, or a thousand people who each owe you one dollar. Only the business owner can determine what sort of work they'd like to pursue and what their business is best geared for; a graph like Figure 3-1 tells you what the average current volume is for each contract you sell.

Let's take Figure 3-1 a step further and add a trend line to show what direction our fictional business is heading. But let's also notice that—as we've seen in many other cases—the sales on a per contract basis in this example run within a *range* of figures. In this case, over the 18 months plotted, they've consistently been between about $1000 and $1500. You can *see* the business cycle at different times of the year.

Figure 3-2 plots the same information we just looked at, with the addition of a trend line that shows the general direction of the data. While we couldn't determine it from Figure 3-1, this example clearly shows a downward trend.

Information of this type isn't necessarily bad, of course; it all depends on where you want your business to go, the jobs you want it to be involved with. More lower-volume installations involve more overhead but perhaps are safer in terms of the severity of on-the-job problems and the collection of

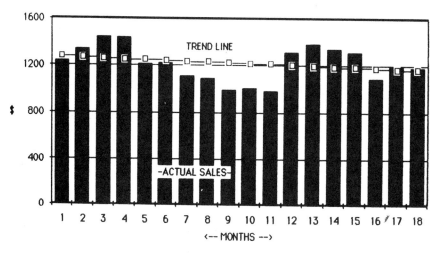

FIGURE 3-2

bills. Larger installations generally consume less overhead (on a percentage basis) and raise sales volume to the point where you can bid lower on other jobs and thus create even more sales. The point is, of course, that graphs like these last two give the business owner a feel for what's happening inside the business, as well as where it's headed.

# More Contract Detail

Since we're examining the subject of contracts in detail, let's look at another way to break down their information. Most businesses do work both inside the city where they're located and outside its limits. The main differences are in travel time and associated costs, and sometimes a difference in the sales tax you have to collect.

Figure 3-3 charts the sales data for our fictitious business over an 18-month period for the contract work it did outside the city limits. It's obvious from this illustration how our sales volume for contracts out of the city is decreasing, even without the benefit of a trend line. Why is it going down? Is that a trend we want to continue, or do we need to do something to increase sales in this area? Naturally, we'd want to examine other data for this part of our business, to see if in fact we are making money on these jobs or not, how

FIGURE 3-3

much they contribute to our total overhead, and so on. We might find that we want to help the current trend continue its downward plunge—perhaps we're not able to properly estimate and/or supervise the work we do outside the city, so we'd be better off to take on only those jobs where we're sure to show a profit. Maybe the contractors we work for out of town are slower to pay than our other customers or more difficult to track down when they do get behind. Once we *know* where our sales are coming from and their dollar value—as we've seen in these first three examples—then we can determine if we're on the right track, or if we want to make an effort to change the direction our business is heading.

# In-shop Work

Just as we've looked at contracts as a part of our total sales and examined the bid volume we write in relation to the sales it creates, it's also helpful to look deep inside our sales at any repair work we do. Your business might have service people who go to a customer's home to repair something, or you might let people bring in their products for you to repair in your shop. It depends on the service work your business does as to what you might want to examine, but for purposes of illustration, we'll look at the work done in the shop area of our fictional business. Not all businesses provide this service for their customers, of course, but if yours does, you know it's one of the hardest to control and make any money on.

A lot of businesses post a sign that tells their customers there's a minimum charge for any work done in the shop. While this is a good idea, it's often difficult to enforce; a customer who's bought from you for 20 years who comes in and takes ten minutes of a service technician's time is hardly a candidate for a minimum charge. Too often, you just tell the customer that there's no cost and let it go at that. A lot of the times, too, you just can't justify your minimum charge for a piddling little job or for finding what's really a piece of scrap material for someone. A customer might call to ask for advice on this or that and ties up one of your people for a half hour; the time's just lost. And there are times when your service technician spends an hour on something only to find he can't fix it for one reason or another, or that the customer needs a part he simply can't afford. It's difficult—and causes hard feelings—when you try to charge for such things.

Because it's such a difficult area to control, it's an ideal one to examine, all with an eye as to how you might improve or change things to make in-shop service profitable. The first step is to break down both sales and costs as they relate to service. What are your sales for the service work you do in your shop? What are the costs involved for this particular area of your business? You need to have some record keeping method to track these things, even though you might not currently record this information.

"IN SHOP" COSTS AS A PERCENT OF "IN SHOP"
SALES

FIGURE 3-4

Figure 3-4 shows the data for our fictitious business for its in-shop sales and their costs, calculated by dividing the labor cost figure by its retail total to arrive at a percent. This chart duplicates the graph you might create for your total sales/cost amounts. You probably shouldn't be too surprised that there are times when this part of your business shows a loss. That's the nature of this type of service, and although you don't want *any* area of your business to lose money, there may be other considerations that you need to keep in mind. For instance, even though this department isn't profitable part of the time, perhaps it creates other work for your business. If someone brings in a product that you diagnose as defective, the customer might want you to go to his home and replace it. That can lead to major sales, too, as other problems are discovered.

The important thing is that business owners realize that this section of their work is difficult to make a profit on; a monthly graph like Figure 3-4 shows exactly how this one area of things is doing. Of course, other parts of your business can be examined the same way, once you take the time to break out their sales and costs, so you can compare one to the other on a graph.

A logical extension of this information is to let your micro create a trend line based on your data and plot it.

Figure 3-5 shows the same information we just graphed, with the addition of a trend line. As often is the case, while we couldn't tell from a chart of the data itself, the trend line makes it obvious that our in-shop costs as a per-

FIGURE 3-5

centage of their sales are rising. This information should disturb any business owner, as it means this one section of the business is going from bad to worse in terms of profit.

Another way to examine this information would be to create a graph with a very narrow scale—perhaps between 60 and 120 percent, as we've done with Figure 3-6.

The trend line shows a steeper rise because of the restricted scale. As always, information like this is designed to motivate the manager to do something to correct the situation.

# Labor Problems

Now that we've examined in-shop labor repair costs, let's expand that same focus and take a more general look at our repair labor and its associated costs from a business-wide standpoint. Rather than just the repair work we might do at our place of business, let's also include any outside repair labor our business sells. Any company that sells labor, either for service or installation, has one of the more difficult tasks that faces the business owner: it's often impossible to make a profit on labor. There are any number of reasons for this, but the bottom line is that much of the time you simply cannot charge the price you need to receive in order to come out on the labor you sell.

There are other costs besides basic salary and fringe benefits that must

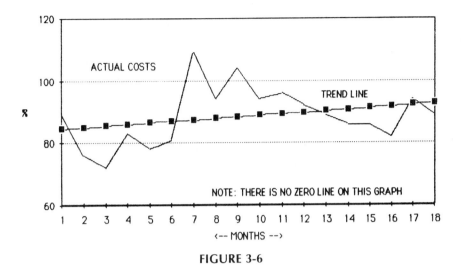

"IN SHOP" COSTS AS A PERCENT OF "IN SHOP"
SALES

FIGURE 3-6

be considered when you examine your labor expenses. There are times when your people cannot work for one reason or another, and yet they must be paid. There are other times when someone can't fix a customer's problem, so you have to send another service technician or two out, at your expense, to find and correct the problem. Something you buy from a manufacturer comes through and needs repair; your costs to fix it total $150, but the manufacturer only allows (if anything) $50. You absorb the rest. A little rise in insurance costs here, an extra coffee break or two there, and a business can quickly find itself in a money-losing position in respect to its labor sales.

Since we've been working with repair labor, let's stay on that same tack and see how our labor should look when we plot its costs along with the sales it produces.

Figure 3-7 is the picture we see when we plot these two data sets; as labor costs rise, so should their associated sales. If one line runs at a direct variance from the other, we know we've got a situation we need to examine more closely. Note that the title for this chart indicates exactly what it plots: retail labor revenue and the cost labor that's charged against the retail price. A similar graph might include any material or equipment these service people install out on the job, but that would skew the picture. We really want to focus on just labor for this example: its costs and its sales. The cost figure you use for this plot would include, of course, any associated labor expenses such as insurance, fringe benefits, and so on.

Although the two lines we see in this example are what we'd expect

FIGURE 3-7

them to be, it's always worthwhile to take a closer look at things. Even though there doesn't appear to be a problem here, a tighter look might reveal something.

Figure 3-8 plots the trend lines for the two data sets we just examined. Whereas Figure 3-7 showed us what was seemingly a problem-free picture of our labor and its costs, this illustration is cause for alarm. The trend lines are running just the opposite of what we'd hope they would: retail labor sales are decreasing while the cost of our labor is rising. There's still a considerable difference between the two lines (they're obviously not going to intersect), but that's because our overhead costs are not included. The data plotted here is for actual labor sales and costs only, without any regard to the overhead required to support things. What sort of a picture would we see if our overhead added $2000 a month to our cost total? All of a sudden, the lines would start to meet, and this department would find itself in the red. What's important about Figure 3-8 is that it is like the warning you'd get from a double-barreled shotgun: *both lines* are going the wrong way, and you'd better get into gear and do something about it.

The logical next step when you find a problem like the one Figure 3-8 illustrates is to look at things on a percentage basis. Figure 3-9 does that, and plots the labor costs as a percentage of the labor sales for our fictitious business, over an 18-month period. As we know, these can represent either the last 18 months or 18 months on a calendar-year basis, whatever we feel is most helpful at this particular time.

TREND LINES FOR RETAIL LABOR REVENUE
COMPARED TO LABOR COST

FIGURE 3-8

What's most striking about this graph of the same information we've been examining are all of those plotting marks we see on the 60 percent line; for fully 10 of the 18 months under study, labor costs amounted to almost exactly 60 percent of the retail price our business received for that labor. The other striking thing is that months 6 through 9 of the first yearly period saw a sharp rise in labor costs as a percentage of its sales. Why?

From this information, it's impossible to understand the *why* behind these increases. When a series of data points remains so stable over a period of time, it takes quite a jolt to knock them off stride, so to speak. In this example, our labor costs as a percentage of their sales rose almost 20 percent in a very brief span of time.

The ideal way to discover the reason behind these fluctuations would be to go back and examine our sales during these periods and compare them to our sales when the line was flat. Who were the service technicians on the job? Who supervised things? Were these times of the year when some of our people were standing around, not able to work (but still being paid) because of weather conditions? Were sales very low while our people were kept on the payroll (which changes the percentage figure we're looking at)? There has to be some reason, and now that the business owner knows *when* there was a problem, he or she knows where to look to find out what happened, determine why it took place, and figure out a strategy to see that it doesn't happen again.

LABOR COST AS A PERCENTAGE OF RETAIL LABOR
SALES

FIGURE 3-9

# Contracting Work

Earlier in this chapter we examined the contracts our fictional business handled, particularly in the way they relate to our sales total. It's also often helpful to get a bit closer to contracting work (or any area, of course, that's important to your business) with an eye to where the work comes from, who we're selling to. Contracts, as you'll recall, is the work our business does for contractors, people who build new homes.

When we want to take a close look at who we're doing work for, the natural starting point is to compare this year's sales to last year's (or the latest monthly period to the same period last year).

Figure 3-10 is a line graph that plots our sales to Bob's Builders over a nine-month period, comparing this year's sales to last year's. It's obvious that early in the year sales were about the same, then split apart in March where this year's figures fell lower than last year's sales. Once we spot this, we'd want to find out the reason behind it; is Bob simply not building as much as he did last year, or is more of his work going to one of our competitors? If the latter is the case, what can we do to change the situation?

In this example, by July our fictional business turned things around, and current sales surpassed those from last year.

SALES VOLUME FOR BOB'S BUILDERS, THIS
YEAR COMPARED TO LAST

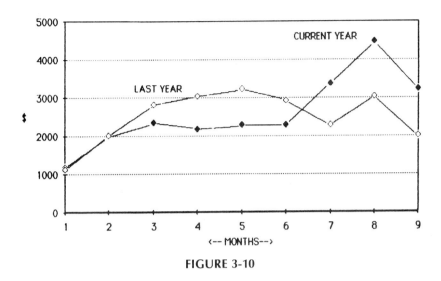

FIGURE 3-10

This comparison is something you'd want to do only for larger volume people (in this example, only for those contractors for whom we do a lot of work).

There are really a number of things this comparison will tell you. In the construction business, for example, where we work with contractors, it gives us a good handle on our pricing policies; unless we're competitive, even the most faithful contractor strays from our fold and buys from the heating and cooling business down the street. A graph like Figure 3-10 helps us know how our prices are. It also gives us a feel for the financial health of the people we work for. Contractors can be funny people: when they owe us money, they seem to have a tendency to not want to come in and tell us they're running behind. Instead, they often shun any contact with us and end up having the competition do their current work. Since we usually have a good idea of who's building how much and where they're building it, Figure 3-10 gives us a feel for how much work our business is getting from the total work a specific contractor has in process.

A logical followup to Figure 3-10 would be to plot a trend line for this year's sales to date and overlay it on a graph of a trend line for last year's sales for the same period for this particular customer. That would give us an indication of how our sales volume for this contractor is heading—lower or higher—and if we project out the trend line information, it even will give us a feeling for how much sales volume we'll do for this customer. If he's slow to pay his bills, this information helps us determine how much cash we may need to borrow; if he pays as each part of a job is completed, it tells us a bit more about the cash we can expect to collect during the coming months.

It might seem to make sense to graph the percentage increase or decrease in the business a contractor gives you. A graph like this doesn't make the figures easier to understand, however. Perhaps you'll find, say, a 10 percent decrease for three months in a row. On the graph, these 10 percent decreases will show up as a straight line—each month's sales were 10 percent less than the prior month's. So, a percentage graph for this sort of data doesn't make it easier to comprehend; you might as well list the percentage increases or decreases on a sheet of paper.

Figure 3-11 plots how the sales our fictional business made to "Ed the Builder" have been doing, on a percentage basis. It's obvious that they've been increasing at the rate of 10 percent per month, but the graph we can ask our microcomputer for doesn't do a good job at telling the story.

This is because the system is working with "raw data" in the form of the 10 percent monthly increase and will plot it just like any other data set—and in this case, a 10 percent rise comes out as a flat line. You could create a semilog chart for this information and see the 10 percent monthly rise, but this is more a case where a graph doesn't tell you as much information as a table with the actual data would.

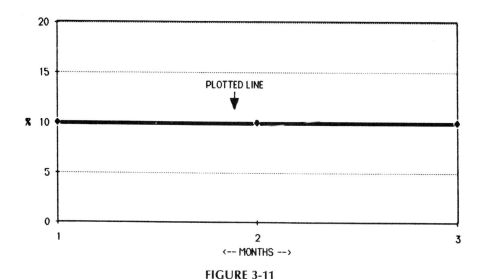

FIGURE 3-11

# Building Pie

A logical extension of a study of those people you do work for is to show how their sales volume connects to your total through the use of a pie chart. As you know, this will give you a feeling of how each contractor's sales volume relates to the total sales you get from contracting.

This examination can be done every month, although you can run into a fluctuation problem when you do it that often. In most small businesses, sales are recorded as they're billed out. For contracting work in particular, invoices sent out don't always match the sales they represent during any given period. This is because a lot of contracting work is done on a draw basis. You estimate how much of a job you've completed at a particular point in time (like the 10th of the month, if that's when you send out invoices), and base the amount of the bill on this estimate. This method lets you collect as a job is in progress, rather than having to wait until it's completed. For instance, when 25 percent of a job is done, it's billed and, hopefully, paid. Often these percentage figures aren't completely accurate. If you're short of cash, the natural tendency is to inflate your estimate (for billing purposes) of how complete a job is. Also, it sometimes happens that you'll want to record as much dollar volume in sales as possible during a specific period of time (particularly as the end of a year approaches), so you might record invoices that really aren't quite due as of their billing date.

Figure 3-12 represents data for the third quarter of a year, based on the

NEW HOMES BY BUILDER, THIRD QUARTER

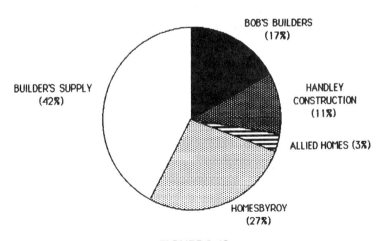

**FIGURE 3-12**

percentage of contract sales each of five builders contributed to the total our fictional business recorded. Builders Supply gave us the largest share of our volume (almost half), while Allied Homes bought the least from our business. Without the same chart over other periods of time, Figure 3-12 doesn't tell us if these percentages will hold true, but once you plot this information over a few quarterly periods, you'll know who's buying from you and who isn't. We'd also want to follow through on Allied Homes' purchases—why were they only 3 percent of our total contract sales? Was it because this particular business simply isn't doing much business, or are we just getting a small piece of their pie?

## Another Group

It's an obvious comparison to make, but surprisingly, while most businesses break down their sales by department, many business owners don't keep a sales breakdown for the different product groups they handle. When the business manager looks at his or her inventory totals, he or she will ask for a breakdown by wholesaler or type of product or department code; it's just as important to extract the data for the different product *groups* you happen to handle.

Figure 3-13 illustrates the sales, on a percentage basis, our fictional business made for the third quarter of a year, for the four major contracting

SALES BY PRODUCT GROUP, THIRD QUARTER

RETAIL SALES (21%)

NEW HOMES (37%)

PLUMBING SALES (25%)

REMODELING (17%)

**FIGURE 3-13**

groups it sells from. In this example, New Homes provides nearly 40 percent of our sales, while the weakest end of the business was our Remodeling group. Why? With four areas to sell to contractors from, we'd expect them each to contribute about 25 percent of our total contract volume, and the only one right on line is the Plumbing group.

As with any other information, this data is only relevant when you relate it to other periods, other graphs. If Remodeling over a period of time stays at its low level, we need to spend some time in that department to determine the reason for it. Perhaps this one chart is derived from data that showed a good increase in sales for the rest of our product groups, while Remodeling remained about the same—thus causing a decrease in its percentage figure.

## Subcontracts

One area of contracting work involves what is called *subcontracts*. One person—a general contractor—will take on an entire job, and hire out parts of it to subcontractors. This can include almost anything, of course, and a new home under construction usually will find itself involved with a number of them—a plumbing company, an electrician, a heating contractor, drywall people, a painting crew, and so on.

While we've examined our sales to contractors on an individual basis (for Bob's Builders in Figure 3-10) and in a pie chart (Figure 3-12) so we can see how each company we work for relates to our total contract sales, it's equally useful to plot the data on a monthly basis as a bar chart. This gives us a unique and useful view to help understand where our sales are coming from for the particular period under study.

For the month of June, Figure 3-14 illustrates the contract work we did for six different builders, running from the lowest in volume (Carter's New Homes) to our best customer for this area, Ram Builders. As always, one month of information doesn't tell us a whole lot but needs to be coupled with a continuous study on the same basis. In this case, since the area of contract sales (with our business acting as a subcontractor) is important to us, we'd want to create this chart every month, just so we can see how things are going. If Ram is consistently our best customer, it should be treated as such. If Carter's New Homes is always our lowest volume buyer, perhaps we need to spend more time with the Carter people in an effort to raise their dollar total. This information, as marked on the graph, is plotted as raw sales totals instead of on the percentage basis we'd looked at before.

There's another side to this coin, too. Just as someone who owns a business like ours (heating and air conditioning) is hired by contractors to work on this job or that installation, so that we track our sales by *builder*, a con-

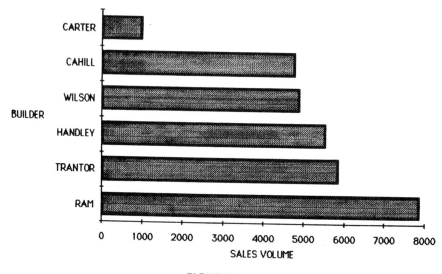

**FIGURE 3-14**

tractor should do the same thing in reverse: by *subcontractor*. The viewpoint is different, of course. For the builder who looks at monthly charts of the people he or she buys from, the idea would be to determine if the supplier who gets most of the business gives the service this large volume deserves.

## Summing Up

Unless your business sells only a single product and/or service, there are sections inside your work that logically will fall into a grouping that makes sense to take a close look at.

Since our business works with contracts—those installations we install for a contractor—we chose to examine them in detail for this chapter. Your work will more than likely be completely different in terms of what you need to look at, but the basic techniques are the same. A good starting point is to break down each item (in our examples, *contracts*) into its average volume. Is it rising or falling for this section of your work? Why? Is the data headed the way you'd like it to be? Add a trend line to the basic information to see its direction.

Think about other ways to break down whatever area(s) you want to study. Do you do some of your work inside the city limits, and other work out of the city? In different cities? Is some of your work taxable, while other parts are not? Does some of it involve major equipment, while other work is based entirely on small parts? None of these comparisons might be right for you, of course; the idea is to examine one area or another inside your work and break it down as much as possible. If you find you don't get valid information from such a breakdown, you don't have to continue tracking the data.

Another group area that many business owners have to wrestle with concerns repair labor. Our examples took a look at the work our fictional business performed on its premises, but the same basic techniques hold true for any examination of labor. This section of your business needs to be split away from the main area, both in terms of its costs and in the sales it creates. The addition of a trend line to your graph lets you know where you're heading. Our study found that while labor and its sales moved about the same when the raw data was plotted, when we charted just the two trend lines, we found a problem.

Within any group, it's worthwhile to examine the relationship your business has with its best customers, the people who buy the most from you. You'd want to look at each customer (we looked at building contractors) in regard to their contribution to your total sales for the group under study, as well as their individual figures for every month or quarter. Conversely, if you purchase a lot of materials or services from other people, chart their sales to you in an effort to determine if you're getting your money's worth.

If you know your line of work, you can often glean more information from these graphs than you'd expect, particularly in terms of your own pricing policies and the cash condition of some of your customers.

## Other Ideas

Since you can combine any logical group of what you sell, or who you sell to, there are an untold number of combinations you might want to examine. Instead of suggesting some specific areas that you might want to look at, it's probably more helpful to give you some general ideas on how to select groups to consider. Anything that's informative should be charted on a regular basis. When you find an area that perhaps sounded good but doesn't tell you anything, stop tracking its information and making graphs of it.

The key to much of this kind of examination is to break things down to their lowest level. For instance, you might want to look at just the sales your business makes for, say, the Plumbing area. You may also want to break this data down, to the sales per truck this part of your work provides. Or the sales created on a per mile basis. Or per service call. You might do much of your work through mail order, or over the phone. Break those sales down on a per delivery or per call basis. The whole idea is to pick a group of logically related sections of your work, break down their contribution to sales/overhead/ profit/costs to the lowest possible level, and examine things. Many times, you'll find the information isn't helpful, and when you do, move on to something else. But inside your work, hidden away somewhere, are three or four groups of things that will give you terrific information when you chart their data.

# Cash Flow

4

*Cash*. It's at the heart of every business transaction, the true bottom line of every company, the way we gauge the health of an enterprise. By any standard, cash is an accurate measurement of our effectiveness as managers: if there's enough left after our sales are totaled and costs paid, we've done well. If not, we've done something wrong. It's as simple as that.

In the old days, it was an easy matter to add up what we had left in the cash drawer at the end of the day. Today we have all sorts of ledgers and journals that we must sort through to find out what we sold, and even more pieces of paper to extract data from to figure out if we made money or not. But the process is the same, and under it all floats (pardon the pun) *cash*. With cash in the bank, we're successful; without it, we're not in business.

## Cash *Flow*

It's important to remember that cash flow means just what it says—cash moves *both* in and out of your business, and the businesspeople who look just at what they expect to collect or only what they owe see things from a myopic viewpoint. So the movement of dollars in your business has to be examined from both directions—coming and going. And it is a *movement*. Every day you receive cash or sell products that promise future cash. Every day you write checks or purchase things on credit that promise a future outlay of funds. Cash is constantly received and spent, juggled and moved, added and subtracted, and with your Macintosh you can get an accurate estimate of what cash you can expect to receive, and how many dollars you'll need next month to pay your bills.

Cash is often confused with *assets,* and while your assets include the cash you have available, cash is a liquid asset, while other things (trucks, office machines, buildings) that are assets are not liquid. Even your inventory isn't fully liquid: you must sell it before you collect the cash. For these reasons, it's important to consider where you put your cash, because if too much is someplace where you can't retrieve it when you need the money (like in the down payment for a new truck), you have a cash flow problem. Likewise, unless you've got the cash you do have available out there working for you, you might be very liquid but probably won't be in business for a long period of time. There must be a balance in the places you put your cash to ensure you have enough for your current needs (payroll, equipment for the job you'll start tomorrow) but still have the proper amount out there working for you.

## Sales and Cash

Any study of cash necessarily starts with sales, as they generate all the dollars you'll receive (unless you borrow money or sell stock in your business). The sales you made last month and the month before (and before that, of course) directly determine the cash you'll receive this month. If you let your customers charge their purchases, the total accounts receivable amount has a direct bearing on the cash you can expect to get. Every business has a historical pattern that reflects how well they collect what their customers owe them. On the average, unless the management changes its policies or credit terms, or business conditions change, this ratio will remain steady over a period of time.

It's a fairly simple thing to go back through your monthly sales reports and/or accounts receivable totals and monthly summaries of cash collected to determine this ratio. You'll find that *on the average* you collect, say, 55 percent of the outstanding receivables, or perhaps 40 percent of the sales total, and so on. Whatever your average ratio is, it can serve as a guide to what you can expect to collect in the future.

## Flowing Graphs

This is where business graphics give us something of a line on the future based on what we've done in the past, and while we can't predict what will happen, the proper dollar amounts displayed in a helpful graphics format can at least show us a picture of what's taken place with an eye to what we

MONTHLY SALES TOTALS

FIGURE 4-1

can expect next month. Let's examine the records of a fictional business that is like many in that it records much of its sales during one period of the year. In this case, let's say it's an air conditioning business, which totals most of its sales during the summer months.

Because *line* graphs help create a feeling of movement and give a bit more life to the image we receive from them, they form a good basis to examine this particular data.

Figure 4-1 is a line graph of just the sales information for our fictitious business. It's easy to see when summer arrived and when it left. There's nothing particularly fascinating about one line of sales information, and even when we add in the accounts receivable total (Figure 4-2), we see about what we expect. Since the amount our customers owe us will depend in a direct way on our sales volume, we can expect these two lines to approximate one another.

Figure 4-2 *does* tell us, though, that this particular business can anticipate that its receivables total will vary in direct proportion to sales, except perhaps during the summer months, where the comparison isn't as exact.

There could be a number of reasons for this, but a logical one is that people who buy summer's big-ticket item (air conditioning) most likely can afford it, and perhaps will send along a check as soon as they receive the invoice. So while the sales can increase dramatically, accounts receivables might not, as a lot of bills are paid before the receivables are totaled at the

MONTHLY SALES TOTALS

FIGURE 4-2

end of each month. When September came along for our fictional business during this particular year, the receivables started to follow the exact line as sales, confirming the relationship predicted by the graph.

Figure 4-3 again shows the total sales line, but now the lower line represents the cash collected each month. However, there are some major discrepancies between the data sets. While the first three months follow a close pattern (coincidence?), the period from month 4 to month 5 started a strong increase in sales. Meanwhile, cash collected started to climb, but at a slower rate. As sales continued their rapid rise through June, July, and August, the dollars flowed in at a much slower rate during the same period.

In the month 9 and month 10 period, we find a reversal of what took place early in the summer. Now, sales show a sharp decline, while the amount of cash the business received continued to increase—still not at the same rate that sales grew, but in direct opposition to the sales pattern for this period. By the end of the summer, cash starts to *catch up* with the volume of sales.

During the last three months of the year, sales still continue to drop but the cash inflow is a higher amount.

In almost any graph that looks at related accounting data, you'll find some correlation in spots here and there. Just as you should be suspect of any graph where *everything* matches exactly, you should be equally suspicious of any where none of the periods seem to follow one another. In this particular case (Figure 4-3), we find only spots of equal movement.

MONTHLY SALES TOTALS

FIGURE 4-3

## Sales = Dollars

But doesn't it make more sense to assume that the monies we collect should *follow* sales by some time period? After all, since our fictional business has an accounts receivable system through which it lets people charge their purchases, we shouldn't expect their payments to arrive at the same time as they would if the business handled everything on a purely cash basis.

Figure 4-4 illustrates what happens when we plot the sales figures along with the cash we collected one month later. In other words, sales for month 3 (about $42,000) are plotted where you expect them—over the 3. But the cash collected plot over that same 3 is the cash this business received during *month 4*—one month after the sales were made and recorded.

In effect, Figure 4-4 shows how this month's sales affect next month's cash. In 'his particular business, there's a direct relationship between the two, much more so than between the raw sales and cash totals for each month we examined in Figure 4-3.

## Receivables and Cash

If you owned this business, you may be able—based on the information shown in Figure 4-4—to reliably forecast what cash you could expect to col-

MONTHLY SALES TOTALS

FIGURE 4-4

lect next month, once you tallied this month's total sales. This has all sorts of implications. Once you know how much cash you'll have available, you can decide what to do with it, when to spend money on this or when to purchase that. But you'd want to take things a step further, to examine the relationship between receivables and cash.

Figure 4-5 shows the accounts receivable totals for each month, along with the cash collected for each monthly period. The relationships here are very similar to what we just examined—receivables rise and fall in almost direct relationship to sales.

Figure 4-6 shows the same figures, with the cash received *advanced* a month in front of the receivable totals. Again, both lines rise and fall in almost direct proportion to one another. In effect, this tells us just what we'd expect, that both accounts receivable and the cash we can expect to collect will follow our sales pattern. Once we know our monthly sales, we can forecast the expected cash inflow.

Because sales compared to the cash received and receivables compared to the cash received both tell us the same story, this particular business can reliably estimate the cash it will collect next month, based on either its sales or receivables totals, *as long as its policies remain the same.* That's an important qualifier, because—if this were your business—you might suddenly decide to limit the access of credit to your customers, or to be more liberal in who you charge to. Either would change conditions. There's no problem with this—after all, if it *were* your business, you'd know what was happening and wouldn't base your cash expectations on sales or receivables totals

MONTH-END ACCOUNTS RECEIVABLE TOTAL
COMPARED TO CASH COLLECTED

FIGURE 4-5

once you adjusted the rules of the game. But as long as things remain on the same basis, this business has an accurate method to forecast its cash inflow.

Your business might be different, of course—your lag time might be two months, or three, or longer. It could also be less; while we've examined things only on a monthly basis, you might have weekly information you could take a look at. The whole idea is to examine what data you have under

MONTH-END ACCOUNTS RECEIVABLE TOTAL
COMPARED TO CASH COLLECTED

FIGURE 4-6

different sets of conditions—move one line or the other forward, over different time frames, so you can see what correlates for you. A line graph examination of cash does exactly that—it gives you a picture of your own data.

## A Two-Edged Sword

The movement of cash is an important consideration, because since it flows both in and out of any business, it's a two-edged sword that cuts both ways. Obviously, if you don't have enough money in the bank to meet payroll, you've got a problem. The solution most often used to combat a cash deficiency is to somehow create more sales. While more volume solves many problems, it also cuts both ways. The worst of these comes along when our sales really spurt, while our collections plod along at the same old rate. The *dollar amount* will rise, of course, as the sales volume goes up, but the problem is that dollars often don't arrive in our mail until long after we've had to pay for the products and/or labor we've sold.

A good illustration of the two-edged sword that cash can become is shown in Figure 4-7. Here we have two new lines, one for the cash our fictitious business collected and another for its costs over the same period.

Let's imagine that our business operates on a 34 percent gross profit

FIGURE 4-7

margin—34 cents out of every dollar we sell (on the average) is left for overhead and profit. Sixty-six percent of our sales dollar, then, goes to pay for the material and labor involved in each sale. Let's also suppose our business has an overhead that comes to 23 percent of its total sales.

The bottom line, assuming that these percentages apply to all sales we make during a given period, is this:

```
DIRECT COSTS  . . . . . . .66%
OVERHEAD  . . . . . . . . .23
TOTAL COSTS . . . . . . . .89%
```

On this basis, our business would have an 11 percent net profit (11 percent of its total sales) before taxes.

The cost line in Figure 4-7 shows our monthly costs for both the materials and labor required to produce and distribute our products, plus the overhead needed to run the business—a total of 89 percent of the sales totals. It should leave a more than comfortable margin of 11 percent for net profit and anything unexpected.

## Can We Pay for What We Sell?

In this case, the cash we received more than matched our monthly dollar needs for the first three months of the year. However, in April our summer sales started to skyrocket (and with them, our monthly cost outlay), and although the number of dollars we received also grew, they didn't arrive in a large enough volume to offset our increased costs.

This isn't a completely accurate image in that a lot of the purchases we make are on, say, a 30-day net basis, and so we *really* don't have to pay for them during the current month. A more correct picture would plot these figures a month ahead of the others, to *lead* them by a month or two. However, since cash collected should come along after the sales are made and payments are required after the items are purchased, rather than plot both lines a month in the future, it's almost as accurate (and definitely easier) to plot them both in the same month. It's important to remember that the purpose of this particular graph is to make a point—a huge increase in sales will *eventually* create a greater inflow of cash, but in the meantime, we can find ourselves in a deficit position, as we do here for the April through September period.

These five months were the best for our business both in terms of sales and in the total cash we collected. Our costs, though, grew at the same rate as our sales, and because cash didn't flow as fast into the business as it went out, we were cash-poor during the best time of the year. In September the situation reversed itself, and cash once again started to exceed our cost requirements.

What's the lesson here? If you find a similar pattern in your business, it's important to try to *conserve* cash during those times when it exceeds costs, to have it available when it will not. This might seem obvious, but the natural tendency is to think, "we have it, so we'll spend it," without enough thought to the invariable changes in future conditions. And we need to be constantly vigilant in terms of our credit policies and collection terms, as they directly affect the flow of cash into our business.

## Seeing Ahead

Where do you spot things like this? While it's helpful to look back over an entire year's figures and think, yes, we should have saved some cash during the spring, it's too late in the game to have any effect on things. For this example, we've used whole-year figures, so let's expand just the first section of Figure 4-7 to see what our position looked like back in May.

Figure 4-8 is the graph we'd have seen in May, if we monitored these two amounts on a monthly basis. It's a close-up view without a zero line, so we can more effectively judge the movement of the data. Early on, we'd probably feel pretty good about things, as the cash for the first three months more than matched costs. However, the situation reversed itself in April, and May finds our costs and cash only a bit closer together. The fact that the two

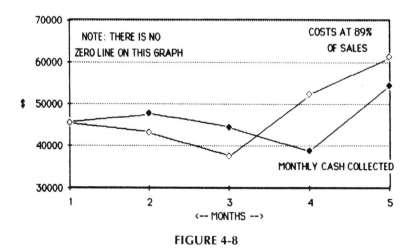

CASH COLLECTED COMPARED TO TOTAL
COSTS

**FIGURE 4-8**

lines *crossed* in the March-to-April period indicates that a significant problem may be right around the corner, and the business owner who's on top of things will immediately take steps to reverse the situation.

While we don't want to slow down the growth of sales, once we realize what's happening to our cash/cost ratio, we can take some measures to improve things. We *know* we'll need cash from somewhere to cover our costs, so we can make plans to borrow it or do something else to raise the money we'll need. We might also want to examine our sales to gauge their quality; perhaps some of the sales growth isn't producing the profits it should—we may just be trading dollars. We'll want to look harder at our costs and overhead, with an eye to reducing them. The point is, when we see this pattern on a graph, it alerts us to a potential and growing problem before it becomes overwhelming. That's the whole function of this sort of graphic analysis—to give the business owner an idea of where he or she has been and where the business is headed.

## Receivables and Payables

One of the most interesting things we can create with business graphics is a moving examination of our financial picture—how we're doing one period compared to another. It's almost automatic to do it with sales, as that's one figure we're constantly concerned with. But it's also helpful to take a look at receivables and payables in the same context.

FIGURE 4-9

Figure 4-9 charts the month-end figures for accounts receivable for last year, along with the first eight months of the current year. For the first five months, the figures were about the same. However, starting in June the current accounts receivable total began to grow, and by August it was substantially ahead of last year's.

An increase in accounts receivable is generally viewed as a sign that business is on the upswing. However, as with any data, a variation from what's expected must be closely examined. Is the accounts receivable total greater this year than last because of more sales volume or because people aren't paying on time? Has the business eased its credit policies to produce more sales only to have them turn into old accounts receivable? While this particular graph doesn't give you the answer to that problem (one like Figure 4-15 will), it signals you that something *might* be wrong, that there might be a problem on the horizon. It gives you this information while there's time to take corrective action if it's called for.

Along this same line, Figure 4-10 tells the same story for accounts payable. Actually, last year's total was greater only during the first two months of this year, which climbed at an alarming rate all the way through August. The difference between the two lines is obvious and signals that the business is either experiencing a great increase in sales (and thus costs) or isn't paying its bills as it should. In either case, Figure 4-10 gives the business owner a strong message that he or she might have a serious problem.

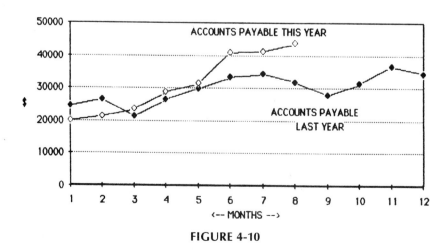

MONTH-END ACCOUNTS PAYABLE THIS YEAR
COMPARED TO ACCOUNTS PAYABLE LAST YEAR

**FIGURE 4-10**

# The Real Secret

While all this gives the business owner some good information (and is based on data you'll want to track), it's well worthwhile to take things a step further and have your spreadsheet compute the ratio between your accounts receivable and accounts payable amounts. Generally, graphics programs can't do this sort of math for you, so you must create your own *data files* with the ratio information, rather than just the raw data. It's just as easy—both in your spreadsheet and in your graphics program—to work with a ratio figure as it is to work with a total dollar amount.

If you owned the fictitious business we're examining here and plotted your receivables/payables ratio for the first five months of the year, Figure 4-11 is what you'd see. Since the first of the year (where you had about a 2.4-1 ratio between the two figures), this ratio has steadily deteriorated. It's starting to bump regularly at or below the 2-1 mark. Confronted with these figures, the alert business owner will know he or she must take corrective action of some sort. The logical place to look is, of course, at the accounts receivable area, to see if more cash can be collected. If you get more dollars in payment and apply them to accounts payable, while still making profitable sales, your receivables total will stay where it should and payables will decrease. This is because while those current sales will add to both receivables and payables (more sales generate more costs as well as charge accounts),

RECEIVABLES / PAYABLES RATIO

**FIGURE 4-11**

RECEIVABLES / PAYABLES RATIO

FIGURE 4-12

receivables increase at a *retail* level, while payables increase on a *cost* basis. Receivables must grow more than payables.

Figure 4-12 represents what happened to our fictitious business for the whole year. It assumes the owner made changes in the operation to the extent the receivables/payables ratio made a marked improvement, and in fact they finished the year at about 2.4-1. Although the scale is stretched out to accommodate 12 months worth of figures, we can see the early-year decline in the receivables/payables ratio, a slight improvement in the July-to-October period (probably the results of mid-term adjustments being made) and finally, a substantial growth in the ratio during the final two months.

## Collecting Your Cash

Anyone with accounts receivable dollars owed them automatically gets a bit of extra baggage with the receivable process. While one class of customer always pays, there's another that never does. In between those two extremes are the people who you figure will pay, but you just don't know when they might get around to it. Unfortunately, the customer whose account ends up as a bad debt or as a candidate for the collection services *passes through* this middle ground, and we don't have any accurate way to determine who's going to pay (eventually) and who we'll have to turn over for collection.

Two things you can do are to track how your finance charges are going and to study the average collection period your business has. All of these calculations, of course, are ideal candidates for your spreadsheet program.

The most accurate and helpful way to examine this information is to calculate and chart it on a monthly basis. In essence, this describes the time period you need to convert your in-stock inventory into cash and includes the time it takes you to get the material, deliver and/or install it, send the bill, and collect for the job.

The first stage is to compute your daily credit sales. It's important to note that you want to work with only *credit* sales, those sales you charge to your customers through your accounts receivable system. To calculate your average daily credit sales, you divide your net credit sales for the month by the number of days during the month. These are in contrast to, say, *cash sales*, where you collect for the purchase at the same time you sell it.

For example, you might have credit sales of $45,000 that you charged to your customers during one monthly period. If there were 30 days in this particular month, when you divide 45,000 by 30, you find your average credit sales, per day, were $1,500.

Your accounting system will also give you your starting period and ending period accounts receivable figures. You'd total them and divide by two, to arrive at an average. For example, if at the end of last month your accounts receivable came to $50,000, and at the end of the current month they total $60,000, you'd add these two figures together (they total $110,000) and divide by 2 for an average accounts receivable balance of $55,000. You divide this by the average amount of credit sales you made each day ($1,500), and the resulting figure (37) tells you the number of days it took your business, on the average, to collect its accounts receivable. If you normally ask for payment on a 30-day basis and find that you have a period like this example—a 37-day time frame to collect your cash—you have a minor problem in this area.

This figure can be graphed, and it's very helpful to examine its fluctuations over a period of time. Once you've gathered enough information on your own business, you'll most likely find that your collection period will run within a specific range of days, except for certain times of the year when someone else gets the payments you should be receiving. You might discover, for example, that on the average your collection period is 30 to 35 days. In effect, this means you can expect payment within that period for most invoices you send out. But you might also find that during certain periods of the year, the slow times, your collection rate might move into the 50- to 60-day range.

Figure 4-13 plots the average collection period for our fictional business over 36 months. The most striking thing about this picture is that for a long time, our collections ran in the 30- to 40-day area. With a *net 30* payment schedule (common for many businesses), that's probably the range

AVERAGE COLLECTION PERIOD IN DAYS

FIGURE 4-13

we should expect to see. Then, about in the middle of the third year, our collection period took a drastic jump. While it's been brought back into its normal range, there had to be some reason for the increase in slow collections, and we need to take steps to see that such a rise doesn't hit us again. Were a lot of our customers during this period those we should have spotted as slow-pay, by using better credit-checking procedures? Were we lax in calling old accounts to ask for payment? Whatever the reason, it would be helpful to know what happened and why.

Although as always, the most helpful comparison you can make is to compare your current collection period with your own past history; a rule of thumb is that the average collection period shouldn't exceed what you request as payment terms by more than 30 percent. If you normally ask your customers to pay on a net 10-day basis, your collection period shouldn't be longer than about 13 days. If you ask for payment within 30 days, your average collection period shouldn't be longer than 39 days.

Along with any discussion of the average number of days it takes your business to collect its receivables, it's important to note there are other considerations to keep in mind. If you feel, when you talk to a potential customer, that he or she is someone who'll pay their bill, it might be worthwhile to extend credit to that person, even if the probable collection period will run considerably longer than what your average is. The point is, you don't want to reduce your sales volume simply to enforce an arbitrary collection period.

There's a happy medium for your business that you need to find and work from.

A logical extension of Figure 4-13 would be to take the same information and ask our plotting program to create a trend line of the data. Once we see it (in Figure 4-14), it seems obvious that we should have done this sooner, as the trend line shows a continual rise over the period under study.

As often is the case, we really can't tell from the data itself that the trend is rising. Even the big jump came back down to what appears to be our normal operating range, but the overall trend is still upward. This picture brings home a good point: we have a problem with the overall trend of our collection period, and we need to do something about it, to reverse the situation, or we can expect significant cash-flow problems in the near future. Perhaps we can screen our credit customers more effectively. Maybe we need to turn down work where there appears to be a credit problem. It might be worthwhile (and almost always is) to get on the phone and call customers just to make sure our work was satisfactory and mention, "by the way, we haven't received your check." Our suppliers don't hesitate to call us if we get a little slow in paying their bill, and we must do the same with our customers. It might be something as simple as letting each customer know, when you allow them to charge, exactly what your credit terms are, and what will happen if they get behind.

FIGURE 4-14

# The Quality of Your Receivables

Any business that has customers who owe it money must consider the quality of those receivables—what percentage of the outstanding amount it can expect to collect. Some businesses have better luck than others, due to the nature of the work itself or the people the business associates with. Sadly, the ones that generally have the most at risk when it comes to bad debts are those businesses that can least afford them.

It seems obvious that the older an account becomes, the less likely it is that you'll collect it. Unless your business is on a completely cash basis, it's important to keep track of things like how old your accounts are, to attempt to control them so you'll eventually get paid. To help this process, almost everyone gets an *aging report,* which lists a numerical breakdown of the age, the quality, of their accounts receivable. Often the business owner sees something like this:

**AGING REPORT FOR JUNE**

| | |
|---|---|
| 0–30 days old . . . . . . . | .$31,965.12 |
| 30–60 days old . . . . . . . | 17,306.36 |
| 60–90 days old . . . . . . . | 11,007.99 |
| 90 days and older . . . . . . | 2,484.01 |

Often it's helpful to convert the same figures to a percentage format and examine them on a graph. Figure 4-15 shows us just that, with the per-

FIGURE 4-15

centage amounts instead of just the raw dollar figures. You want to use a complete scale for this display (all the way from zero to one hundred) as it gives you a better feel for the actual size of the data represented.

While you can't use a graph like Figure 4-15 for monthly comparisons, if you create one every month on a regular basis, you can quickly find out—by leafing through them—if one particular area is getting worse as the months go by.

It's possibly just as useful to examine the same information in a pie chart format. While the bar chart of Figure 4-15 shows us how each figure relates to the others, Figure 4-16 illustrates how each part of our accounts receivable relates to our *total* accounts receivable.

Figure 4-16 uses the same percentages we just examined in Figure 4-15 but puts them into the pie chart format to give us a feeling how each particular area relates to the total of our accounts receivable. It's obvious that the biggest share—more than half, by a little bit—is in what we'd consider the current area. The smallest slice of this pie is also what we'd expect—the 90-day and older category. The other two slices are where we might be the most disturbed by this chart; almost one-third of our accounts receivable are in the 30- to 60-day section, and nearly one-fifth are in the 60–90 category. Combined, we find we've got almost half of our outstanding accounts older than 30 days.

You can equate this information with your own ability to pay your bills when they come due. If half of your customers can't pay their bills until they're a month or two old, you should be aware that you're in exactly the

AGED RECEIVABLES BY PERCENT FOR JUNE

90 DAYS AND
OLDER (4%)

60 TO 90 DAYS
OLD (17.5%)

0 TO 30 DAYS OLD
(51%)

30 TO 60 DAYS
OLD (27.5%)

**FIGURE 4-16**

same situation: you won't be able to pay *half of your bills* until they're just as old. Unless you can collect the cash, you can't pay your own bills.

## Charting Their Age

You can take things a step further, too. Every business has a historical pattern that a little study can discover. If you go back through your aging reports, you'll soon find in what range your average figures should be. Let the numbers themselves tell you what's important (and what's not) for your business.

For instance, you might discover that your old accounts (defined as older than 60 days) historically average about 20 percent of your accounts receivable total. It's a worthwhile project, then, to create a graph like Figure 4-17. This chart displays the percentage of your receivables total that is older than 60 days, on a monthly basis. It's done for the first nine months of the year. With this sort of guide, the owner can see that old accounts were being reduced early in the year, but the situation started to change back in month 4. By month 5, more than 20 percent of the total showed up in the "old" area, and stayed there through September.

It's obvious that the owner isn't taking the steps he or she should to reduce this growth in old accounts, and if it remains unchecked it will cause a

FIGURE 4-17

serious hardship for the business in terms of cash flow. If this trend continues, the amount in *old* accounts receivables will continue to grow every month.

A graph like this one not only makes it easy for the business owner to *see* the situation, but he or she can instantly do the math in their head to get an approximate value for these old receivables. It's one thing to realize that 20 percent of your receivables are old, and quite another to multiply that 20 percent by (for example) total accounts receivable of $70,000, and suddenly figure out that there are 14,000 real dollars sitting there, getting older by the day. It motivates you to do something to try to collect some of these overdue accounts.

Along this same line, it might be worthwhile to go back over your records to determine exactly what percentage of old accounts your business historically collects. You might discover that once an invoice gets more ancient than 60 or 90 days, it's almost impossible to collect it.

## Searching Assets and Liabilities for Cash

While sales and accounts receivable are the logical places to look for cash, the business owner can get a line on his cash position from the balance sheet he receives every month or quarter.

There's a distinct relationship between the amount of available cash (working capital) and the debts (liabilities) a business owes. Working capital is the excess of current assets over current liabilities and serves as a measure of the business's ability to pay its current debts. Your balance sheet, for example, may show that you have $100,000 in current assets (generally cash and things that can be quickly converted into cash, including inventory), and $50,000 in current liabilities (debts due now or within one year).

The difference between the two is called working capital; it's the amount of cash you have to *work* with. The "current ratio" reflects the relationship between these two figures. If you *divide* your current assets by your current liabilities, you end up with what accountants call the current ratio. In this example, you'd divide $100,000 by $50,000, which gives you a 2-1 ratio. Like the comparison between accounts receivable and payable, a 2-1 split indicates the business is probably in good condition. A ratio less than this is a danger sign: the business might not have enough cash to do business.

Like any accounting item converted into a ratio, the unusual must be examined, whatever direction it appears in. For instance (assuming that 2-1 ratio applies to your line of work), you'll obviously be concerned if you find your business with a 1.5-1 ratio, or a 1.4-1 figure. But you might not be as concerned if this ratio started to grow and in fact may be quite pleased if you checked last month's figures and discovered you had a 2.7-1 ratio between current assets and current liabilities.

However, *any* aberration should be examined in detail to find out what caused the change. For instance, that high current ratio might be caused by too many slow-paying customers (current assets include your current accounts receivable total). If that's the case, the ratio indicates a problem rather than a reason to be content with things as they are.

## The Acid-Test Ratio

A harsher look at the current state of your cash examines the ratio between *quick assets* and current liabilities. Inventory and any prepaid expenses are removed from total current assets; quick assets are what is left in the asset account—cash, net receivables, and any marketable securities, only those things we can expect to convert *quickly* into cash. The excluded items (like inventory) are left out because you might not be able to change them rapidly into funds. This ratio tracks the current *pool* of cash, the actual dollars that are available to pay current debts.

One other consideration arises here—the quality of the marketable securities and the net receivables included in the total. How good are the receivables? If you sell the securities, will you incur a loss? As with any financial figure, you often have to look a bit deeper under the surface information to discover the truth about your condition.

## Liquidity Ratio

All of this leads to a ratio we feel is important to keep track of. The comparison is a bit different than the usual and that perhaps is where it gains its validity. Yes, it's necessary to look at the current ratio (current assets divided by current liabilities) and the acid-test ratio (quick assets divided by current liabilities) as both give you a feel for your current cash position. But in addition, you might also keep monthly tabs on the liquidity ratio of your business. This simply divides your total assets by your current assets. If you have $70,000 in total assets and $35,000 in current assets, you have a .5 (50 percent) ratio here—exactly one-half of your total assets are in a *liquid* form. If you had only liquid assets, then you'd be 100 percent liquid.

Is a lot of liquidity good? Do you need a lot of cash around, or would it be better to have those same funds out working for you? That all depends on your cash requirements, and business graphics can help you know your own. For example, we saw earlier in this chapter how one business experienced a terrific sales growth during the summer months, but at the same time, it didn't have the cash to cover its anticipated costs. The knowledgeable manager looks at his or her liquidity ratio in view of the estimated cash needs of the business. If it appears that business conditions will cause a cash-flow problem, then he or she will want to *increase* the liquidity ratio to compensate. The worst thing that can happen is to have both a deficit in the cash we need *and* a low liquidity rate, where many of our dollars are tied up in fixed investments of some sort. They can't come to our rescue, then, when the bills start to accumulate.

Figure 4-18 is a column chart that covers the first half-year of a business and shows the month-end liquidity ratio, with the figures multiplied by 100 so they're shown in percentage fashion. January's, for example, indicates this business had about 53 percent of its assets in a liquid form—about half its assets were in cash or something that could be quickly converted into cash. However, with some minor fluctuations, this percentage steadily decreased throughout the first half of the year. In June, only about 40 percent of the business's assets were in a form creditors will accept for invoices—cash or its equivalent.

How do you think this business would fare if it had the same cash-flow problems we examined earlier? Could this business handle a rapid rise in sales? Would it have the cash available to cover the necessary costs? The sad part of all this is that even if the business has the assets to handle a change in sales (in *either* direction), they're of no use unless they can be easily

LIQUIDITY PERCENT

FIGURE 4-18

converted into cash. The wise manager looks at *all* ratios, with a particular eye to his or her liquidity position both now and down the road a bit.

## Finance Charge Dollars

At first glance, the finance charges you add to past due accounts might seem to be a blessing. After all, it's money you didn't really have to go out and earn.

While that sounds fine, we'll bet all those customers who don't complain don't always *pay* the finance charges that you put on their statements. They might pay their bill, but often ignore that $1.57 late charge. If your business is like ours, the finance charges you add to your old accounts are really an extension of your own credit situation; you have to borrow money to carry your customers, so any past due charges they do pay just help offset the interest you have to pay your banker. And in reality, there probably isn't a business owner around who wouldn't prefer to handle everything in cash, both for what he or she purchases and for the work he or she sells. It not only simplifies things like accounting and payables and receivables (there won't be *any* of the latter two), but eliminates the cash-flow problem every business faces from time to time.

Probably the worst thing about finance charges is that they simply mean one thing: someone's not paying their bills when they should. When you have *any* finance charges to add to your accounts, it means those accounts are older than they should be. That's a problem for any business, because even as you add those finance charges and watch their total accumulate, invoices are getting old, customers who haven't paid are leaving town, and those customers with available cash are sending it elsewhere. If you were getting paid on time, you wouldn't have any finance charges to record.

All of this doesn't mean you shouldn't add finance charges to your old accounts. These days, people expect it, and it does help offset the interest you have to pay when you borrow money so you can stay in business while you wait for people to pay their bills. A much better way to handle the situation is when you find a customer (preferably before you install or deliver what you sell) who appears to have a cash problem, to consider financing the sale yourself. This gives you a written agreement (that can be legally recorded) that the customer will pay so much every month. This method is much easier to enforce than the "open account with interest if you're late" many of us offer our customers.

Figure 4-19 is a simple line chart that plots the monthly finance charges that were added to old balances over a nine-month period, for last year and this year. It's obvious the monthly finance charge totals are greater this year than they were last year, for every month. Unless we increased the

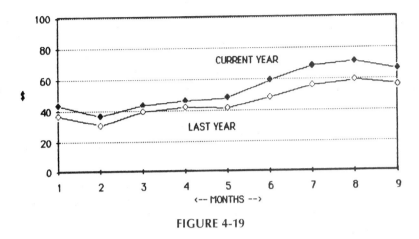

FINANCE CHARGES THIS YEAR COMPARED TO
FINANCE CHARGES LAST YEAR

**FIGURE 4-19**

rate at which we calculate our finance charges, it tells us we've got more dollars tied up in those past due accounts receivable. Our collections aren't as successful this year as they were last year.

We can also do a quick calculation to tell us how many dollars were old during each period. For example, let's say we add a 2 percent interest charge on all accounts over 60 days old. For month 7, our total finance charges last year were about $55. $55 is 2 percent of $2750 (you calculate this by dividing 55 by 2 and moving the decimal point two places to the right (55/2 = 27.5—when you move the decimal point two places to the right, you end up with 2,750). This year our finance charges during month 7 were $75. When we do the calculations, we know we have $3,750 in accounts that are 60 days old or older.

You can get the same information, of course, with a chart of your monthly accounts receivable totals, if you break down their amounts by age. However, even this rough estimate presents us with a disturbing picture. At a 2 percent finance charge rate, each additional dollar in monthly late charges is equal to $50 in old receivables. As we saw above, an increase of $20 in finance charges (for month 7 from last year to this) means we've got an additional $1,000 in accounts that are 60 days old or older.

## More Finance Charges

Another way to examine this same information is to plot it as a percentage of your total accounts receivable. If you do this for your business, you'll usually find it will run within a specific range, and so if you see it leave this area, it's an indication your collection methods have changed and are either better or worse than they've been.

Figure 4-20 presents a 24-month look at our fictional business and plots its finance charges as a percentage of its month-end accounts receivable total. In this case, this percentage stayed in the 1 percent to 1.5 percent range until just recently, where it took a sharp jump. It's a warning signal that the total we've got in old accounts is growing (unless we recently raised the rate at which we add finance charges, or changed the terms as to which accounts are charged late charges). In any case, this example warns the business owner that there is a potential problem and he or she needs to find out why it's happening and take steps to correct it (restrict credit, call more of the old accounts to collect more of that old cash, and so on).

It's interesting to note that this same picture can tell you a lot about the state of your accounts receivable total. If, for example, you assessed a 1.5 percent late charge and produced a graph like Figure 4-20, you've got a definite problem, as it appears that *all* of your accounts are overdue. In this example, where our business charges a 2 percent late charge to its past-due customers, the business owner has cause for concern, as his or her late charges are approaching 2 percent of the outstanding accounts receivable balance. If it reaches that 2 percent level, then *all accounts are overdue.*

A logical extension of this illustration is to carry its data a step further and add a trend line, as shown in Figure 4-21. The trend line tells us that if

FINANCE CHARGES AS A PERCENTAGE OF
ACCOUNTS RECEIVABLE

FIGURE 4-20

FINANCE CHARGES AS A PERCENTAGE OF
ACCOUNTS RECEIVABLE
WITH TREND LINE

FIGURE 4-21

we really want to have more old accounts, we simply have to do nothing; they'll most likely grow without any help from us. However, that's the last thing we *want* to happen, and so these last two examples serve as an effective warning that our collection procedures aren't working. We need to change things, to get those old accounts back under control.

It's important to note that the quality of everyone's accounts receivable total decreases as an account gets older. *Quality* in this sense means the probability that the account will be collected in full. The older a balance gets, the less likely it is that you'll collect it all. Associated with this, in Chapter 8 we'll cover accounts receivable from a collection standpoint, to find out how to calculate and graph the collection period for your business.

## On the Good Side

Not everything is wrong with the occurrence of finance charges, of course. For many businesses, they provide a substantial source of income. If you carry your own contracts (and have good methods to screen out poor credit risks), you'll make sales to people who otherwise couldn't be your customers. Many businesses can get a higher markup, too, if they have liberal credit terms—people who can't qualify to borrow money (except from you) aren't in a strong position to argue about the price of the merchandise.

The key here is to create some systematic accounting method to track your credit costs so you can compare them to the cash inflow your credit terms bring into your business. It's easier if you consider your finance charges as a separate income account, just as you now track things like labor sales, material sales, and so on. The idea is to separate it and keep track of both the income you get from finance charges and their associated costs.

Your costs must include all of your expenses to handle your credit sales, including the extra postage and paperwork involved, and need to incorporate the collection costs and bad debt write-offs you incur. Once you do this over a period of time, you'll have a good handle on exactly what effect your credit policies are having on your net profit. You might find that even when you add in the cost of your bad debts, the total you collect in finance charges more than makes up the deficiency.

## Summing Up

Nothing works without cash, but all too often the business owner thinks of just incoming cash and doesn't pay enough attention to what'll be going out the door to pay that stack of bills he or she has accumulated. Cash *flows* both directions inside every business.

Whereas there's a definite relationship between sales and cash and between accounts receivables and cash, it's different for every company. A graphic look at these figures is often the only way to see what kind of collection cycle your business has. By moving one line on a chart one direction or the other, the business owner can usually determine *exactly* how today's sales or receivables total will affect tomorrow's cash. Once you know how much cash will be available, you can plan properly.

But cash flow is a two-edged sword, since it does move both in and out of any business. It's important to track the cost of sales (including overhead items), as we must have the cash available to pay them. While an increase in sales will raise cash and accounts receivable, it also increases what we owe. Often, those bills will come due before our customers pay us, which puts the business in a deficit position.

This all leads to the fact that it's necessary to examine cash flow not only from both directions, but also with an eye to *when* we'll need a specific amount of money, and whether it will be there at the time it's needed.

We also should chart accounts receivable and payable, as it's important to compare this year's totals with last year's, to see if there are any variations. If there are—in either a positive or negative direction—it's a sign to investigate further. We need to look at not only just the rise or fall in these totals, but also at the relationship between the two, the ratio between payables and receivables. And in fact, this is the real secret of any examination of this sort—to plot the *ratio* that's important to our business.

We must particularly look at a growing accounts receivable total to determine *why* it's getting larger. If it's because our sales are higher, that's fine. If it's because more people aren't paying their bills, it's not so good and in fact might pinch our cash position down the road. So the quality of our receivables is important, and we can judge their quality by their age—the older they are, the less likely we are to collect them.

Finally, we need to keep track of our working capital, our current and acid-test ratio, and—perhaps most useful of all—our liquidity ratio. All these must be examined in light of our anticipated cash requirements. The liquidity ratio in particular tells us what shape our dollars are in and gives us the chance to take corrective action before we start to get calls from creditors demanding they be paid.

It's also important not just to add finance charges to those past-due accounts we all have, but also to track them in a meaningful way. These late charges often give the business owner good information about the state of his or her accounts receivable condition.

## Additional Ideas

There are some extra ideas it might make sense for your business to examine on a regular basis. The way to determine this is to look at your own figures for the items suggested, to see if they may be valuable for you.

For example, you might want to create a column chart that tracks your working capital. Depending on when you get your financial statements, you can do this monthly or quarterly. A column chart will give you a good feeling for what's happening to your working capital, whether it's increasing or decreasing.

You might want to track sales on one line of a line graph and working capital on another line. If your sales increase, does your working capital? Or does it go down? Why?

We used the example of a business with an 89 percent total gross cost percentage. From your financial statements over the past few years, gather your own percentages and graph them. Is your gross margin decreasing or increasing? Why?

Another way to look at accounts receivable and/or accounts payable is not just with their raw totals, but at either the volume of change or percentage of change. An examination of last year's receivables to this year's totals is important, but you might learn more from a look at what the *rate* of change is. Plot the percentage difference for each month and see what it tells you.

Through all this, keep in mind that since cash moves both in and out of your business, it's a primary concern of every business owner. The right selection of cash-flow charts for your business can help put cash in the bank.

# Estimating/Warranty Expenses/Truck Costs

# 5

There are some areas of anyone's business that don't require hard and detailed study, where every month we calculate and examine all the data we can get our hands on. These sections of our work are important and need to be looked at, but perhaps not as frequently or in as much detail as others. We'll examine three such areas here—the estimating we do, the warranty repair costs we incur, and the truck expenses many business owners pay each month.

Many of us work on a bid basis, and for us, most (if not all) of our sales volume comes directly from the estimates we make. To be successful, our prices have to be right, our quotations presented in a professional manner, and we have to do our work in a way that the customer will call us the next time she or he needs something in our line.

The obvious thing that a Macintosh brings to your business is the capability to combine the quotations and estimates you make with some supporting graphic images. If what you're proposing to a prospect will save money, why not include a graph that illustrates his expected savings right in the body of your quotation?

Macintosh also gives you—because of its inherent ease of use—the capability to make as thorough a presentation as you wish. Other than charts or graphs that support what you're selling, you can extend this concept a bit—away from visual images—to the entire bidding process. For instance, it's almost always useful to create a bid breakdown sheet that details the cost of each individual item you're proposing. Once a prospect sees what each

Bid breakdown sheet for Mr. and Mrs. Robert Porter
covering the installation of a new swimming pool for their home.

| | |
|---|---|
| Engineering time | $150.00 |
| General Survey | $200.00 |
| Backhoe work | $475.00 |
| Excavation | $550.00 |
| Hauling old dirt | $150.00 |
| Concrete cost | $1,355.00 |
| Form | $675.00 |
| Pump & its parts | $900.00 |
| Cooldeck | $275.00 |
| Ladder, Diving board | $150.00 |
| Painting | $200.00 |
| Extra landscaping | $175.00 |
| Lighting | $300.00 |
| Trim-out | $100.00 |
| Extra Supplies | NO CHARGE |

-----------------------------------------

| | |
|---|---|
| TOTAL | $5,655.00 |

FIGURE 5-1

piece of your total job costs, he is more likely to accept it. Rather than looking at just the total price, he can concentrate instead on all the smaller items that make up the total. In essence, this makes the price easier to understand and accept.

If you design and construct swimming pools, for example, you can present your proposal one of two ways. The first is to simply write a quotation that outlines what you'll do, with the total price listed. The second—and often the more effective approach—is to also break down the cost, so your prospect can see exactly what he or she is paying for. You might end up with something like Figure 5-1.

The worksheet shown in Figure 5-1 was done with Microsoft's Multiplan℗, and is simply a guide to the type of thing we're suggesting you try.* The whole idea is to give your customer not just a bottom-line price for what you're trying to sell, but a detailed item-by-item breakdown for that same job, so he or she can see how each individual price adds up to the total.

* Multiplan℗ is a trademark of Microsoft Corporation.

If you want to take the process a bit further, this does a number of other things for your business. For instance, this example is done as a retail price list. Why not start, as most of us do, on a cost basis, and create an in-house worksheet to estimate your jobs? You can even use Multiplan to create a blank form you can fill in with the details about each installation of [whatever you sell] and then transfer it to a Multiplan file. Then you can ask the program to automatically put the markup you use on your cost amounts to create a retail price breakdown, as we've done here. This cost data, if you save it, gives you a good worksheet to use after the job's been completed, to compare your estimated costs to the actual costs you incurred for the work. It's a good place to calculate how you came out on the job, to find out whether you made money or not.

Naturally, you can create templates of most of these worksheets—on both a wholesale and retail basis—and simply change the names and amounts for each customer. You don't have to create a new worksheet for each quotation you provide. You can use this same idea to make alternate estimate sheets, to show your customers the available options they might consider, and the effect on the bottom line price if they buy one set of options but not another, get the deluxe unit rather than the standard model, and so on. This gives you a chance to increase the total volume of each sale, but with minimal work on your part. Once the template is designed, you just plug in the name and numbers for your current prospect and your Macintosh will do the rest. Let's now move into more detail on estimating from a graphics standpoint.

## Bids by Quantity

Although it's vital to examine the estimates you make in terms of how they relate to the sales those estimates produce, it's often equally helpful to look at the raw number of bids you write from a couple of directions.

Figure 5-2 is a column chart that plots a 12-month picture of the number of quotations our fictitious business created. While this illustration doesn't tell us anything about the quality of those bids (How many did we sell? What was their volume?), we can see that the general line is rising—a good sign. It's important to realize that many businesses derive the bulk of their sales from the estimates they put out. If we study the right information, we can get a pretty accurate idea of what our upcoming sales will be, based on the bids we write during the current period. Let's take this example a step further and have our plotting program add a trend line.

Figure 5-3 illustrates the same information we just examined and adds a trend line to show the direction of the data. It's a good picture, and the kind we'd hope to see when we examine our own information.

NUMBER OF ESTIMATES PRESENTED, LAST 12
MONTHS

FIGURE 5-2

NUMBER OF ESTIMATES PRESENTED, LAST 12
MONTHS

FIGURE 5-3

# Bids and Sales

Another useful way to look at the total number of bids you produce is to link them to the number of sales you make from those estimates. If, during one month, you write 30 quotations and eventually sell 15 jobs, you had a 50 percent success rate for that particular group of bids. You can have your spreadsheet do the calculations for you and ask your graphics package to keep a running visual total of your sales success.

Figure 5-4 covers the data for our fictional business over a three-year period, and plots the percentage of quotations that eventually turned into sold jobs. The range our business shows on this historical basis appears to be between about 60 percent and 70 percent—that's the number of jobs we sold out of each 100 quotations we presented. It's interesting to note that at no time during this period did we do better than 80 percent. Why not? That would be a good goal to work toward. It's also interesting that we never hit the 50 percent mark, either, so we always (during this time) sold more than half of the estimates we created.

The logical next step is to have our plotting program add a trend line to this information, to see if our overall percentage is rising or falling.

Figure 5-5 narrows the scale of our graph considerably and plots the

THE PERCENTAGE OF BIDS SOLD, FOR THE LAST 36 MONTHS

**FIGURE 5-4**

FIGURE 5-5

information we just examined within a 40 to 75 percent range, along with a trend line. The trend line, as noted on the chart, is based on 36 months of information.

While it's nothing to shout about, the general trend of the percentage of bids we're selling is on the upswing, growing slightly as time goes along. It's not a really rapid rise, but this steady growth is probably preferable and indicates that we're on the right track, that our sales methods are working.

With this much information, the direction of the trend line should be accurate. Again, this is exactly the picture we'd want to see when we examine our actual data.

## Bidding Dollars

Although a close examination of the number of estimates we make is good, and is better when we relate that information to the number of sales it produces, it's equally useful to take the same basic information and look at it from a dollar standpoint. You can have your spreadsheet program take the number of bids you make during a specific period and divide it into the total bid *value*. This will tell you the average amount for each estimate you make. Once you have that information and plot it over a period of time, you'll know if your quotations are just rising in terms of quantity—the raw number of bids you type up and present—or if they're also increasing in dollar value.

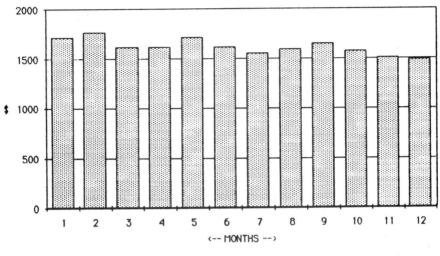

AVERAGE BID AMOUNT, OVER THE LATEST 12
MONTHS

FIGURE 5-6

Generally, of course, the more quotations you make, the more jobs you'll sell. Likewise, the greater the value of those bids, the greater your sales volume will be.

Figure 5-6 takes the number of quotations our business made over the latest 12 months and divides that figure into the total dollar value those bids represent. Since we saw in earlier graphs the total number of bids we presented were on the increase, we should expect that their average value might decrease. Naturally, we'd hope for a rise in value along with a rise in quantity, but it would be unusual if that really happened.

There are two things you'll notice in Figure 5-6. The first is that our average quotation ranges between $1500 and $2000. Second, the recent drop in value is obvious, even without a trend line. We get a feeling from the entire graph that the dollar value is decreasing. However, to really understand what's going on between our bids and the sales they produce, we need to back up a bit historically and examine things from a longer viewpoint.

Figure 5-7 plots the amounts, on a monthly basis, of the average dollar value for estimates our fictitious company presented to its customers, over a 36-month period.

As we saw when we examined just the most recent 12 month's worth of information, the historical picture we see in Figure 5-7 finds our average bid running in the same $1500—$2000 range. We can also see the latest drop to the $1500 level, and we might be a bit comforted to note that two other times

AVERAGE BID VALUE, OVER THE LAST 36 MONTHS

**FIGURE 5-7**

in the past, our average estimate value dropped to the same low. Even without the benefit of a trend line, though, the general information seems to be heading downward; let's add a trend line and see what it tells us.

We've tightened up the scale a bit in Figure 5-8 to eliminate the zero line, so, as we know, the picture of our data is a bit changed, and the line that charts our average bid volume rises and falls much more sharply. However, the process serves its purpose as we see the trend line that represents the value of our average bid has been dropping for some time, and at an alarming rate.

The information Figure 5-8 gives us may not be disturbing; we in fact might want our business to work with lower volume jobs, and, at the same time, hope to sell more of them. The important thing is not whether the trend line rises or falls, but that it heads in the direction you feel is right for your own business. In this case, Figure 5-8 tells the owner that the average dollar value of each estimate the company makes is dropping, and fast. That's going to mean a drop in sales volume, unless the business can convert a greater percentage of its bids into sales.

Any look at the bids you make in relation to the sales they produce should be done on a percentage basis, as shown in Figure 5-9.

Figure 5-9 lets the spreadsheet program where we store our sales and bid information calculate the percentage of bid volume that actually turned into sales. For example, during one particular month you might present es-

AVERAGE BID VALUE, OVER THE LAST 36 MONTHS

NOTE: NO ZERO LINE ON THIS GRAPH

TREND LINE

ACTUAL DATA

<-- MONTHS -->

FIGURE 5-8

SALES AS A PERCENTAGE OF TOTAL BID VOLUME,
OVER THE LAST 48 MONTHS

<-- MONTHS -->

FIGURE 5-9

timates to potential customers with a total value of $50,000. If you eventually closed $40,000 worth of sales from these estimates, this means you sold at an 80 percent rate. You calculate this by dividing what you sold (40,-000) by the total sales volume you estimated (50,000), which comes out to 80 percent.

This is an interesting long-range look at things, and the mathematics involved are simple. You just divide your sales volume by your bid volume, for each monthly figure.

The basic information we can glean from this chart is that we generally get more than 75 percent of the total we bid on, in the form of sales volume. Also, there are months where we get more than 100 percent of our bid volume, which is to be expected—we'll always get work based on bids we created months ago, so there will be times when the total adds up to more than the potential volume we've bid on during one monthly period.

Another way to look at this data would be to plot the percentage of sales our business records based on how old the quotations are: we get X percent during the month the bid was made, for example, less than one month ago; Y percent when the bid is between 30 and 60 days old; and so on. Let's add a trend line to the data in Figure 5-9 and see how our sales staff is doing.

Figure 5-10 plots the same 48 months of information we just examined, with the addition of a trend line. The interesting thing about all this is that once you determine roughly what percentage of your bid volume you normally record as sales and get some idea of the time frame involved between when you present a quotation and when the sale is actually recorded, you

SALES AS A PERCENTAGE OF TOTAL BID VOLUME, OVER THE LAST 48 MONTHS, WITH A TREND LINE

FIGURE 5-10

can make an accurate prediction of what's going to happen to your business. For instance, you might find—with a study of your own bid and sales volume information—that you generally sell about 75 percent of your bid volume, with a 30-day lag time. If you write $50,000 worth of quotations in March, you can estimate that April's sales will come in at about 75 percent of that—about $37,500. Once you chart this information for a long enough period to have an accurate base, you can total up the bids you made during the current month and just about know what your sales volume will be next month.

That gives you all kinds of lead time to plan what you'll need in the way of more people, extra cash, material for installations and inventory, and so on.

Figure 5-10 also tells us a comforting story about our salespeople (even if the total sales staff is just you): it's doing a good job. Although we couldn't tell from the actual data (as shown in Figure 5-9), the trend line on this picture shows a nice rise; we're recording more and more of our bid volume as sales.

It's also gratifying to note that we don't even need to reduce the scale for this graph to see how the trend line is rising or falling—we can see that our sales performance is improving even with the wide scale we have here.

# Warranty Problems

Whatever we sell, we have to provide some guarantee on it, often on both the material itself and on the labor it might take to repair the product during its warranty period.

It's important to realize that all warranty costs we might incur may not be a total loss. Instead, by taking the best possible care of our customers, we improve our chances for future business from these same people. So it pays any company to go out of its way to ensure that its customers are happy, even if that means it has to absorb in-warranty expenses that it really shouldn't have to.

For instance, you might provide first-year in-home service for the products you sell. Any parts are probably guaranteed by the manufacturer, so during the warranty period you have to pay the freight to get the new parts to your store, the freight to send the bad items back to your supplier, and pay your cost labor (and its fringe benefits) to handle any warranty problems.

This data is fairly easy to track. If you don't have much warranty repair, you can even keep it on a legal pad, with columns for the information. A larger business might want to use a simple file-handling system on its Macintosh to track the costs of the information along with other data—what items cause the most problems, what product groups have the greatest warranty expense totals, and so on. When your billing people find a warranty situation, the work order is voided (since you won't send a bill to your customer), and the data is transferred to your record keeping system.

The important thing here is to track all the information. Often, labor is so obvious that we keep a record of its cost, but we also need to list freight, phone call expenses, the cost of equipment we loan to our customer while we're waiting for parts, as well as any other costs that might be involved. Once we have an accurate picture of our warranty expenses, we can start to examine them with an eye not just to understanding where the dollars went, but to make an attempt to lower their total.

The first comparison to make is to relate your total warranty costs to your sales volume. Each business will vary, of course, but once you track this data over a period of time, you'll have a good idea what yours should average. In this case, Figure 5-11 plots a nine-month picture of the warranty costs as a percentage of sales for our fictional company. As always, we need some supporting information to determine how things look on a long-term basis, but at least for the nine months shown in Figure 5-11, we know our warranty costs ran about 2 percent of our gross sales volume.

If we know—from enough study of our warranty information—that 2 percent of our sales is about what we should expect to spend on warranty costs, then this example tells us we may have an upcoming problem, as our

FIGURE 5-11

warranty costs jumped a bit over the past four months and currently are running away from the 2 percent level.

To help put things into perspective, if the owner of our fictional business examined these nine months of information and knew that 2 percent of sales was the maximum he or she should spend for warranty repairs, the logical thing would be to do something to correct the problem. Perhaps one brand of equipment is causing the most difficulty; let's stop selling it. Perhaps one grade of equipment *inside* of a brand we handle is where most of the problems start; let's find out where and at least not continue to sell those specific products.

Once we found ourselves with a terrific brand of equipment, except for their line of heat pumps. Unknown to us (and probably most others in the dealer network), these particular units were not built by the company we purchased them from. Instead, they had another manufacturer build this line of units for them, put their name tags on, and sold them as their own equipment. Once we discovered where all our problems were coming from, we stopped selling that specific unit.

Figure 5-12 illustrates what the warranty repair cost graph should look like, once the business owner found he or she had a problem and took the proper measures to correct things. By the end of the 12 months shown, warranty costs as a percentage of sales were lower than the 2 percent mark. As always, with all graphs, these were created so the scale marks will help us

WARRANTY COSTS AS A PERCENTAGE OF SALES

**FIGURE 5-12**

understand the information. In these examples, 2 percent was the (fictional) figure the business wanted to keep its warranty repair costs under. So, we asked our plotting program to scale with that 2 percent figure in mind, so it would show up as a grid line of the chart.

## Equipment Warranty

Most major brands of equipment, whether they are in our line (furnaces, air conditioners) or another (washers and dryers, appliances, electrical equipment, and so on) have a factory warranty. As anyone in business knows, some brands are better than others in how they support their dealers when it comes to first year (or even first month) warranty repair labor. Some manufacturers don't say a word when you charge them for sending a service technician out to fix a factory defect, while others complain and may only reluctantly agree to pay part of your bill to them. What this means is that you'll end up absorbing some of the warranty repair labor the factory should reimburse you for.

A logical thing to examine, then, is your cost of repair for each brand of equipment you handle. It might be worthwhile to use the examination for total warranty costs (including those the manufacturer pays for), but it's

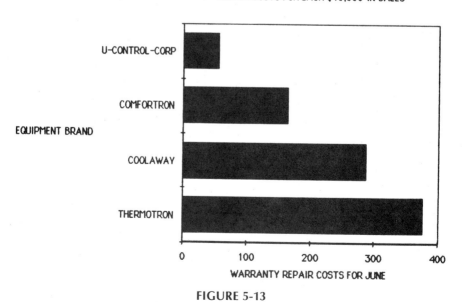

FIGURE 5-13

more meaningful if you work only with the dollars that come out of your pocket.

Figure 5-13 uses a bar chart to show the warranty repair costs for each of the four brands of equipment our fictional business handled during the month of June. The figures shown, as noted on the graph, are not raw dollar amounts. Doing that might distort our graph, because if we sell twice as much of one brand than we do another, we should expect to have double the in-warranty costs for the first than we do the second.

In this case, the dollar amounts shown are the warranty costs our business had to put out for every $10,000 in sales for each brand of equipment. That's an easy calculation to make and puts each brand on the same basis, so our comparison is accurate. The equipment we bought from U-Control-Corporation performed well during June. The Thermotron equipment, on the other hand, cost us almost seven times as much for in-warranty repair. Why? Was it because we had many more problems with Thermotron, or because the U-Control-Corporation people paid for nearly all the calls we had to make to repair factory defects? Whatever the case, we obviously need some supporting information to know if we have a problem or not, and that data can be as simple as creating this chart over a period of time. If Thermotron is consistent in its warranty costs, we'd better do something to change the situation (sell less of it, add more when we bid to use it on a job, fight with the factory for the money they should pay, etc.). If, over a period of time, U-Control equipment is consistently best, maybe we should start to use more of it. If this data holds true over a few years, it's obvious when we specify U-Control material that we'll have lower costs. Why not use more U-Control equipment, so we can bid a little lower and perhaps sell a bit more?

# People Problems

We've looked at warranty repair costs in the context of total sales and in light of the equipment we handle, but it's also important to take a look at your people and how they're performing. Since this section is about warranty repair work, the people who'll do it for you are your service technicians, so we'll examine their performance.

From a labor standpoint, it's worthwhile to calculate the total sales each service technician produces, as well as his total cost (including any fringe benefits and callbacks for mistakes he made). From a warranty viewpoint, it's helpful to simply track the callback rate per service technician. You don't want to look at the raw data, as one service technician might make more calls over the period under study than his or her counterparts do. So, like the warranty repair costs we looked at for each brand of equipment our fictional business sold, let's break down the number of callbacks each of our service people had, for every 50 calls they made during June.

It's important to keep track of each callback based on the original person on the job. Often, a different service technician will go back to correct the problem, but the cost of the callback must be charged to the technician who originally went to the customer's home.

It's also interesting to note that this information (as contrasted to simply a study of the dollars a service person produces or costs) gives us a feeling for how well our people are doing from a customer satisfaction standpoint. The more callbacks, the more dissatisfied customers we've got out there. For the one-month example shown in Figure 5-14, Al obviously did very well, while Bill and Bob show rates three times as high. Why? A bar chart is used for this comparison, as we want to see how each person is doing in relation to his or her peers. It also gives us a good feeling for the quantitative difference among the technicians shown.

As always, more information over a longer period of time is needed before you decide to give Al a raise or let Bob and Bill go, but the basic concept is what we want to illustrate here. With any of these studies you can accumulate the data and add a trend line to a long-range group of information, to see which direction you've been heading and project what you can expect the future to bring. If you create this bar chart comparison each month for

FIGURE 5-14

your service technicians, you'll soon know who has the best (and worst) callback rate. This particular method of examination doesn't include the dollar cost of these callbacks. Not to ruin the reputation we just gave Al, but his callback problems might be terribly costly, so it's important to look at that, too. The ideal way is to examine your people's data jointly—on a dollar basis, and as their callback rate. The dollars tell you just what you've spent, while the callback rate shows you how satisfied your customers are.

# Truck Expenses

As anyone who operates even a single truck knows, there's nothing that runs up total costs more than his vehicles. They're often a necessary part of your work, whether it's just for delivery or sales, or whether your people work out of them for the service and/or installation your company does. One of the best ways to keep track of truck expenses is simply to examine them on a cost-per-mile basis. It's nice (and often a good idea) to track each vehicle's mileage, or how many service calls it makes on the average, but the bottom line is still total cost—those dollars you put out every month for gas and tires and insurance.

Figure 5-15 is a worksheet that calculates the average cost per mile for

| | |
|---|---|
| Truck cost information as of................ | Sept. 30th |
| Truck # 7, 1/2 ton Chevy pickup (Blue) | |
| Total maintenance costs this year to date....... | $957.29 |
| Total gas costs this year to date.............. | $1,957.01 |
| Insurance costs this year to date............. | $159.80 |
| Other costs this year to date................. | $0.00 |
| Total costs this year to date................. | $3,074.10 |
| Starting Miles.............................. | 65,654 |
| Ending miles............................... | 93,838 |
| Miles driven this year so far | 28,184 |
| Current cost per mile....................... | $0.11 |
| Average cost per mile for all trucks.......... | $0.16 |

**FIGURE 5-15**

this particular truck. By entering the year-to-date costs and the starting and ending mile figures, the program figures out the net cost per mile for this truck. It also has a spot—the last line—to indicate what your average vehicle costs per mile.

At a glance, the business owner can see that this truck is better, at least for the period under study, than the average cost per mile for all the other vehicles the business owns. Let's take things one step further and examine a summary of this information over the latest nine months.

While Figure 5-16 shows the kind of picture we'd hope to see—a steadily decreasing per-mile cost—it's presented here as something of a reverse example. The business owner who owns this truck would probably be very pleased with this image, and perhaps he or she should be. But like all financial information, any aberration should be examined with care. In this case, you'd want to ask *why* the per-mile cost for this vehicle is going down. Perhaps you just paid for the truck and so removed the comprehensive insurance coverage you were required to have because you'd financed it (so your insurance cost is lower). But maybe whoever takes care of this vehicle is neglecting the maintenance on it. Perhaps he or she is driving on bald tires. The worksheet (Figure 5-15) doesn't specify what maintenance or other costs are for our fictitious company—what would they be in your business?

AVERAGE COST PER MILE, TRUCK 7

FIGURE 5-16

The point is, *any* major expense—and vehicles are certainly that—needs to be looked at once in a while, just to see if any of its figures are out of line from what they've been in the past.

## Summing Up

Since many of us work on a bid basis, where we have to provide estimates to potential customers, the quantity of our sales volume is directly related to the number and potential sales value of the estimates we present. Because sales volume depends on bid volume, that's an important comparison to make. It's often equally valuable to look at the sheer quantity of bids we present, especially in relation to the number of jobs those quotations produce. Are we creating more or fewer bids than we did last year for the same period? How's our sales success? At what rate are we selling our jobs? Is the trend line up or down for this information? In other words, is our selling getting better or worse?

We also need to know the average value of the estimates we present, as the volume of sales we'll create from those quotations will have a direct relationship to it. Is the trend of this information—the potential dollar value of our average estimate—going up or down? Why? Let's look at a trend line based on this information and project what our average volume will be a few months from now. Does it look like it's heading where we'd like it to be?

Warranty repair costs are a real headache for many businesses. If they contribute substantially to your cost of doing business, then it's worthwhile to track them, starting with a look at their total as a percentage of your sales. Once you know, historically, how much you should spend on warranty repair labor, you'll be able to see immediately when you begin to have a problem in this area. It's also helpful to examine the trend of warranty repair costs, which gives you a feeling for the quality of the equipment you sell.

On the plus side, a good warranty program means happy customers, so you want to strive for a happy medium. You need to make sure you collect for any just claims against the product suppliers you work with, while at the same time making sure your customers are satisfied.

Along the same line, anytime you have labor repair costs, you'll have people problems. Some service technicians are terrific—few callbacks, good profits—while others are just the opposite. Those two are easy to spot; it's the marginal ones that are more difficult to discover, but you can do it if you track their service data and graph it.

Any major expense—we chose truck costs—should be examined from time to time, not with the detail at which you look at your financial statement information, but often enough to see that the figures stay in line.

## Other Ideas

Since any business is constantly *doing* business, it's always a good idea to monitor your work in progress. If you use a spreadsheet on your Macintosh to create cost worksheets, why not use them to evaluate how each job is going?

For example, most businesses operate on a draw basis, where the work is billed as it progresses. Once a job is 25 percent complete, you send your customer an invoice for 25 percent of the total price. This helps keep your cash flowing and is actually easier on the customer because he or she gets to pay in smaller increments.

You can monitor the progress of each job you do by comparing your cost worksheet with the details your people record as they make out their actual materials list, and adding in the labor costs you've incurred to this point in time. If you've billed a job as 50 percent complete and find that your material and labor costs—to date—add up to 60 percent of what your costs are expected to total, you've got a problem. In effect, this gives you a running check against each job's progress, from an actual versus estimated cost standpoint. If you find that you've got a job where the costs are considerably higher than they should be at that point in time, perhaps you can change things before the situation completely collapses and you end up losing money on the whole project.

Every business has hidden expense areas that can add up to a considerable sum, and if we try to find and examine them once in a while, perhaps we'll be able to save some of that money. For example, almost every company spends a good deal of cash on freight and phone calls. These two dissimilar items share a common bond in that they often can be charged directly to a specific job. Whenever you place a special order for a customer, you probably have a long-distance call involved, as well as the freight cost to get the item to your store. Why not try to pass along these costs?

# Cutting Costs for Higher Profits

# 6

While the words *sales* and *gross* and *net profit* are music to the ears of every businessperson, words like *direct labor* and *material costs* are not. They conjure up images of cash spent, wages paid, dollars going out the door. But since they're something we all have to deal with, we'd better be aware of how they work inside our own businesses and have some insight as to what trends to look for that might cause future problems.

Probably the best thing about direct costs is that there usually aren't many of them to worry about—often, we have just labor and materials, with perhaps a bit of freight or outside services thrown in. But for what they lack in numbers they more than overcome in dollar amounts; in any business, direct costs are the second-largest item on your income statement, right after your sales total.

## What Are Direct Costs?

Simply put, direct costs are the dollar totals you can assign directly to the production, delivery, installation, and warranty service costs of what you sell. You test for direct costs by asking if the item *varies* in direct proportion to the number of things produced and sold. The more you sell, the greater total of your direct cost items. If you don't sell anything, you don't have any direct costs.

Generally, things like material and labor are pretty easy to track. *Your* salary is obviously not a direct cost; you'll (probably) take home a check regardless of how much the business sold this past week. However, if there were no sales, you shouldn't have any direct labor or material costs.

There are also some gray areas where you and your accountant might have to dig a little bit to put into their proper places. A salesperson who works for you might receive a salary plus a commission bonus of some sort. If he or she gets paid whether he or she sells anything or not, the salary belongs in the overhead column. If salespersons receive a bonus based on their sales, the standard salary is still an overhead item, but the bonus—since it can be directly tied to sales—is a direct cost amount. Freight on any materials your company buys should show up as a direct cost item; freight on office supplies should not. You can get quite involved here, so most business owners leave the chore of what to put where up to their accountant; the dollar figures you get from yours will almost always have things in their correct place.

## Where to Start

All direct cost totals are shown on your income statement. Direct labor is usually listed just as that, often with any extra payroll tax items shown separately. The materials you used are derived by taking your beginning inventory, adding any purchases you made during the period the statement is for, and then subtracting your current inventory. The figure you arrive at is the amount of material you used for this period. Other direct cost items will also be listed as part of your cost of sales, and can include things like freight, equipment rent (if it can be charged to specific jobs), outside services, and so on.

## The First Picture

Since direct costs should vary in a direct proportion to your sales, the first place to look is at a picture of these two items.

Figure 6-1 charts our fictitious business over a 12-month period. It's pretty obvious that both lines show about the same ups and downs with one apparent oddity: costs seem to lag behind sales about a month. However, this isn't unusual, as often sales are recorded one month while the invoices for at least some of the materials used aren't received and tallied until the following month.

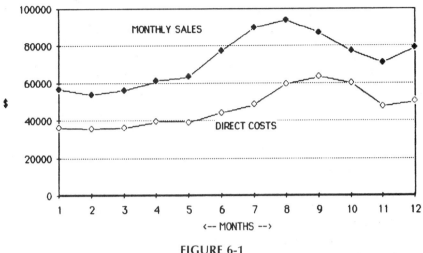

MONTHLY SALES COMPARED TO MONTHLY DIRECT COSTS

**FIGURE 6-1**

While the sales line climbs at a faster rate than the cost figures do, that's to be expected. The dollar totals are greater for sales than they are for costs, because sales are recorded on a *retail* basis, while direct costs are totaled, of course, on a *cost* basis. In all, Figure 6-1 is the picture we should expect to see from a comparison of our sales to our direct costs. Any variation—particularly if the two lines head off in opposite directions—might signal a problem.

## Labor vs. Materials

The next logical thing is to examine direct labor and the cost of materials on the same chart. Each business has its own trends that apply on a historical basis. In many companies, when the cost of direct labor exceeds the cost of the materials used, the business cannot make a profit. For those periods where it spends more on material than it does on labor, the bottom line is black rather than red.

You can find how this relationship works in your own business with an examination of your financial statements. Perhaps you'll end up with figures like those shown in the following table:

| YEAR | COST OF MATERIALS | COST OF LABOR | PROFIT (LOSS) |
|------|-------------------|---------------|---------------|
| 1 | 156,092 | 191,092 | (11,092) |
| 2 | 163,373 | 151,872 | 3,003 |
| 3 | 161,762 | 147,044 | 11,098 |
| 4 | 171,092 | 151,091 | 12,404 |
| 5 | 173,092 | 179,092 | (4,202) |
| 6 | 167,020 | 152,095 | 17,093 |
| 7 | 171,009 | 149,094 | 27,092 |

For every year in this fictional example, when the cost for labor exceeded the cost of the materials used, the business lost money. While no percentage will hold true 100 percent of the time, based on its recent financial statements, *this* business can pretty well figure that when labor costs are higher than material costs, it will lose money.

In your own business, a study of this kind might tell you that when *your* materials cost more than labor, you won't make a profit. Or when labor is 15 percent higher than materials, you have a profit problem. But the answer is in your figures somewhere, and an examination like the one above will help you find the answer as to what's true for you.

This generally is correct on a quarterly or semi-annual basis, too, which gives the business owner who doesn't get a monthly income statement a chance to visually see how he or she is doing.

## One at a Time

Since direct labor and your cost of materials will make up the greatest portion of your direct costs (in some cases, *all* of your costs), it's worthwhile to examine them in a little more detail.

In our own business, we not only discovered that we had to keep labor costs lower than material costs (as outlined above) to make money, we also found that we could only make a profit when those labor costs wcrc 30 percent of sales or lower. Since we have a sales figure every month as well as a total for direct labor costs, it's an easy matter to plot this percentage on a monthly basis.

Figure 6-2 charts the direct labor as a percentage of monthly sales for our fictitious business over the first three quarters of the year. If we assume this business works on a similar basis to our own, it probably made a profit during any month where direct labor totals 30 percent or less of its sales volume. During those months when the labor costs got carried away and rose above that 30 percent line, the business most likely lost money.

This particular chart can also be used for any *other* comparison(s) that you find are important to your business. You might find that you only make

DIRECT LABOR AS A PERCENTAGE OF SALES

FIGURE 6-2

money when materials are less than 35 percent of sales, or when labor and materials *together* are less than 67 percent of your sales total. The percentages are different for every business, of course, but once you get a feel for what they are, you'll find they generally hold true over a period of time. It's also worthwhile every three months to examine these figures on a quarterly basis; the data gives you a different impression than it does when you see it every month.

Figure 6-3 plots a trend line for the direct labor as a percentage of sales for our fictional business. The actual data is also plotted. The disturbing thing about this picture is how the rate of the data is growing—it's going in exactly the direction we don't want it to. While we had an idea from Figure 6-2 that our labor, as a percentage of our total sales, was rising, this illustration confirms it and serves warning that we'd better take some corrective action to lower our labor costs (as a percentage of our sales).

# Zeroing In

Since direct labor costs for this business are volatile and form such a large part of its costs, it's helpful to examine any *associated* costs. For our fictional

FIGURE 6-3

example, we've grouped *all* other costs that are directly concerned with labor and called them payroll taxes.

There are all sorts of things you can classify as payroll taxes, including unemployment taxes at the federal level and that large expense that employers must match what their people contribute: Social Security. In your business, they are anything that *varies* in relationship to your direct labor costs—the more checks you write for payroll, the more these extra taxes add up. Most businesses also have to carry some type of workmen's compensation insurance, in case an employee gets hurt on the job. Others must pay a state unemployment tax. For this example, we've lumped them all together and called them payroll taxes.

Figure 6-4 plots two widely variant figures, but ones that have a direct relationship. Because payroll taxes (in this example) approximate ten percent of the total direct labor costs, it's an easy matter to multiply them by ten. They can then be charted on the same scale as direct labor, and the business owner can get an idea of the *rate of change* between the two lines (if any). You could get much the same impression by using a semilogarithmic chart, although (at least to our minds), this seems a bit clearer.

Figure 6-4 plots the direct labor costs for this business for the first five months of the year, along with its payroll taxes multiplied by ten. For the first three months, the amounts varied at about the same rate. From March to April the gap closed a bit. A little change like this might be attributed to

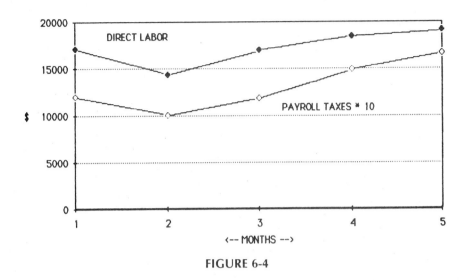

DIRECT LABOR COMPARED TO PAYROLL TAXES
MULTIPLIED BY TEN

**FIGURE 6-4**

part of the payroll being recorded in one period, while the business might have been slow to pay some of the taxes that were due.

However, the movement of the two lines made a marked change in the April–May period; the two lines look like they're on a collision course. While payroll costs flattened out a bit, the taxes *rose*. The business owner who spots something like this needs to discover why there's been a change; perhaps compensation insurance rates went up and payroll taxes as a percentage of costs increased. As always, these two lines are directly related to each other and as such, should rise and fall at the same rates. If they don't, we need to find out the reason.

## Total Costs

Once you add together all your direct costs, it's helpful to compare their total from last year to this. However, since your sales will be more or less than last year's (and so will the dollar value of your direct costs), it's usually more useful to examine the figures as a *percentage* of sales. If you look at them on a percentage basis, it doesn't matter if sales rise or fall; direct costs as a percentage of sales should be about the same. You know what this percentage was last year, and if you made money or not during that time. So, you should

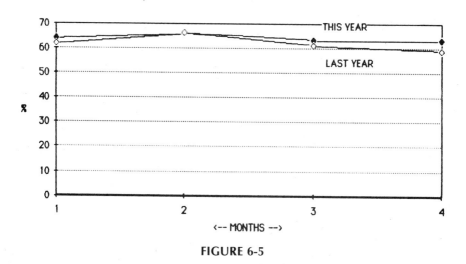

FIGURE 6-5

have some feeling as to how you're doing if direct costs are a higher or lower percentage than they were last year.

Figure 6-5 plots the direct cost percentages over the first four months of the year. We can see an obvious rise in the figures for the current year.

For some reason, the business this year is spending more of its dollars for direct costs, on a percentage basis, than it did last year. Have wholesale prices gone up without a corresponding increase at the retail level? Have the employees slowed down? Did the business put a major labor raise into effect, without incorporating it into its pricing structure? Has some component of direct costs (like freight) taken a big jump?

To get a better idea of the seriousness of this increase, it's a good idea to again expand the graph to get a clearer picture of what the figures are doing. Figure 6-6 eliminates the zero line (as is noted on the graph), and because it's plotted over a narrower scale, we can get a better idea of the *rate of change* of the data.

While January's figures looked about the same on Figure 6-5, the expanded image of Figure 6-6 shows that this year's were definitely higher than last year's totals. We can also see that during the February–April period *last year,* our direct costs as a percentage of sales decreased, while the opposite is true for this year's work. In fact, both Figures 6-5 and 6-6 show the two lines heading off in opposing directions.

This is precisely where business graphics can help us. Once the business owner sees that he has a discrepancy in two similar data sets, he

DIRECT COSTS AS A PERCENTAGE OF SALES,
COMPARING THIS YEAR TO LAST

<-- MONTHS -->

FIGURE 6-6

needs to examine his information to determine its cause. When something as critical as direct costs increase on a percentage of sales basis, any business faces a serious problem.

## Another Way to Look

While they're not useful for everyone's applications, a *stacked bar chart* presents a unique picture and is particularly suited to manufacturing businesses. In effect, this graph lets you combine two or more data sets into one column of information. For our purposes here, where we're examining direct costs, they have their own helpful niche when it comes to taking a look at our costs on a per item basis.

While each business that fabricates things in quantity has a method to track all of the costs that go into their products, it's often difficult to picture where those costs are changing (if they do) over a period of time. Although Figure 6-7 illustrates only two broad categories of expenses, the basic concept is what's important: the use of a stacked bar chart gives us a feel for what's happening to the costs for our fictional business.

As with our other graphs, this one is designed so the grid lines assist us when it comes to understanding the information. Since both labor and materials—the two categories this graph plots—each consume about $15 of cost per item produced, the logical grid line to use scales at $15 increments.

FIGURE 6-7

There's a definite limitation to this type of graph, in that if *both* data sets jump around a lot in terms of their dollar amounts, you can get a good reading for your total costs, but it's impossible to understand each individually. If that's the case, you're better off to graph each component of your product cost on a separate chart. Figure 6-7, however, finds our fictional business with a pretty steady cost-of-material line. With the help of the grid line located at $15, we can see that our material costs remained pretty stable for the eight months charted.

Since the total cost per unit is creeping up, albeit slowly, we know the problem is in our labor area. And in fact, if we kind of let our eyes believe that the $15 grid line is the bottom of the *labor* part of this picture, we can really see the monthly variations in the cost of our labor, on a per unit basis.

Although the stacked bar chart is useful only in certain areas, it's very helpful to the manufacturer who needs to examine not only the total cost of each product the business produces, but also needs to know how each component part is changing.

# Payday Costs

Odd as it may seem, you can pick up almost any accounting book and not find even a mention about *payroll*. Things like cash flow and balance sheet items and net profit are covered, but for some reason, that bane of the businessperson that comes along every Friday is often ignored. Since payroll is such a large part of anyone's total cost picture, we need to examine it in detail.

And *you* know about payroll, don't you? Probably more than the experts, at that, who may never have had to meet a payroll. Whether you sell anything this week or not, whether you collect any cash today or not, whether your bank account on payday morning shows $10 or $10,000, your employees still must be paid, and it's difficult for someone *not* in the position of a business owner to appreciate this fact.

Associated with payroll are any number of problems. The most obvious is the collection of enough cash to cover our payroll checks, but along with this difficulty comes the payroll function itself (keeping track of every penny, creating correct checks) as well as a confusing array of government tax forms to fill out and send money along with.

Thankfully, your Macintosh can help with just about everything, including making a suggestion or two on better cash management so you will have the cash available when you need it (see Chapter 4 on Cash Flow). But payroll often appears to be a dead end from an analysis viewpoint: it must be paid (as must all its associated taxes); there's really no way to *analyze* payroll, other than to track its total; payroll amounts are difficult to relate to other parts of the business; and, it's most often done on a weekly basis while other costs are computed monthly, which makes comparison difficult.

## Payroll Comparisons

However, while payroll certainly doesn't have all the implications and variations the businessperson can find in his or her balance sheet or overhead figures, it does have its own niche and unique ways it can be examined, with an eye to making the act of paying as painless as possible.

Since all cash ultimately comes from sales (even if you borrow or invest money, it still must be repaid with sales revenues), it's the logical place to start your examination of payroll. Generally, your payroll total should rise and fall in proportion to your sales or production volume. This won't be the case if you compare your total payroll to gross sales, because total payroll includes office and perhaps sales salaries. Your overhead wages must be paid whether there are any sales or not.

So while you'll want to track your total labor figure, if you need an accurate estimate of how labor relates to sales you must remove any overhead salaries from its total. You also should compute and *add in* any fringe benefits that apply to this direct labor. Only then will you get an exact summary of your labor costs as they relate to sales. When you've calculated this figure (usually on a monthly basis), it can serve as a means to make a number of helpful comparisons.

## Payroll's Relation to Profit

Payroll has, of course, a definite affect on the bottom line. If we can somehow cut our total payroll, we'll make more money. If our people slow down and payroll costs increase, we'll find less money in the till come the end of the year. Every business has a historical figure for payroll—if labor's percentage stays below X amount, the business will make money. If not, if the payroll total is above X percent, the business will end up in the red.

While it's helpful to compare payroll and labor to other amounts, one of the best comparisons is to the sales figure itself. If you go back through your records, you'll find that for those periods where your labor was less than a certain percentage of sales you made money, and where it ran over that percentage figure, you lost money. The actual percentage will vary, of course, with every business, but in most cases you'll find it's a surprisingly correct number to use.

Once you know that, it's an easy matter to create a line chart like Figure 6-8, which shows payroll as a percentage of gross sales, on a monthly basis.

Figure 6-8 tells the businessperson a number of things. First, for some

FIGURE 6-8

reason the payroll as a percentage of sales took a big jump in May. While it started coming down in September, there was a four-month period where it was considerably higher than it'd been earlier in the year. The sign that it's coming down in September can be viewed as a positive one, perhaps as the direct result of the management's efforts to reduce it to a lower percentage.

Now, if this business's historical average indicated that it made money whenever its payroll averaged less than 40 percent of gross sales, the business owner would feel pretty comfortable. While the percentage started to rise in May and almost got to the breakeven point in August, the drop in September is an encouraging sign.

What if this business only made money when its payroll percentage was 30 percent or below? Early in the year it flirted right on the edge of major problems and jumped off when May arrived, as its payroll as a percentage of sales took a huge leap. Even with the slight drop in September, this business has a real problem because its direct labor percentage is still up around 38 percent. Even the bit of profit it made during the first quarter of the year cannot compensate for the money it has lost since.

It appears that whoever managed this business missed a significant warning back in May and has ignored it ever since. But perhaps that's too harsh a judgment; the owner might not have *known* the relationship between sales and payroll and, sadly, just didn't realize what was happening to the business. Again, that's why we spend the time to dig out the information and chart it—it can act as an early sign of approaching danger.

An obvious way to improve the warning these figures might give you is

TREND LINE BASED ON PAYROLL AS A
PERCENTAGE OF SALES

FIGURE 6-9

to let your plotting program calculate a trend line, based on your own figures. This will give you a sense of which direction those amounts are heading.

Figure 6-9 charts a trend line based on the latest nine months of payroll figures. While this is too short a time span on which to base any major decisions, it at least is a starting point, and tells you that payroll, as a percentage of your total sales, is going in the wrong direction. Since it's based just on recent data, it has the benefit of being current.

## Payroll Pie

Once you have the departmental totals, the first thing most businesspeople will do is to create a sales and profit breakdown so they can see where their profits come from. A pie chart is ideal to display this. While this chapter is on payroll, we can get a helpful comparison if we use the pie chart breakdown of profits alongside a pie chart of payroll costs for the different divisions.

Figure 6-10 is a profit picture for June for each individual department. The percentages listed represent the share each department contributed to the total profit the business as a whole produced. If that profit was $10,000,

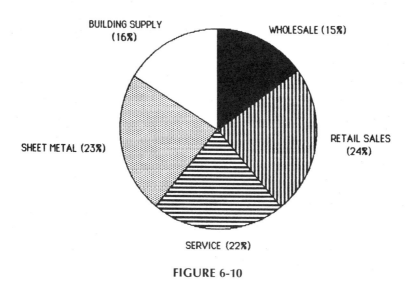

NET PROFIT BY DEPARTMENT, FOR JUNE

**FIGURE 6-10**

then sheet metal provided 23 percent, or $2,300 of the total profit. While this picture is one every business should create and tells a story all its own, it's even more revealing once you put it next to the payroll picture.

Even though pie charts aren't really designed to compare things, when you have two similar pies (two data sets representing the same branch or type of information), they can be used to compare data sets.

Figure 6-11 takes the payroll figures for this business and breaks them down into its five departments, by percentage. Again, this chart can stand alone and tell its own story. Wholesale, as you might expect, gets the smallest share of the payroll dollar. Building supply, which produced the highest dollar volume, also ate up the largest amount of the payroll pie. Again, you'd expect that.

What turns out to be a surprise is that four of the departments produced a profit percentage in excess of the payroll percentage they drained from the business. Each of the four did better than its payroll share. Building supplies, though, while it still produced a profit (which after all, is better than a loss) took 33 percent of the labor dollar but only provided 16 percent of the net profit.

While each of those pie charts can stand on their own and still give us a comparison, we can combine their information in a column chart like Figure 6-12.

PAYROLL BY DEPARTMENT, FOR JUNE

FIGURE 6-11

FIGURE 6-12

Now we can see a direct comparison on a percentage basis of our payroll costs to the profit produced for each department for this particular business. Four of the five parts of our enterprise are making a profit percentage that's *higher* than its percentage of labor costs. This combined column chart makes things even clearer and easier to understand. Unless the figures are normal, there's a definite problem in building supply.

## Where to Look

What this comparison gives you is an indication that something might be wrong out there in building supply. Perhaps it's not; some areas of any business will not produce the profit they should. What we see here might be perfectly proper for this particular department. It might even be a loss leader of sorts—a necessary area to have available for your customers, who you hope will come in to shop in building supply but buy from another department.

However, this same graph might tell the business owner something he or she didn't know before now—there appears to be a problem in the building supply department.

The point is, of course, that without this sort of visual communication, the business owner might not be aware of the situation in building supply and continue along with one major area of his or her business that doesn't make anywhere near what those invested dollars could be producing.

## Inside Payroll

With any payroll the businessperson inherits a number of things; one of the most significant is lumped together and called fringe benefits. These can include anything from vacation pay to insurance to letting someone take home a company vehicle at night. In all cases, they add up to dollars that too often aren't considered when payroll is examined. One of the purposes of any sort of analysis is to get the business owner to consider areas that perhaps haven't been as fully explored as they should be, and your fringe benefit amount is one such cost.

We're no different than anyone else: when we get our paycheck, we look at the take-home pay, the bottom line. Sure, we know all the deductions are listed on the check stub, but who pays much attention to them? It's the same with any fringe benefits you provide to your people. Too soon, they not only don't think of them as a part of their pay, but *expect* to receive this or that and create all sorts of problems when the business tries to cut expenses by eliminating a benefit or two.

## Our Sad Story

A few years ago, for example, we allowed each employee to drive a truck home at night. Our thought was that it would eliminate vandalism to the vehicles and provide a good fringe benefit at the same time. We initially calculated that it would cost us about fifty cents per employee per night, considering gas and wear-and-tear, and so on. We took things a step further and let each employee know that this fringe benefit in effect added X amount to their pay per hour.

Then along came the oil embargo, and a decision by Uncle Sam that he should control and allocate gasoline. The price per gallon skyrocketed, and with it, our monthly gasoline bill. The condition was aggravated when two of our people moved about 20 miles out of town. But, you can't tell an employee where to live, so we didn't think too much about it. By then the practice of taking a truck home at night was expected. The employee drove the company truck, while the spouse got the family car.

The situation rocked along for some time before we created a graph that showed us our monthly gasoline bills in relation to the prior year's amounts. The difference was astonishing! Our monthly cost for gas had just about doubled, and we really didn't realize it. Well, the trucks were soon back on our lot (vandalism or not) and you can imagine the picture our graph of gasoline usage showed then: *it plain dropped.*

## Charting Fringes

The point of all this is to make you aware that fringe benefits have a way of not only entrenching themselves in our everyday work, but of growing while we don't see their increased cost. Part of the problem is that often—in dollar amounts—fringe benefits are considerably smaller than the payroll figures we work with and so have a tendency to be forgotten. As we know, this holds true for both management and labor; graphs that chart fringe benefit costs let both parties know what's going on.

The business owner would look at Figure 6-13 and wonder why the lines were about the same for five months and then made a significant change. Did everyone start to take their trucks home? Were some people given an extra vacation day or two during this period? Did a big raise go into effect? While the raise itself won't directly add to the cost of fringe benefits, many of us have agreements that affect this fringe or that based on the pay

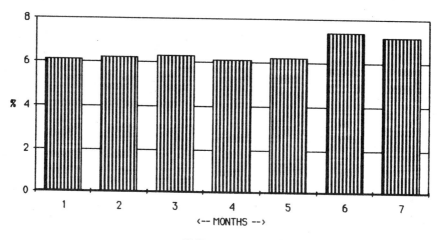

FRINGE BENEFITS AS A PERCENTAGE OF TOTAL PAYROLL

**FIGURE 6-13**

rate. If these benefits are on a percentage basis, a jump in pay might cause a significant difference in your fringe benefit cost. The alert manager will note the change in the monthly figures and set out to discover why it happened.

# Payroll and Cash Problems

As anyone who's had to meet a payroll knows, you must have the cash in hand on payday. With most other bills, a delay of a few days might cost you some interest and a black mark in your credit file, but little else. With payroll, though, your employees expect their checks, and the business must be able to cover them. Because of this, there's a distinct relationship between cash flow and your payroll requirements.

In the chapter on cash flow we saw the results of a situation that happens to many small businesses, and often they're not aware of it. They'll get a terrific spurt in sales, but since the customer payments for those sales *lag* a bit behind the sales themselves, the business owner is put into a cash-poor situation. Payment must often be made before the cash is collected for the work.

This same thing exists for payroll, but on a more definite basis. While material suppliers can often be put off for a time until your anticipated cash arrives, your employees expect their checks on payday. So every week or every two weeks (whenever you pay), the cash in your bank account must cover the cash outgo for payroll and its associated taxes.

The next illustration assumes a few things about some of the amounts we've used as examples. In this case, it's based on the assumption that the costs for this business average half material and half labor. It follows, then, that one-half of its *net cash* will go for payroll. The term *net cash* can be defined as the cash you have left once your overhead amount has been removed.

This is, of course, exactly backwards from the way some business owners look at cash—they think once they've received X amount of dollars, if they pay their material and labor costs, what's left is for overhead and profit. But in real life, the overhead amounts *must* be paid along with materials and labor. The phone company won't wait for its money with any more patience than your material suppliers will.

In effect, this means you need to go through the following simple calculations to determine how much cash you'll have available for payroll, and then with a graph you can quickly see if it'll be enough.

You start with the cash you expect to collect (or did collect) for the period you're working with. In this case, we're doing things on a monthly basis. Let's imagine that your cash inflow for March is $36,307. Let's also suppose the overhead for your business runs 23 percent of sales, so you can expect to spend about 23 percent of your cash (since it's based on sales) on overhead: 23 percent of $36,307 is $8,351.

If you deduct this amount from your available cash, you have:

```
total cash  . . . . . . . . . . . . .   $36,307
− cash for overhead  . . . . . . .   − 8,351
net available cash  . . . . . . . .   $27,956
```

Each business varies, of course, in how it distributes its money for labor and materials, but as noted, let's assume this business has about a fifty-fifty breakdown. Half of the total available of $27,956 could pay labor costs and the other half will be used to pay for material used. This means that $13,978 is the total available during March for payroll purposes. If your net payroll is more than this figure, you have a problem.

Figure 6-14 tracks the payroll amounts and the cash available for payroll for the first eight months of the year. The payroll is the actual monthly payroll cost for our fictitious business, and cash plotted is what's left when you remove 23 percent (for overhead) of the total cash collected and then divide by two—as this business uses 50 percent of its cash for labor and 50 percent for materials.

For the first quarter of the year, there's a bit of a cash surplus in the payroll account. However, when sales start their summer spurt in May, pay-

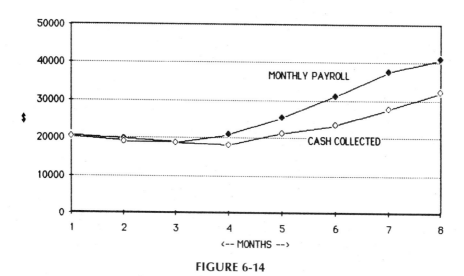

PAYROLL COSTS COMPARED TO CASH COLLECTED

FIGURE 6-14

roll also takes a huge jump. Throughout the summer the situation gets worse as the need for payroll dollars constantly outstrips the available funds.

In effect, since you *must* make payroll every week, dollars are stolen from other areas of the business (material purchases and overhead) to make up the difference. These other areas suffer, of course, because then there aren't enough dollars to handle their cash requirements.

While this example might appear exaggerated, even if we split the total cash in half (and assumed we'd pay the overhead out of leftover funds), this business will *still* be cash-poor from May on.

When the situation reversed itself after the first quarter, the smart businessperson would take some steps to increase the cash available for payroll. Perhaps you can ask for a partial payment when the contract is signed, or work on a draw basis where you can collect something every month based on the percentage of completion. This isn't a *total cash* problem—it will eventually catch up—but a *cash flow* problem.

## Summing Up

Direct costs are also called *variable costs* because they vary in direct relation to what you sell. In most businesses, you can chart sales and direct costs, and they'll rise and fall at the same rate.

One key to any examination of direct costs is to look at their various components in relationship to sales. The knowledgeable businessperson will plot both material and labor costs as a percentage of sales, because these usually combine to make up the largest share of total costs. He or she will also look at any major component of direct costs in relation to the sales total, and also as a percentage of direct costs themselves. Put a profit line on the images to track the movement in relation to the other data.

Since labor was one focus for this study, we also found it instructive to examine it in relation to its associated costs. To simplify things, we lumped all the fringe benefits (taxes, etc.) together and multiplied the total by ten. That let us put this data on the same chart as direct labor. As always, these two lines should rise and fall at the same rate; any aberration is a cause for more investigation.

A helpful graph to create to examine payroll is a line chart that plots sales and direct labor payroll costs. If either line has decided to head off in its own direction for one reason or another, we'll be able to see it and note its rate of change. A minor shift or two probably means little; a major variance between the lines might signal an upcoming major problem.

We also want to examine direct costs as a percentage of sales. As our sales volume goes up or down, so do our direct cost dollars. Direct costs should remain about the same *as a percentage* of sales from year to year. If this percentage goes up, it's a signal to look closer. If we can decrease direct costs as a percentage of sales, we'll add dollars directly into the profit column. Here, too, an expanded chart can be of help, because we can focus on the *rate of change* between the two data sets. In certain instances, particularly if our work involves two major cost items, a stacked bar chart gives us helpful information.

## Other Ideas

Since direct costs form such a huge portion of any business's dollar outlay, it's well worthwhile for the business owner to look at his or her own figures to determine what's important and valid for his or her particular line of work. If your business uses 800 items and very little labor, you'll naturally want to pay more attention to your cost of materials than you do to your labor expense. If freight is a major expense every month, then it pays to chart it, always with an eye to somehow reducing this particular expense.

While we plotted payroll taxes in comparison to direct labor, it's often useful to get a year-to-year picture by charting this year's payroll taxes compared to last year's or a historical long-range look at payroll taxes as a *percentage* of direct labor.

If you're in a manufacturing business, it's a terrific help to plot labor against the number of units you produce each month. Along the same line, chart your material cost along with the units total. You might have to multiply one of these figures (as always, by ten or a hundred) to get them both on the same graph, but they should go right along the same line, shouldn't they?

If gasoline or delivery costs are a major expense, break them out of your direct cost total and plot them compared to last year. Chart them in relation to sales—as you do more sales volume, you can expect your gasoline/delivery costs to increase. But they *should* move right along with sales, and if they don't you'd want to look closer to find out why. You can expand this to total vehicle costs, and compare it to your sales volume. Learn the significant ratios and comparisons for your own business and plot them on a regular basis. If you do, you'll reduce your costs.

# Reducing Your Overhead Burden

The worst thing about overhead is that it's *always there*. Whether we sell anything or not, overhead goes on and on, and often seems to grow with a life of its own. There are a lot of different things that make up our overhead total, often a number of small items that by themselves are insignificant, but together add up to a lot of dollars.

It's important to note, though, that while overhead is usually considered something of an independent item (we have to pay its costs even if sales are poor), it's still related to the sales our business makes. How do you measure and talk about your overhead? As a *percentage of sales*. As our sales increase, we can expect our overhead to take something of a jump at the same time. To create those sales, our overhead will rise as its total grows from its many pieces: advertising, office supplies, phone calls, rent. So while much of our overhead must be paid regardless of our sales picture, it's vital to understand that there's still a relationship between sales and overhead.

Any examination of overhead should concern itself with (1) ways to reduce the overhead amounts, and thus its total, and (2) a look at the direction the various things that make up our overhead costs happen to be moving up or down at a particular point in time.

## Wrong Images

It's important to know in advance that we're never going to get a perfectly accurate overhead picture. For example, telephone costs are commonly included as an overhead item; it's true that our business will (probably) have a phone whether it sells anything during a specific period or not. However, as our sales increase, so will the cost of our long-distance calls. This same line of reasoning lists our utility costs as an overhead expense. In actual practice we may find that our gas (or oil) and electricity costs increase as we do more business, for we might stay open longer, work on Saturdays, and so on.

In truth, too, many small businesses simply charge their entire phone bill to telephone expenses without removing the cost for advertising in the Yellow Pages and charging that to their advertising expense account. Freight is often lumped together and posted into one category, without regard as to whether a particular freight charge was for delivery of a new desk (overhead) or for delivery of the products we sell (direct cost).

## The Choice

While none of this matters a whole lot to the bottom line, it has a tendency to distort some of the pictures we see. Often, too, when we start a detailed examination of a specific area of our business, we'll discover that our expenses aren't being broken down as they should, so we have to make a choice. We need to decide whether we want to *change* the way costs are distributed, to be more accurate, or whether we should leave them the same so we can compare them to other periods. Once we change things, we can no longer make valid comparisons (either numerically or graphically), because the data is based on different criteria.

For instance, for years we've lumped all of our truck costs into a category called *"auto."* Once gas prices started to jump, we wanted to know how much of that auto expense was for gasoline alone. We could also break it down into the money spent on repairs, the cash spent for tires, for maintenance, and so on. In another area, we put all our office expenses into a category called "office." These days, it'd be nice to know exactly what our postage costs are, without including all the other amounts for legal pads, pens, scotch tape, and so on.

Probably the best solution to this problem is that when you find some numbers from your own business that aren't in the form you feel they should be, *leave* the old breakdown as a general heading and create new, more detailed areas to track. For example, you might have a file where you store information for your vehicle costs. Once you start examining it in detail and with graphs, you may find you want more information on your vehicle repair costs. This amount may not be broken out of your *total vehicle* account, so you'd have to go back through old invoices or checks to find its total. An examination of this information might make you want to search further, perhaps to look at your repair costs on a per truck or per mile basis. This doesn't mean you should stop tracking the original vehicle cost account, but rather use your *new* ideas as an adjunct to the main file.

# Overhead Details

Our examination of overhead in this chapter will focus on the general, overall picture of this expense as a whole, and then we'll break things down into a few smaller parts and see how they look. Since there are so many different areas that add to the total overhead amount a business reports, we cannot touch on them all. However, the same approach and methods of examination and types of graphs will work for each section of your own overhead. The idea is to examine overhead as a total cost, and then you'll have to determine which areas of your total overhead are important for you to take a closer look at.

While it's helpful to create a graph that compares overhead to total sales, and perhaps equally as useful to examine a chart that shows this year's overhead compared to last year's, let's take things a little further and see what a picture of nine months of overhead along with a trend line shows us.

Figure 7-1 is a column chart for the first nine months of a year, for our

OVERHEAD FOR 9 MONTHS, WITH TREND LINE

FIGURE 7-1

fictional business's monthly overhead. Overhead includes office salaries, postage, rent, accounting fees, and so on—anything that doesn't directly relate to the creation of sales. The graph also uses the capability of our plotting program to create a trend line, based on the nine periods of data. This line shows the *trend* of our numbers—obviously upward.

At first glance, we see a disturbing picture. None of us like to see our costs increase, and that's especially true in the case of overhead. Anything we can save and not spend on overhead goes directly into the profit column.

Although overhead exists whether our business does any business or not, this overhead figure is rising. Why? Unless we've recently increased our office staff or advertising or some other expense, overhead should remain pretty stable. This picture tells us this one isn't, but it's something of a false reading in that it shows raw overhead data but tells us nothing about sales during the same time.

## Overhead and Sales

If our sales dropped during this period, this business has a definite problem, especially since the overhead trend is up. But once we see a picture like this one, it's important to link the overhead amount to sales, to get a better idea of exactly what's happening inside our business.

A more accurate way to gauge how our overhead is doing is to make a comparison of it to our sales, and plot overhead as a percentage of sales. Figure 7-2 does so, again over a nine-month span.

Let's say that this business, over the years, has determined that it must allow 24 percent of its sales dollar to cover its overhead expenses, and this could be called its *maximum* overhead percentage. Anything higher than this seems to put the business into the red. A lower figure, of course, is a worthwhile goal. In any case, this company must keep its overhead at 24 percent or below, or it'll lose money. This figure is noted on the graph. One of the best things about this sort of picture is that the business owner can instantly *see* where the business is making money and where some adjustments need to be made. During the first few months of the year, its overhead as a percentage of sales rose to where the business was probably in the red every month; something was done to correct this situation, and the line showed a marked drop in the months 5-6 period. Since then, although it's been rising slowly, it's still under the break-even point.

It's also helpful to scale a graph like this as we've done here. The scale from 0 to 32 might seem odd, but since it scales in increments of 8, it allows us to plot the 24 percent break-even line and draw it on our chart.

Any important line should be indicated with a side scale mark and grid

OVERHEAD AS A PERCENT OF SALES

ANYTHING OVER 24% IS TOO HIGH
FOR THIS BUSINESS

<-- MONTHS -->

**FIGURE 7-2**

line. To do this, you often must instruct your plotting program to scale things according to the range that will be of the most help to you. In the example above, once our fictional business determined that its overhead should stay at 24 percent or below as a percentage of its sales, a grid line on any graph that tracks the overhead percentage immediately shows any rise or fall in the data. You can do much the same when your information generally runs within a specific range of figures. If your overhead, as a dollar total, runs between $3,000 and $3,500 per month and you're plotting it, ask your graph to scale in increments of $500. The grid lines will *outline* the average range of your information and make it easier to spot any deviation.

# A Closer Look

Figure 7-3 examines the same information that Figure 7-2 plotted, with the addition of a trend line based on that data. The maximum overhead (24 percent) this business can have and still show a profit is noted on the graph. The scale marks are the same, but note that there is no zero line plotted. While the graph is physically the same size as Figure 7-2, it covers only the data points between 16 percent and 32 percent—a much narrower scale. This gives us a different picture, as the data points will rise and fall at a much more severe angle, since the scale is expanded. What's important

**FIGURE 7-3**

about Figure 7-3 is that the *trend* of our overhead as a percentage of sales is dropping.

What can we figure out about this business so far? For the first nine months of the year under study, its overhead rose in terms of raw figures. It also rose as a percentage of sales for five months, then took a drastic plunge, to back below the break-even point. The last few months see the overhead as a percentage of sales rising slowly. However, the overall *trend* is downward. In effect, this means that sales are rising at a faster rate than overhead is, and when we project our overhead percentage a few months down the road, it's well below what this business can stand and still produce a profit.

## Specifics

Once you have a feel for what total overhead looks like, you need to go inside your business and see where your overhead dollars move. We're going to take a close look at utility costs (at electricity in particular) and office salaries. These same concepts and methods of examination are valid for almost any overhead item. *You* might want to look at phone costs, or office expenses, or what you spend on fuel oil every month. Most overhead costs can be viewed the same way, first with an examination of the general area (auto costs, insurance, and so on) and then a move to a more specific section *within* the general area.

## Utility Costs

Certainly it's valid to create graphs that compare our utility expenses this year with what we spent last year; that at least tells us how we're doing in terms of any cost-cutting measures we've adopted. Once we're a few months into a year, another way to examine our monthly utility bills is to plot their total costs along with a trend line. Often, because the actual amounts rise and fall from period to period, it's hard to discern the trend of the data until we plot a trend line.

Figure 7-4 is a column chart (to give us a good feel for the actual dollars we're spending on costs) for the first six months of the year, for our major utility expenses. If we looked at this data alone, it'd be pretty obvious that it's a growing expense. Once we add a trend line, we can project that this part of our total overhead is growing at a very rapid rate. Unless sales are growing at about this same speed, we need to do something about our utility costs. This should include an attempt to discover which part of their total is increasing (or are all our utility bills?) in an effort to determine *why* as well as *where* the dollars went.

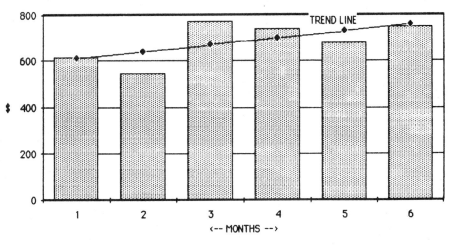

MAJOR UTILITY COSTS WITH TREND LINE

**FIGURE 7-4**

## Utilities and Sales

Probably the first place to look is to see if the rise in utility costs matches a similar increase in sales. Since utility costs aren't anywhere near as large as our sales total, we can multiply them by a factor of 10 (10,100, etc.) so we can plot both data sets on the same chart.

Figure 7-5 plots our monthly sales figures for the first six months of the year, along with our total utility bills multiplied by 100, so they're on the same scale. We can see that while they matched each other in their movements for the first two months of the year, we had a huge jump in utility costs over the next two months. Why? Did we use more gas or electricity or incur more telephone charges? In effect, Figure 7-5 tells us that sales were not the cause for the jump in utility bills.

## A Closer Look

While you might want to examine each amount that makes up your utility expenses, we're going to examine electricity—its use and cost. This may or may not be the area that caused the huge jump in this part of our overhead, or it might be part of a larger problem. The important thing here is to re-

FIGURE 7-5

FIGURE 7-6

member that you can look at any similar area in much the same manner, examine it with the same graphs and ideas.

Figure 7-6 charts the cost of our electricity as a percentage of our total overhead. For the first four months of the half-year period shown, our relative cost for electricity remained about the same—about 20 percent of our total overhead. It took a significant jump in month 5. Have we started to use air conditioning? Was there a rate increase? Were we able to reduce our total overhead while our electric bill remained stable (which would, of course, cause it to rise as a percentage of overhead)? If this were your business, you'd probably know the reason.

If we plot these same figures as a column chart on the same scale, we can get a better idea of their growth rate. Figure 7-7 does this, and adds a trend line to the chart. This doesn't tell us that our monthly electricity bill is the cause for the total rise in our utility expenses, but points a finger at our local utility and/or our own use of this product. Let's look at our usage.

One of the best ways to examine the usage for anything our business consumes, whether it's gallons of gasoline or therms of natural gas, is a historical line graph over a two- or three-year period. Figure 7-8 charts the average number of kilowatt-hours we've used on a *daily* basis, for two full years plus part of the current year. This is calculated by taking your total kilowatt-hour usage figure (for example, 3,300) and dividing it by the days in the month (say, 30). This example means your business used 110 kilowatt-hours per day, on the average, for the month under study. This particular illustration is an excellent one to use if you have any tenants for whom you pay utility costs—it's often hard for them to appreciate total costs (since

FIGURE 7-7

they only rent a part of your building), but easy to see the total used as a daily average.

Both the first 12 months and the second 12 months show a similar picture—a mid-year rise (air conditioning in use?) with a drop in the fall, to a yearly low around January. Year 3, beginning at month five, started out much the same, but for some reason our usage really took a spurt and reached a new historical high in April. Sadly, it remained at that point for the next two months. It seems obvious from a long-range vantage point that

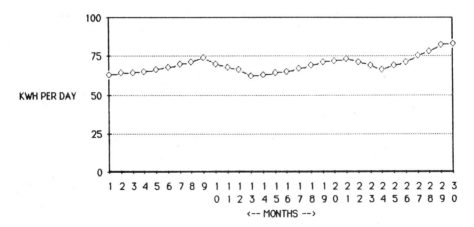

FIGURE 7-8

something drastically changed for our business in terms of our actual kilo-watt-hours of *use*.

The next logical step is to examine how we've used electricity over this same long period of time by adding a trend line to our picture. Figure 7-9 does this.

This particular example shows a trend line, based on 30 months worth of information—long enough to tell us where our business is heading. While no scale numbers are listed on the right side of the graph (and the horizontal grid lines were left off to make the plotted lines easier to see), it's obvious that we started back in January of year 1 with a use of about 60 kwh per day, and by the end of the period the trend line forecasts our daily use at about 76 kwh per day. This 16 kwh difference is a 26 percent rise (16/60) in daily use; if our electricity costs .07 cents per kwh, it will raise our monthly bill by about $34.00.

Perhaps the worst thing about the trend line we see in Figure 7-9 is that the increase has been constant; we should have seen and done something about it before we found ourselves in the middle of the current year with a growing and harder-to-solve problem on our hands.

This example is a good one to show the *seasonality* of certain costs. Just like what we sell (and how much we sell) varies by the time of the year, our costs often do the same. If you have higher electricity costs during the summer (perhaps because of air conditioning), they'll show quickly in a graph. Likewise, you'll be able to spot any change from your historical trend.

**FIGURE 7-9**

## Office Salaries

A major part of anyone's overhead total is that of office salaries. Even if you are your only employee, your salary probably contributes a huge share to your total overhead cost. A logical thing to track plots both your monthly overhead figures and your monthly office salary total. Figure 7-10 charts these two items over a 12-month period. As we know, these 12 months can represent the *last* 12 months, or the latest calendar or fiscal year, whichever is the most helpful to us.

What Figure 7-10 tells us is that our overhead rises and falls at a greater rate than office salaries, although when our overhead total increases, it does so at least in part because we expended more cash in the office salaries area. This is shown by the little bumps in the data for months 7 and 8.

While this comparison is helpful, it's often of more use to have the spreadsheet we use take our data and do the math to compute what our office salaries are as a percentage of our overhead figure.

Figure 7-11 tells us that over the past 12 months, our business has made some significant improvement in what we spent for office salaries, at least in terms of its percentage of our total overhead. Obviously, if all the *other* areas of our overhead took a big jump, this percentage will go down, so the alert businessperson has to look at his or her total overhead, too, as well as this percentage figure.

**FIGURE 7-10**

OFFICE SALARIES AS A PERCENTAGE OF OVERHEAD

**FIGURE 7-11**

Once you're satisfied that your overhead isn't out of control and its growth is causing your office salaries to drop in relation to the total amount, you could be generally satisfied with what Figure 7-11 tells you. While office salaries were high on a percentage basis during the early part of this period, they've been brought down and since May have been in the 30-40 percent range.

## Who's Best?

For a business with more than one location and/or department, it's helpful to chart office salaries as a percentage of your total overhead figure on a department or location basis.

Figure 7-12 shows us the overhead information broken down on a percentage-of-overhead basis for each of the five locations of our fictional business for the month of June.

A bar chart gives us a good feeling for the relationship of each store's overhead in relationship to its peers. The figures illustrated in Figure 7-12 show a wide variation in overhead percentages for each of our locations. The Metro store is considerably higher than any of the others; why? The Moonvalley store has the lowest overhead percent; why?

One way to help discover the answers to these questions is to break

FIGURE 7-12

FIGURE 7-13

things down a bit, to examine a major part of anyone's overhead—office salaries, as shown in Figure 7-13.

If we use a bar chart for this display, it's easy to transmit the information to our office managers. While each store is shown as to how it relates to its peers, no one *individual* is singled out, so our people as a group will accept the data. Those who work in Moonvalley should be pleased with their performance for June, while the Central and Metro locations are running way out of line compared to the three others. Why?

One month's comparison of this sort isn't a long enough time period on which to base any management decisions, of course, but if you create this chart every month (or every quarter), you'll soon *know* which locations or departments spend more on their overhead than they should.

## Payroll Pie

It's also a useful tool if every quarter you create a pie chart to display your salary data, but base it on a different criteria. While the bar chart of Figure 7-13 shows the relationships between the data, a pie chart like Figure 7-14 shows how each item relates to your total office salary expense as a *whole,* on a per-person basis.

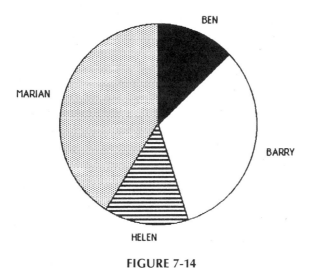

OFFICE SALARIES BY PERSON, FOR THE FIRST SIX
MONTHS OF THE YEAR

**FIGURE 7-14**

Figure 7-14 gives the business owner a feel for who in the office is getting what share of the salary pie, in this case, over the first six months of the year. Do you see any of your people who are making more than they contribute? Less? The point is, with this breakdown, the owner or manager can understand the figures more effectively.

# Advertising and Sales

The only reason to spend any money on advertising is to create more sales. A lot depends, obviously, on the business you own as to what sort of advertising makes sense. If you get a lot of work over the telephone, the Yellow Pages might be vital to your success. Perhaps just some *institutional* advertising in your local paper is all you need. A lot of businesses run weekly or monthly specials and/or coupons to promote sales for one product or another.

If advertising does create sales for your business, it seems logical that you ought to be able to plot that relationship, always with an eye to determining *when* your advertising is effective as well as *what type* of advertising works for you.

In most cases, the advertising you do today won't bring people into your store tomorrow. There's almost always a time lag between when an ad appears and when you feel its effect on your business. This period varies by the type of advertisement as well as where you place the ad. This book isn't the place to discuss what sort of advertising is best for any specific purpose; rather, we simply want to give you some tools to help discover what works for you, and in what time frame you might expect some response to the ads you do run.

Because of the time lag involved between when a prospect sees your ad and when they respond to it, in order to chart the effectiveness of your ad budget you almost always have to move your advertising information forward into the future just a little. Then, for example, you can plot March's advertising at the same point as April's sales. That gives you a one-month period between the time the ad ran and when you recorded sales based on that ad. You might also want to move your advertising two (or even more) months ahead in time; your business is different from others in terms of how long it takes your prospects to respond to your advertising.

Once you find a correlation, though, you can measure future advertising against this norm, which in turn lets you know how your current advertising is working. Perhaps you discover that historically your business increases its sales roughly two months after advertising appears. Let's say you recently ran a major ad campaign and your business volume *decreased*. Since you know there should be about a 60-day period between when an ad runs and when it affects your sales, you'll know the first place to look is at the ads you ran two months ago. Weren't they effective? Where did they run? Did you change your ads or the media or the general approach? Since you expected those ads that appeared 60 days ago to create sales during the current month, if your sales decrease, you probably can blame it on the ads and/or where they ran.

## Converting the Numbers

Because your sales dollars are much higher than those you spend on advertising, an adjustment must be made in the figures so they'll fit on the same chart. As we've done in other cases, you can often multiply the smaller figure by ten or one hundred, to get it into the range of the larger amount. That lets you examine and *see* both data lines and how they move. But perhaps a more conventional way is to translate your advertising dollars into a percentage of your total sales. If you examine this over a long period of time, you get a good feel for what the percentages should look like.

Figure 7-15 covers a 30-month period in the life of our fictional business, plotting the advertising costs it incurred as a percentage of its total sales volume. It's obvious that we recently experienced a breakthrough in the percentages of our sales that we spend for advertising—our historical av-

ADVERTISING AS A PERCENTAGE OF SALES

**FIGURE 7-15**

erage runs between 2 and 3 percent of sales, and over the last few months we've started to spend considerably more. There's nothing wrong with an increase of this kind, and in fact it might be something we intended to happen in an effort to create more sales. This graph is simply a signal that our pattern has changed, and it only makes sense to find out why. What perhaps is the most revealing image we glean here is that at two other times our business flirted with a higher than 3 percent figure—back around month 9 and again around month 22. But each time—whatever the cause—we dropped this percentage back down. Recently, though, the reverse has happened, and the situation appears to be on a continual upward line. This recent aberration may not be cause for alarm, but certainly should prompt you to find out *why* your ad budget as a percentage of your sales is rising, and to determine if you want it to continue to do so.

## Advertising Pie

Any business should be able to measure—in some way—the success of its advertising. Large corporations have an advantage along this line: they can afford major marketing studies and reliable testing. The small businessperson doesn't have the cash to fund such complex research, but still has perhaps the best method of all: a simple question of each customer.

You wouldn't be offended if the salesperson you bought your last car

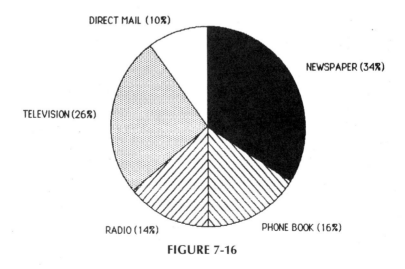

ADVERTISING BY MEDIA – FIRST SIX MONTHS

**FIGURE 7-16**

from asked you why you came into his place of business. Or if the plumber you called to fix that leak asked why you called his company. You can do the same thing, and if you don't want to ask on a person-to-person basis, you can simply print up some postcards and send them along with your invoices. Let your customers tell you why they called you.

Figure 7-16 details the advertising expenses for our business for the first six months of the year. A pie chart is ideal to plot an example like this, as it gives us a feeling for where our dollars went in relation to all the money we spent on advertising.

There's no way to know if this particular ad mix is right or wrong without some associated data. That's why you need to take your customer survey, to find out as best you can which ads are working and which aren't pulling their weight.

Figure 7-17 shows the results of a mini-survey, and when it's examined at the same time as Figure 7-16 is, tells us exactly what's effective (and what's not) for our advertising. Note this graph is called "sales by media," and means just that—the sales *volume* was tallied up, based on what our customers reported to us, and converted into percentages of the whole amount. Again, we use a pie chart to get a feeling for how each individual total relates to the whole picture.

We can visually see that our newspaper ads produce more on a percentage basis than we spent on the ads themselves. The phone book's Yellow Pages didn't do so well during this period, and the dollars we spent on radio

SALES BY MEDIA, PER CUSTOMER SURVEY

DIRECT MAIL (6%)

NEWSPAPER (40%)

TELEVISION (34%)

RADIO (10%)

PHONE BOOK (10%)

**FIGURE 7-17**

provided about the same (percentage-wise) as the percentage of our advertising budget we spent there. Television is the big surprise—we spent 26 percent of our advertising dollar for television ads, but it produced 34 percent of our sales. Direct mail didn't work.

What conclusions can we draw from this? While we don't want to eliminate the poor performers out of hand, we need to examine them in more detail. For instance, perhaps direct mail did so poorly because of the advertising literature we sent. Or because of the mailing list we pulled prospective names from. Perhaps television did so well because of the *times* the ads ran, or because of the quality and focus of the ads themselves.

There are obviously all sorts of variables, and it might seem impossible to make a decision based on this set of data. That's true. However, it's a starting point, a place that gives you something of a benchmark for the future. It also motivates you to change the direct mail prospect list or whatever advertising information you're sending out. When you run the same kind of test six months from now and produce the same set of graphs, what if they tell you exactly the same thing? *Then* it's probably time to eliminate direct mail and put the money you were spending there into television. The whole idea of all this, of course, is to put your advertising dollars where they're the most productive. Business graphics can help you see exactly where that is.

## Sales and Overhead

We're going to end the discussion with overhead right where we started—with a note on how overhead relates to sales. Did you ever wonder why the more successful you are, the harder it seems to make money? The more you cut costs and lower your overhead, the more difficult it seems to be to stay in the black? There's a paradox in business that involves both our sales and our overhead totals.

Most of the time when we think about sales and overhead, we automatically divide the overhead total by the sales amount, and so get a percentage figure. $400,000 in sales with $100,000 in overhead means we perform this equation: 100,000/400,000, which gives us a 25 percent figure—overhead is 25 percent of our total sales. But the same line of thinking runs both ways. If we divide our sales volume by our overhead figure (400,000/100,000), we come out with $4. This is the amount of sales we have to make to justify a $1 increase in our overhead total, if we want to keep our overhead *as a percentage of sales* at its new, lower level.

If we want to give our office staff (whose salary is included in our overhead total) a raise of $10,000 per year, we'd have to increase sales by $40,-000 *just to break even*. This is because of the 4-1 ratio this business has now (an overhead of 25 percent means the overhead dollars will divide into the sales total 4 times). To keep its overhead at the *current* percentage level, this business must sell $4 for every $1 it adds to its overhead total. If we want to buy a new truck that really won't increase our operating efficiency, and this year's share of the payments will run $5,000, we'll have to sell *four times* that amount—$20,000— just to break even.

All of this assumes that same 4-1 ratio, based on sales of $400,000 and overhead of $100,000. But let's say you really work at reducing your overhead and drop it from $100,000 to $80,000. Your overhead as a percentage of sales goes from 25 to 20 percent, a drop any businessperson would be pleased with. But the reverse figure moves from 4-1 to 5-1 (now you divide your sales of $400,000 by your new overhead of $80,000). Now to justify a $1 increase in overhead, you have to somehow raise sales by $5.

Therein lies the paradox: the more successful you are at reducing overhead also makes the basic problem a bit tougher to cope with. It's something not enough businesspeople are aware of and can be a crucial factor when we have to decide whether to buy this or that, approve a raise for one employee or another, and so on.

Figure 7-18 covers one year plus the first two quarters of the following year. For most of year 1 and the first quarter of year 2, our reverse overhead figure ran in the $3.75-$4 range. We knew that if we wanted to buy something, we'd have to raise sales by $4 just to maintain our current profit percentage. Naturally, if what we bought increased our productivity and sales jumped *more* than this amount, it would be a good investment.

SALES DIVIDED BY OVERHEAD

(NOTE: THIS IS QUARTERLY DATA)

<-- QUARTERS -->

FIGURE 7-18

The second quarter of year 2, however, finds us with a lowering overhead and/or rising sales figure, which causes a major jump in our reverse
overhead amount. Now, we see that any increase in overhead will require a
4.75-1 rise in sales; each dollar we raise in overhead must have a corresponding $4.75 increase in sales, or we'll head toward the red end of the
profit picture.

There's obviously nothing wrong with trying to reduce overhead; in
fact, it's a major goal of any business. But it's equally important to know that
as we're successful in lowering our overhead total, we also make it more difficult for our business to stay profitable. Any *increase* in overhead must be
matched with a higher rise in sales, if we want to stay at the lower overhead
percentage. It's a paradox we have to deal with, and if we plot it on a regular
basis, we'll be able to see the exact figure as well as the trend of our numbers. We'll be able to make more reliable decisions.

## Summing Up

Overhead lives in every business and while much of its costs are fixed,
others vary at least in some respects as to sales. As our sales increase, we can
expect overhead to also take a jump. There are ways to examine different
overhead areas and at the same time take a concentrated look at overhead as
it relates to sales. We not only need to know what our overhead percentage
is, but also what its trend line tells us. We need to look hard at utility costs
(and at any part of them that contributes to the total cost). Other expenses
of this sort can be examined in much the same way. We want to examine
things like this on the basis of their historical trend and a forecast based on
their long-term performance.

Office salaries often form a major part of anyone's expenses and so
must be examined from the inside out, including making charts of our people individually, to gauge if someone is over- or underpaid. Office salaries—
since they are much of anyone's overhead—also can be examined on the
basis of department and/or location. Often, we'll find that the store with the
highest overhead percentage can blame much of that on having the highest
salaries for its people. There's a graphic way to explain this to our people,
without pointing at any one person in particular.

Advertising is another expense most of us have, and we need to take a
close look at it. Where is our advertising working? Where are we spending
cash for little return? Should we do more advertising? How can we find out?
These are all areas where business graphics can help.

Finally, the relationship between sales and overhead cuts both ways,
and we can gain knowledge about what's happening inside our business by
dividing one into the other from both directions. There's a paradox not all

businesspeople understand, yet it's one that holds true for all businesses: the more successful we are, the more difficult it is to make money—all because we lowered our overhead. We need not only to discover, but to chart exactly how much we have to increase sales for every dollar we raise our overhead figure.

## Other Ideas

There are lots of ideas associated with overhead, because it forms such a huge part of anyone's business. There are all sorts of little entries that may or may not be important to you and your work, so we simply want to suggest a few you might examine.

Office supplies are a major expense (as is postage) for many businesses. How do yours compare this year to last? As a percentage of your total overhead?

Telephone costs are an expense that's always there, yet rises and falls (at least partly) with your sales volume. How can you cut your phone bill? What are your phone charges as a percentage of overhead? Are they better or worse than last year's?

While we looked at advertising only as it related to sales, it also can be compared to what we spent last year on advertising. How about a five-year graph that charts sales and advertising, with the ad dollars placed behind the sales totals, so they'll plot on the same month? Are there other ways to chart the effectiveness of your advertising?

Since there are many things that make up your overhead totals, it's often worthwhile to examine them as a percentage of that overhead, and plot it over time. The more you can dig back into past data and plot this information over a long period, the more helpful it will be.

# Financial Statement Analysis

# 8

The best thing about an examination of your financial statement data is that you work with ratios, measures of comparison most business people are familiar with and can easily find out more about. Unfortunately, the *worst* thing about a look at this information is also that you work with ratios, for a couple of reasons.

For some reason, business people are expected to know about ratios for their business. When their banker or accountant mentions the *quick ratio* or the *acid test,* they assume we know what they're talking about. Sadly, even if we're one of the lucky ones who went through business school, a real understanding of ratios often escapes us, perhaps because the only real basis of comparison are the facts and figures we can gather from industry-wide sources. While that data is helpful, it still is related to our business only because those people are in the same line of work that we are. But their market is different. Their product lines are different. The ways they do business, handle their customers, work with money, pay their bills—they're all different than the way we do things. To be sure, we share the common bond of a particular industry with many of the same problems, but the most accurate things we can compare our business to are its own ratios, based on a history of the business itself.

National statistics—as the people you get them from are the first to admit—sometimes are based on incomplete data. It isn't that the information is incorrect, but rather that it's (sometimes) drawn from too small a sample to get a statistically correct picture of things. When you combine that with the fact that your local business conditions are widely different than those of a business even in a neighboring town, it's obvious that if you can extract and track the proper financial information from inside your own company, and examine it in the right ways, it will be more valuable to you than entire books of national averages.

This isn't to say that you should ignore those industry figures. On the contrary, your banker will have a copy of them and probably will compare their averages to your own numbers when you ask for a loan. How extensively they make their comparison varies by how much they know about you (and probably by the amount of the loan you request). The vital thing is that you're aware of the fact that your banker will use industry-wide figures, and since he or she is concerned with them, you must be, too. If one ratio varies significantly from what appears to be the norm for your industry, your banker will probably ask you to explain why. There can be all sorts of good reasons why your business heads away from what the national average is, of course. If you have your own internally generated information, you'll be able to provide a logical explanation, (hopefully) in a manner that will convince your banker that there's nothing wrong with this specific variation.

Ideally, then, financial ratios should be examined from two points of view: how they're performing from a historical perspective, based on information generated from inside your business, and how they compare to national averages for other businesses like yours. The first examination—based on your own past history—will be more useful to you, while the latter—when you compare your figures to industry averages—will be helpful when you talk to your banker.

# A Look at Reports

There are all kinds of reports your accountant might create for you, each with information gathered from your business records. The problem is in its presentation. Not that it'll be incorrect (your accountant will make sure everything balances), but rather that all the data you might find important to keep track of may not be easily available.

In our own business, for instance, we have an account that tracks how much we spend on office supplies. The data that flows into this area includes everything from paper for the copying machine to postage to cash register tapes to the money to make up the cash when the pop machine comes up short. There are times, though, when it would be helpful to look inside this area and find out exactly what we spent on postage during a particular time. While all the information is there, it's not broken down separately. For us to figure it out, we have to go back through our cash disbursements journal and manually find and add up every check we wrote for stamps and postage.

In other words, while the information is inside our accounting system, it's not always available in the breakdown and/or formats we need. Some digging is often required to extract the data that we want to track.

There's also the problem of the sheer volume of information we have available on our financial statements. We always look at the bottom line to see how we did profit-wise, but once we know that, we find all kinds of other data there. What's important? What should we pay attention to? What should we graph? Why? While businesses vary, you'll almost always get a period-end and year-end balance sheet that shows your financial position at that particular moment in time, and an income statement that explains how you did from a profit standpoint over the period of time covered. This distinction is important, because the balance sheet captures a day in time, while the income statement covers your performance over a period of time. There are other associated reports, including a flow of funds statement, that indicate where your cash came from during the period under study, as well as where you spent it all.

Because there's a lot of information, it might seem overwhelming to attempt to study it. If you try to cover it all, it can become an impossible task, so the secret is to determine what areas are important for you to understand in terms of running your own business, and follow them closely. One way that helps you know which areas are vital and which are not are business graphics; a few charts can help you determine what's important, and what's not, for you, personally. Your accounting people are a terrific help here, too, as they can suggest places for you to start; since they know your business from a financial viewpoint, they'll have a good idea of what's important to its proper operation and can make suggestions on which areas to examine.

# Assets etc.

This book is not the right place to explain how you value your assets (what you own or can turn into cash) or how to evaluate your liabilities (what you've got to pay, someday). Likewise, we're not going to cover how you'd set about gathering the information for your income statement, where your overhead comes from, or suggest you use a certain type of inventory valuation. Those subjects are more properly served in accounting books. We will look at their relationships, how one sometimes affects the other, and so on, but for a basic knowledge, two suggestions: The first is to ask your accountant. That might seem obvious, but even though we pay his or her bill, we often feel that we should know enough (somehow) to understand all those pages of information he or she gives us. The accountant wouldn't spend the time to figure out all those things and type them up if we didn't understand all of it, right? If there's something you can't figure out, swallow a bit of pride and ask; your accountant won't mind and probably will be pleased that you had enough interest to want to know. The other area is to pick up a good accounting book or two, and take a look at those areas that you're not quite clear on. One recent good one is *How Accounting Works: A Guide for the Perplexed,* by James Don Edwards, Roger H. Hermanson, R. F. Salmonson and Peter R. Kensicki. It's published by Dow Jones-Irwin (Homewood, Illinois 60430). The book is well written and explains things clearly.

While it's important that you understand how things work inside your business before you attempt to chart its information, that doesn't mean you need to know how this or that operates as well as your accountant does. After all, that's his or her business. In many cases, the graphs we'll use as example illustrations will also serve as a guide to how one part of your business relates to other areas, how one thing affects another, and so on.

You'll find out how efficiently you're using the cash you have invested in your business, on a basis that you may not have thought of. While you may calculate how your profits are as a percentage of your sales, you might not figure out how they are in relation to the investment you have in your business. Would you be better off with that cash in the bank than you are with it invested in your own business?

Since you've got money invested in your company, it's important to know who else does, too. If you're the sole owner, you might think that you've made the total investment, but that's (sadly) not correct. Those folks to whom you owe money have an interest in your business, too, and if you don't believe it, don't pay them and see how they remove their share. There's a definite relationship between what you've got invested in your business and what others should have; you'll find out how to figure that out and graph it.

The important thing is not to be afraid of financial ratios and their associated data; like anything else, they're simply a tool to help us be better at what we do: business.

## The Bottom Line: Profits

Probably the logical spot to start any examination of your financial statement data is right at the place where everyone's eyes go: the profit line. While there may be more valuable places to look—in terms of information to tell you how you're managing your business—that bottom line is still all-important.

Figure 8-1 shows us the picture of a business in trouble. It's a line graph that plots 24 months of information, and even without a trend line, it's obvious this business has a problem. At the start of this particular period of time, the business had a net after-tax profit that amounted to three to four

NET PROFIT AFTER TAXES, IN PERCENT

FIGURE 8-1

percent of its total sales volume. That's nothing to shout about, to be sure, but it's still a profit, and one many businesses would be glad to make.

During the next few months, the profit line went steadily downward, until by month 8 the business was doing little better than breaking even. A small recovery took place, followed by a long period of profit in the 1 percent range. Again, nothing to be particularly proud of, but at least the business was still in the black. A trend line done during this period would most likely have shown a downward trend. By months 19 and 20, the profit line plunged again, to where the business was losing money. By the end of the 24-month period (which, as we know, can represent either the last 24 months or a two-year period on a calendar basis, whatever's the most helpful to us) the business had somehow managed to climb out of the red, but was producing a zero profit.

In all, this isn't a particularly good picture and indicates the business has serious problems of one kind or another. It doesn't tell us where those problems might be, of course, but if this were your business, you should be disturbed by this graph. Probably the worst thing about it is that things are seemingly getting worse almost monthly.

However, a business owner who saw this graph at the end of the charted period is still *in business* and so has the chance to pull the company out of the difficulty it's in. More sales, a better effort to cut costs in all areas, a strong drive to reduce overhead to its lowest possible level, a close look at

NET PROFIT AFTER TAXES, IN PERCENT

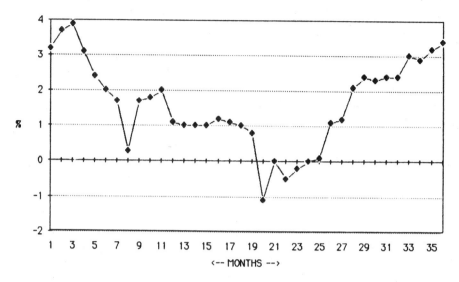

<-- MONTHS -->

**FIGURE 8-2**

employees and how they're doing—all are methods the business owner must use to change the condition of his or her profit level.

To bring things into the right perspective, Figure 8-2 shows you the result you'd hope for, if this were your business. It plots the same information you just looked at, along with another 12 months of data. In effect, it shows you the position the business found itself in after another year had gone by. Something was done (again, the graph doesn't tell us *what*, but rather shows us the result of the action) to change things. Perhaps more sales were created, overhead was lowered, employees were motivated to be more efficient, costs were cut, but whatever it was, the business turned its profit situation around.

This is a good picture, because it shows you how the business climbed out of its depressed condition and restored its former profit level. The end of the three-year period finds this business at close to its original profit percentages. Further, the rate of profit seems to be improving; early in the graph, the trend was obviously downward, while the current trend is rising.

## A Long-Range Trend

It appears that business is on the upswing for this company, but as with most things, it's worthwhile to take a closer look at the data. Figure 8-3 plots a trend line, based on the 36 months of information you've been examining.

**FIGURE 8-3**

Because of the long time frame (36 periods of data), you can expect the trend line to give you an accurate picture of things.

The original information is also plotted on Figure 8-3, as just a background line to the trend line. While that trend line appears to be pretty straight (a closer look on a narrower scale would confirm this observation), even with this wide scale you can see a slight fall in the line. In effect, while the data fell to a level where the business lost money and then pulled itself back up close to its original condition, the trend line indicates a slight drop in the overall picture. This means that even with the current rise in profits, the business still needs to do more to bring its profits up. Ideally, the trend line for net profit will rise, and this one shows a small fall late in the data. It tells you that the overall *drop* of the data was greater than the total gain it made. To get things on an even keel (and, hopefully, to get that trend line heading upward), the profit picture needs to improve even more.

# Profits and Assets

While you need to compare your profits to your total sales (this is the most common way to look at profits), it's equally useful to examine the relationship between the profits your company makes and the total assets of your business. This gives you a feel for how effectively you're managing those assets.

Assets in this example are the total assets a business has at a particular time—cash, inventory, buildings, equipment, vehicles, and so on.

Figure 8-4 plots 10 quarters of information for our fictional business and shows the net profit the business produced divided by its total assets, at the end of each quarterly period. The net result—a percentage figure—is a measure of how well the business is using its assets. Remember that assets in this sense are what a business owns (including financed items), so in essence, these assets are what the enterprise has available to do business. If the manager is doing his or her job properly, the assets are being used in their most effective manner and this line will rise. Conversely, if the manager isn't handling assets well (poor scheduling, sending people and equipment out to a job when it's too late in the day to accomplish anything, keeping too many dollars invested in slow-moving inventory but not enough available to pay current bills), this line will fall. Even without the benefit of a trend line, this data seems to be rising. In effect, this tells us the business is doing something right: it's producing a profit that is growing in relation to the dollars the business owners have invested in assets. There are averages for any industry, of course, as to where this line should be, but in general, it should run between 5–15 percent.

Since this ratio compares the net profit a business makes in relation to everything a business owns, including both owner-invested capital and borrowed money, it probably is the most accurate way to find out how a business is managing its money. Not just cash, but the use of all assets are taken into account, so in effect the focus is on how effectively you, as the business owner, are controlling the assets you have.

FIGURE 8-4

# Profits and Net Worth

Another way to look at profits is to examine them in relation to the net worth a business has, over a specific period of time. Assets—what we just compared profits to—include all that a business owns. Net worth, on the other hand, is what the business is worth, once you subtract any liabilities (what the business owes) from its assets. As such, net worth is a smaller figure than assets (unless the business doesn't owe anything to anyone), so we should expect the profit percentage in relation to net worth to be higher. Net worth is, in theory, the amount the business owner would receive if he or she sold the company; it is, as the term implies, the *worth*, the value of the enterprise. Again, each industry has an average; this figure generally should be higher than the cost of borrowed money, and a well-managed business should be able to earn 25 percent on its invested capital.

The reverse of this would ask the business owner(s) what kind of a return they'd expect on their investment, if they sold the business and had its net worth in the form of cash, ready to invest. What would you consider to be the minimum rate of return you should receive? Whatever it is in your own mind, that's the least you should expect your business to produce for you. If it's not, it's not being managed as well as it should be.

Figure 8-5 is an example of the picture you want to see when you examine your business. This particular illustration covers ten quarters of infor-

NET PROFIT AS A PERCENTAGE OF NET WORTH

<-- QUARTERS -->

FIGURE 8-5

mation. While the business was doing poorly at the start of the period under study (in about the 12 percent range), from quarter 5 on it's been producing profits in relation to its net worth at a greater than 20 percent rate. Since it's unlikely the business owner could take that cash out of his or her business and invest it at a higher rate, he or she should be pleased both with the progress this business has made since the first plot on this graph, and also with the current level of return on his or her investment.

Even without a trend line, this two and one-half year's worth of information is obviously heading upward, and lately the business is making about a 25 percent profit on the investment the business owner(s) have in their company.

## Assets and Liabilities

One ratio your banker will want to examine as soon as he or she gets your financial information is one we've all heard about—the *current ratio,* the ratio between current assets and current liabilities. Current assets are described as cash or things that you can reasonably expect to convert into cash during one operating cycle or within one year. An operating cycle is the time it takes for you to put stock into your inventory, sell and/or deliver it, and, ultimately, convert the sale into a payment from your customer.

As such, the most common things you'll find in your current asset figure are cash, inventories, prepaid expenses, temporary investments, and accounts receivable totals. There are some fine lines here; your accountant is the final guide as to what should be included in current assets. For instance, you might have an old piece of machinery that you want to sell. While you fully intend to sell it during the current period, unless you have a sales contract with a purchaser for the equipment, it really isn't a *current* asset, as you might not be able to convert its value into cash during the current operating cycle or one-year period. Likewise, an investment in the stock market might be considered current, as you simply have to phone your broker to convert it into cash. However, if the market value for this particular stock is severely depressed, you probably won't sell it during the current cycle. It, then, shouldn't be included in your current asset total.

Current liabilities are considerably simpler to understand: they're the bills you must pay during the next year. Current liabilities include accounts payable, any notes due during the year, any taxes due and payable, and the current portion of your long-term debt. As such, you'll most likely pay them from the funds you receive from current assets; thus the relationship between the two amounts.

Current assets compared to current liabilities are a direct measure of your capability to pay your bills. The general rule of thumb says you should have twice as much dollar value in current assets as you have in current liabilities. Short-term lenders consider this to be an important guideline to the health of your business, as they expect to be paid from the cash you collect from current operations.

On the flip side of things, you also don't want to have *too high* a ratio, especially if it's caused by slow-paying customers or nonmoving inventory. For instance, you might have (at the end of one period) $30,000 in accounts receivable plus $30,000 in other current assets—a total of $60,000 in current assets. At the same time, you might have a total of $30,000 in current liabilities. Your ratio, then, is 2-1 (60,000 to 30,000).

At the end of the next period, let's say you were hit with a slew of slow-paying customers and poor collection procedures; your accounts receivable total $60,000, while other current assets come to $30,000—a total of $90,-000 in current assets. If your liabilities stayed the same, you find yourself with a 3-1 ratio (90,000 to 30,000). In this case a higher ratio is not better, as it simply means you've got a lot of customers who aren't paying their bills.

Any study, then, of the current ratio calls for you to watch for a variance from what your established pattern has been. If your business has been doing fine with a 1.8 to 1 ratio, then you want to examine things more closely whenever that ratio varies in *either* direction.

There's an associated ratio called the *acid test* or *quick ratio* that examines much of this same information but looks more at what can be called "instant liquidity." It's a more uncompromising test than the current ratio because it compares cash or what can be quickly converted into cash (and doesn't include inventory, because you might *not* sell it right away) to your current liabilities. In effect, then, it gives you a picture of your business at a moment in time with its liquid assets compared to the obligations you have to meet during the next year. As such, it's like comparing the cash in your wallet to your total expenses over the next week, so it's a harsher look at your bill-paying capability. Since the acid test ratio is directly concerned just with cash, you'll find more detail on it in Chapter 4 on cash flow. Usually, a value here of less than 1-1 indicates that you must sell something from your inventory to meet your current obligations.

There's another reason to note that the 2-1 figure most people want their current ratio to have isn't correct for all businesses. This is especially true when a large part of your current assets are made up of inventory, because this is an area that, depending on your industry, is hard to evaluate. Some businesses, like ones in the food industry, move their inventory almost daily. Others, perhaps in an industry like machine tool parts, might have things sitting around on their shelves for months at a time. The important thing is that if you have a large percentage of your current assets tied up in inventory, the 2-1 ratio figure probably won't apply to your work. As always, it's necessary to discover the right level for your own business, and base any corrective action you take on that figure.

CURRENT RATIO (CURRENT ASSETS DIVIDED BY
CURRENT LIABILITIES)

FIGURE 8-6

Figure 8-6 is a long-term look at the current ratio for our fictional business. It plots the information over a 36-month period (either the latest 36 months, or the last three years on a calendar basis—whatever is the most helpful to us at this time). This isn't a particularly good picture, if we assume this business needs to maintain the *average* current ratio, a 2-1 breakdown. This graph, since it's designed like the others we've shown, is scaled to help the user understand it. In this case, the scale is set to indicate the 2-1 ratio level. Early on, during the first 12 months, the business kept its current ratio above the 2-1 mark, but from month 16 until just lately, the current ratio fell below 2-1. At one point it got all the way down to an even mark: 1-1.

The whole idea of this ratio is to measure a business's capability to pay its bills on time. The ratio of 2-1 is a generally accepted basis that allows a margin of error, and takes into account that all current bills don't get collected during the current period. Current assets include things such as inventory, which may not be converted into cash for some time to come. Current liabilities include payments due within a year from when the ratio is calculated. When this ratio approaches the 1-1 figure, though, there's no margin of safety for the business. If this were a purely liquid asset measurement (the cash you have compared to the cash you owe), this low ratio might be acceptable. In this case, because you don't know *when* your inventory will turn into cash or *if* everyone who owes you money will pay, you need a safety margin.

One of the major limitations of the current ratio is that it only indicates the position of the business in respect to paying current liabilities through the liquidation of current assets. While we can estimate some future performance with a trend-line analysis of the ratio data, it is *not* as accurate when it comes to predicting future performance as, for example, a study of cash flow can be. It's important to understand the built-in limitations this ratio has, but equally necessary to track it, because of its widespread use, particularly among the bankers you'll do business with.

Figure 8-7 plots the trend line of the current ratio for our fictional business, based on 36 months of data. Since it's based on a long series of data, we can expect that it's pretty accurate, and that this ratio concentrates on current information only (which, judging it by its name of current assets, we should expect it to do).

This chart confirms our feeling that our fictional business has a problem with its current ratio, and confirms what our first impression was: the current ratio is getting worse by the month. Even the recent rise in this ratio isn't enough to change the momentum the trend line has built up. Even if we keep in mind the limitations that are built into any study of the current ratio, we still find an image like the one we see in Figure 8-7 to be disturbing, and (hopefully) it will motivate us to change conditions, to correct the direction our current ratio seems to want to go.

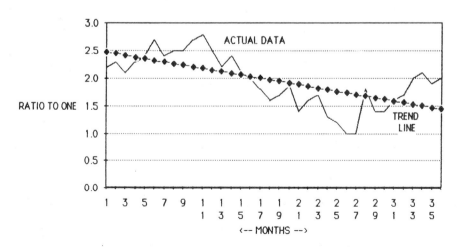

FIGURE 8-7

## Liabilities as Assets

It's also interesting to note that liabilities can be *sources* of assets—a seemingly odd relationship that we often don't understand. The asset and liability accounts in your business aren't to be confused with net worth, the value of your business, which grows or shrinks based on your profit performance and investment total. Assets and liabilities can *offset* one another; when you increase your assets (through the *use* of a liability) one cancels out the other, while your net worth position remains the same.

For example, your business might borrow $5,000 on an open line of credit with the payment due in 90 days. You've created a liability (the $5,000 loan repayment) but at the same time you've increased the total of your current assets. Likewise, when you purchase items (on credit) for your inventory, you increase the asset value on that inventory total. At the same time, of course, you increase your current liabilities. In either case, the net worth amount remains the same.

The pair—assets and liabilities—compose a unique duo that when you work one against the other in the proper manner, can add to your cash flow, when you need them to.

## Asset Pie

At the end of a year (or any specific period that's helpful to you), it's a good idea to plot your assets as they each individually contribute to your total asset base.

Figure 8-8 is a pie chart created at the end of a yearly period that illustrates how the four breakdowns our fictional business keeps track of each look in relation to our total assets. Without other supporting information we can't, of course, draw any conclusions from this one chart, so we'd want to make this graph at the completion of every quarter or every year. We don't know if the inventory total of 19 percent of assets is where it should be, or if fixed assets (23 percent of the total) are larger than they should be or not. Only a long-range study of this information will tell us that, and a pie chart doesn't lend itself to an examination of time series data. It does, however, give us a guide to each asset's contribution to the total asset base at this specific time, which is useful information.

Since all the data is shown on a percentage basis, and those percentages are listed on the graph, the business owner can both see and read how each asset contributes to his or her total. Since the manager will know what the dollar amounts of their assets are, it's usually easy to convert the percentage figures listed into a dollar value. Cash, for instance, amounts to 7

CURRENT ASSETS AS OF THE END OF THE YEAR

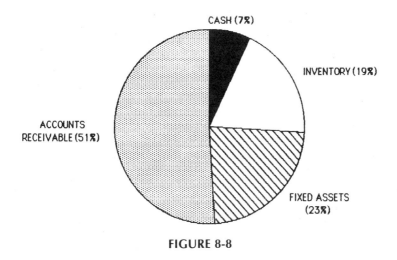

**FIGURE 8-8**

percent of the business's total assets. If those assets totaled $100,000, the owner would know that—at this particular moment in time—he or she had about $7,000 in cash or cash equivalents.

One thing we can see from this picture is the large percentage of our business's assets that accounts receivable total. Since they amount to slightly more than half of all the assets this business claims, they'd better be *good* accounts, dollars the business must be able to collect. If a study at the same time indicates this company had, say, 20 percent of its accounts older than 90 days, this business has a real problem.

The conversion process can be taken a step further, of course, in that once you know what percentage of your accounts receivable are in what age bracket, you can calculate pretty easily (or have your spreadsheet do it) what percentage of your total assets are tied up in receivables that grow older by the day. Again, this information can motivate the business owner to do something to correct a bad situation.

# Fixed Assets

One problem many businesspeople have is a tendency to invest too many dollars in what are called fixed assets, trucks and machinery and equipment that never get sold but rather are purchased to make the business more productive. Your Macintosh is an investment as a fixed asset—termed that not because it is *fixed* in place but rather that it represents a fixed obligation that must be paid over a period of time and/or a dollar investment that took a fixed sum of cash (a liquid asset) and converted it into machinery or equipment when you wrote the check.

Along with most fixed assets comes depreciation, which in effect adds cash back to your business and most often, interest costs that must be paid (anytime the purchase of an asset is financed). The problem comes along if sales slip a bit, and cash flow is impeded. Suddenly, the business owners find they don't have enough cash to cover the payments they'd contracted for when they bought all those trucks and expensive equipment. But how much of an investment in fixed assets is too much? A balance must be found, as always, since without enough fixed assets (and their associated costs), the business won't be able to do business.

Figure 8-9 plots a two and one-half year period (10 quarters) of the percentage relationship between fixed assets and the net worth of our fictional business. Even without a trend line, we can see that our fixed assets as a percentage of our total net worth is increasing. In effect, this means either we've been putting more dollars into fixed assets, or our net worth is decreasing for some reason, or we have a combination of the two conditions. While each business is different, a rule of thumb is that a business shouldn't have more than 75 percent of its net worth in fixed assets, as it begins to get

FIXED ASSETS AS A PERCENTAGE OF NET WORTH

<-- QUARTERS -->

**FIGURE 8-9**

top heavy with the machinery to produce sales, but without the cash—the liquid assets—and inventory to sustain those sales.

If this were your business, you might want to put a trend line on the data illustrated in Figure 8-9 just to give you a better idea of how serious a problem you have. You'd also want to take a long and hard look at what you've been purchasing in the way of fixed assets and whether they're really improving your sales and/or production efficiency. Perhaps the high ratio won't hurt your business. In any case, a graph like Figure 8-9 sends a warning to the business owner that perhaps he or she is spending cash where it shouldn't be spent.

## Measuring Efficiency

While we all strive for more efficiency and are constantly looking at our people to see how they're doing, you need to turn the examination around and see how you're doing, in your role of business manager. How efficient are you?

In a sense, when you break things down inside your business, you have in effect a number of assets and are asked to do business with them. You have a certain sum of cash, a specific dollar amount in inventory, an amount that customers owe you, trucks and equipment, perhaps a building, and so on—a quantity of assets. While you can change the mix of these (take some cash and buy a new copy machine), you only add to your assets when your business creates a profit or you increase your investment (or, if you operate another business form, like a corporation, when others increase their investment in the business). Likewise, your assets decrease when you suffer an operating loss or when you remove assets from the business (a dividend payment, the purchase of a personal vehicle).

That might seem elementary but in essence at this particular point in time, your business has a combination of assets that together are listed on your financial statement along with their specific dollar value. The way you use your assets has a direct bearing on whether you show a profit or a loss. If you handle things right and keep the proper dollar amount in inventory (so you have the right stock on hand at the right time), have the proper equipment (so your people can be efficient in their work), handle your accounts receivable correctly (so you get paid when you should), and so on, your business will show a profit. Since your assets have to be manipulated properly for your business to be successful, you can gauge your performance not only by using the profit amount as a yardstick (as we saw earlier), but also with the movement of your assets—what's called the *asset turnover rate*.

Turnover of assets simply means the number of times your operating assets can be divided into your sales, during a particular accounting period.

Operating assets are those you use to create sales in the usual operation of your business (as contrasted to, say, a building you own but rent to someone—it doesn't affect your business operation).

Figure 8-10 plots the asset turnover rate for our fictional enterprise over a 36-month period. Just as we examine our inventory turnover to see how it moves through our business, this illustration plots the same type of image and tells us how often our assets *turn* during the normal course of operations. Unless our inventory is turning, being sold, we won't make a profit. Unless we're effectively using our assets, the bottom line will be red, too.

Lately, our business has been improving and has made quite a comeback from where assets weren't turning even once a month. What's the proper asset turnover rate? Only through a long-term examination of your information will you know what's right for you. This particular chart is unusual in that it's normally only done on a yearly basis, while Figure 8-10 covers things from a monthly standpoint. Turning over your operating assets only once or twice during a *year* would probably not be a particularly good performance, while turning them over at that rate on a monthly basis, as this example shows, is a completely different picture and probably means the business owner is doing his or her job well. The higher the ratio, the better the performance.

You can carry this approach a step further and create an *earnings power* ratio, a comparison that puts an exact figure on your efficiency as a

**FIGURE 8-10**

manager. You multiply the rate of profit your business made (in comparison to its sales) by the asset turnover rate. The more a business can sell and the more it's capable of earning on each sales dollar in relation to the cash it has invested in operating assets, the higher will be the return on each invested dollar. This figure shows how effectively you, as a manager, are using the assets you have available.

## Liabilities and What You're Worth

Just as we looked at fixed assets in relationship to the net worth of your business, it's useful to make the same comparison between the liabilities you have and what your net worth is. You can examine your total liabilities or your current liabilities in relation to your net worth; we'll use current obligations.

Figure 8-11 illustrates the value of our current liabilities as a percentage of the total net worth of our business, over a 36-month period. As often is the case, even without a trend line we can see this business is heading toward difficult times, as its ratio of current obligations to its net value is constantly rising. Simply put, this is a comparison of what is owed on a current basis to the net worth of the business. As a rule of thumb, anything over

CURRENT LIABILITIES AS A PERCENTAGE OF NET WORTH

**FIGURE 8-11**

CURRENT LIABILITIES AS A PERCENTAGE OF NET WORTH

FIGURE 8-12

about 75 percent is probably too high. Let's add a trend line to give the bad news a bit more force.

Figure 8-12 plots the same data we just examined, with the addition of a trend line that shows its average direction and narrows the scale to 50–100 percent.

Unfortunately, the trend line predicts that our current liabilities could approach 100 percent of our net worth, so in effect we'd owe the same amount as what the business is worth. And the liabilities for this example are *current* obligations—part of what we have financed over a long period of time isn't shown as a current liability. So, our condition is even worse than what we'd expect from these pictures, and we might even be in a position where outside creditors own more of our business—through the obligations we have to them—than we do. Let's add in those long-term liabilities and see how bad the picture really is.

In Figure 8-13, we can see the relationship between everything we owe (total liabilities) to what we own (net worth), and it's a discomforting look. Lately, in fact, we have reached that stage where our creditors own more of the enterprise than we do, and if we were to liquidate at this particular time, we wouldn't be able to pay all the outstanding obligations of our company. A business in this position often finds itself with severely restricted credit (who wants to loan money to a business that owes more than it's worth?) and will have truly difficult cash problems if sales slow down even a little.

TOTAL LIABILITIES AS A PERCENTAGE OF NET
WORTH

<-- MONTHS-->

FIGURE 8-13

# More Interest Problems

If the business owner with the company that has all the poor financial information we've been examining can turn things around and finds a bank that
will consider a loan, he or she might find his or her banker requesting an unusual figure: the business's *times interest earned* data.

In effect, the ratio is simpler than it sounds. If your business made
$15,000 in profits last year and had total interest expenses of $1,500, it can
be said to have *earned* its interest costs ten times. This is calculated by dividing the net profit (usually after taxes) by the total interest expense for
the period under study.

Anyone who might loan you money is a candidate for this information.
Since they'll expect repayment out of the operating funds your business produces, a primary concern for any lender is to consider how safe their loan is.
If you can display the capability to earn many times over the amount of the
interest you'll have to pay, your loan will be a better gamble.

A normal guideline calls for this figure to be at least ten to one, although the higher it is, the more likely you'll get any loan you might request.
The obvious danger is, of course, that if a business has a low ratio, if it's not
earning enough profit to cover the interest, the loan is in danger of not being
repaid at all.

FIGURE 8-14

Figure 8-14 is another look at a business with an upcoming problem. For the first four quarters under study, the times interest earned ratio was at least 10–1, but since quarter 5 it's been steadily dropping. Since this is something of a long-range look at things (two year's worth of information), this is a picture that should disturb any business owner. It *will* bother a banker who examines it, so it's important for us to understand and track.

## Summing Up

There are probably 100 ratios you could track and graph that will be helpful to you. We've tried to suggest some of the more obvious, along with a number of unusual ones, as they often give you useful ways to examine your information other than the *acid test* and *quick ratio* and other things you're so accustomed to.

Ratios for balance sheet and income statement items are only tools, and while they can be compared and graphed and examined, they remain just that: a method to help you understand where your business has been, and (perhaps) in which direction it's going. You need to be aware of industry averages for each ratio, mainly because the financial people you deal with must use them as a judge to gauge the quality of your business. After all, they're not around to see the daily operation of things and can only estimate your capability to repay a loan based on your past performance and any financial information they have access to.

Three sources that can be of help for information about your own industry and what ratios should be examined and what they should look like are:

1. Your own accountant. He or she has the knowledge and often the information on what to look for and how to examine it.

2. Robert Morris Associates (Research Department, Philadelphia National Bank Building, Philadelphia, PA 19107). This firm gathers and summarizes industry averages, which you can use as a basis of comparison for your own business.

3. Dun & Bradstreet, Inc. (99 Church Street, New York, NY 10007). Get to know your local D&B people; they have all sorts of financial information you'll find helpful.

Ideally, you'll have access to past information from your company that you can go back through and find data for a long-range look at your personal financial picture. This is the best comparison you can make, of course, and once you chart the information you'll be able to see exactly when there's any deviation from past trends.

The logical place to start any examination of financial information is with your profit line. It's useful to compare profits to sales (that's the standard comparison we all make) and also to assets, as that gives you a measure of how you're managing the assets you have available.

Profit also can be compared to the net worth any enterprise has, to give you a feel for how well your investment in the business is doing, as an investment.

One comparison any banker will make when he or she examines your financial information is to look at your *current ratio,* a guide to whether or not you can pay your current obligations from the resources you have available now. You need to know, then, what current assets and current liabilities are, as well as the historical trend of this ratio for your own business. Although it's worthwhile to compare its performance to industry averages (which your banker will certainly do), if you know what your long-range current ratio shows, you can better explain any deviation from what appears to be the norm. It's vital to know what your own current ratio has been in the past, as either too high *or* too low a ratio is a sign that there may be a problem.

It's also helpful to remember that liabilities can be sources of assets;

when cash flow becomes a problem, you might be able to help things out by creating a liability (a loan of $10,000 means you have to pay it back, with interest, but also gives you the $10,000 to use in the meantime).

Since assets are the total of what your business owns, it's helpful to take a look at their distribution—*where* do you have your cash invested? Are accounts receivable a major portion of your total assets? If so, it's vital that the business owner makes sure those receivables are collectable. You may also want to track individual asset groups over time, to see if their value, as a percentage of your total asset base, rises or falls.

No examination of assets is complete without tracking and taking a hard look at the fixed assets your business has. Since many businesspeople have a tendency to put too many of their dollars into fixed assets (thus locking up cash that perhaps will be needed elsewhere), this is an area that needs constant vigilance.

While we looked earlier at assets in relation to liabilities and as part of their own pie, it's also useful to examine them from another direction to see how rapidly they *turn* inside our sales. This comparison measures the efficiency at which the business owner manages his or her assets—the more use you can make of your assets, the more successful your business will be.

It's also necessary to look at the other side of the balance sheet, at the liabilities your business has. One good way to examine what you owe is in relation to the net worth, the *equity* you have in your company. While we chose as an example a look at current liabilities compared to the net worth value, it's equally useful to examine your total liabilities in relation to this figure. This ratio tells the business owner how much outsiders—in the form of creditors—have invested in the company.

Anyone who loans you money has one major concern: whether you'll repay the loan on time. One way they gauge your capability for this is to see if your business is earning enough cash to support its operations and make enough profit to pay the interest on the loan amount. This is often done with something called the *times interest earned* ratio, which simply divides the total interest obligations of a business into its net profit, usually over a one-year period.

## Other Ideas

Within the whole area of your financial statement information are all kinds of things you might find it helpful to examine, and we've just scratched the surface in this chapter. Some of the ratios that could logically go here have been extracted and are covered in the chapters on specific areas. Here are some additional ideas.

You may want to compare your net worth (owner's equity) to just the long-term debt your business has, and plot it over a period of time. This gives you another view of how much you have invested in your business as a comparison to what other people have, on a long-range basis.

One thing many business owners take a hard look at is their gross profit margin (gross profit as a percentage of total sales). Since your overhead and net profit must come from your gross profit, it's an important thing to track and chart over a period of time.

Within the profit area itself, you may find it useful to break down your profit and look at it from a couple of directions. Examine your operating profit before taxes as a percentage of sales, and profit after taxes as it relates to sales. Chart profit (either before or after taxes) over a length of time, on a this-period compared to last-period basis.

You might want to examine your accounts receivable as a percentage of your total sales, and/or to find out what percentage they are of just the credit sales you make. All this with an eye to determining if you have too much in your total accounts receivable (poor collection procedures, easy credit) or too little (too stringent credit policies). As always, you need to strive for the balance that's right for your business.

While we looked at fixed assets in relation to the other assets our fictional business carries on its books, it's often useful to examine fixed assets in relation to total sales, as those sales are what you produce through the use of the fixed assets you have available. How about a look at other assets in relation to sales? Is there any correlation?

The *equity ratio* examines how much of the total value of a business is owned by the people who own the company. You calculate this by dividing the total assets into the owner's equity amount. Since assets include the value of everything a business owns (including financed items), this gives you a measure of the proportion of the total assets you—the owner—have invested in the business at any given time. When this percentage is subtracted from 100 percent, you're left with the percentage that others have invested in your business, either through loans or payments you owe them (accounts payable). From the viewpoint of someone you ask for a loan, the more you have invested in your business, the safer he'll feel. However, if you, as the business owner, can effectively use borrowed funds to create profits above the cost of those funds (the interest you must pay), then you may want to do so.

We haven't touched on corporations, where any number of people might have cash (or other assets) invested in a company, but if you operate this form of business and have outside investors, you may want to keep track of their return on investment (per share of stock), dividend payments, the price-earnings ratio per share of stock, and so on.

Probably the most important thing about all this ratio analysis is to simply look around and examine each area until you can determine what's most important to your business and its successful operation. Don't be afraid to ask your accountant, to buy and read accounting books, to send away for more information. Track the data you find most useful over a period of time, put trend lines on it to get some idea of where you're headed, and you'll find that a study in this area—financial statement information—will produce real results in terms of real profit dollars.

# Inventory Analysis and Control

Any business owner fights a constant battle with inventory: you worry over what to order and when to order it, have to work to get it delivered on time, wonder if it will sell once it's in stock, have to care for and insure it until it's sold, and then you worry if you'll get paid once the items are gone. While it's a truism for any business that without inventory you'll soon be out of business, it's equally true that without the *right products* to sell, at the *right price,* your business will be on the ropes just as fast.

Often, a business owner whose retail sales are minimal assumes that a lot of things about inventory don't apply to his or her work. The feeling is that only *retailers* have inventory problems. But oddly, it's often the company that doesn't have racks filled with products that need the most help in understanding inventory control. Even a real estate company (that markets something hard to define—customer service) still must have the right product available for each prospect, at the right price. They must have the right inventory in terms of the listings they carry, the best financing contacts (to help prospects *buy*), the proper people to create and present contracts, and so on. The insurance company (who sells more of an intangible than an insurance business?) must have the right inventory for its prospects, plans and ideas that people are interested in and will buy today, the right prices, good merchandising and so on, or it, like the retailer, will soon be out of business.

Someone on the wholesale level faces many of the same inventory problems the retail store owner does, with one added difficulty: the quantities a wholesaler works with (and thus the costs) are often huge. Order dates sometimes must be months in advance of when you feel you'll need the products, because of the quantity of merchandise involved. While the wholesaler has little customer *shopping,* cost is often more of a factor than in the retail world—and so, then, is the price at which the wholesaler buys his or her merchandise. An extra percent spent at the time of purchase may mean thousands of dollars in lost sales because buyers in the wholesale market are so price conscious.

## The Nonretail Business

Often, too, the company that relies on major equipment sales for much of its sales volume finds itself with inventory problems. Not in the sense that they don't have the right equipment on hand, as customers often expect that their purchase (car, air conditioning system, custom-made bookcases) will have to be ordered or produced, but since they don't see day-to-day operations in the same light that retailers do, they have problems looking at inventory the right way. Since "we have to order that, you know" is the byword, he or she feels they don't *have* any inventory difficulties.

The retailer watches as customers come into his or her store, notices how they examine this or that piece of merchandise, note how they weigh its price against a value picture they have in their mind, and make a buying decision. If the customer walks out and leaves the item still on the retailer's shelf, the business owner knows (1) the product was wrong for this customer, (2) the price was too high for this customer, or perhaps, (3) this customer was just shopping. Whatever the case, the sale was not made and the businessperson knows it instantly. Once they see a particular item examined and not purchased time after time, it's clear the price is incorrect according to what the prospects feel it should be and/or the people who do consider the item aren't really prospects for it.

But the business owner who must *order* most of what he or she sells just doesn't see this daily interaction between merchandise and potential customer. If your business operates on a per order basis, it's vital to understand that the same relationship exists between your products and your prospects as there is between the retail store and its customers. Even though you don't have everything on hand—it has to be ordered or produced to order—you still must have access to the right merchandise, the right inventory, at the right price.

In our heating and air conditioning business, for instance, it's impossible (from a financial standpoint) to keep every size of every furnace and/or air conditioning unit on hand. They have to be ordered, and our customers usually don't have a problem with this process. These days, one major concern of anyone who's considering this purchase is *energy efficiency.* "How much will it cost to operate?'' is a question we get every day, from nearly every prospect we talk to. They want to know what the most efficient unit is, why it'll cost less than another brand or system, and focus on that during the buying/selling process. Even though we don't have these units in stock, we *must* be able to talk intelligently about what's available, show a prospect why he or she should purchase this or that system, and so on. While we don't have a warehouse filled with merchandise of all assorted shapes, sizes and efficiencies, we still have to have it available, know about it, be able to price it right, and so on—exactly like the retailer.

## Sales and Inventory

Although it's obvious when you think about it, one of the primary functions of management is to make sure there's enough of whatever you sell *on hand* to supply the needs and wants of your customers. Surprisingly, many businesspeople tend to ignore this part of their operation, and turn over the control and management of whatever inventory system is in use to someone not qualified in any manner to determine what to buy, where to purchase it, and when to place the order. Too often the duties of inventory control fall to the person who puts away the stock: he or she is left to record what came in and went out, is required to fill out purchase orders, and so on. Or business owners simply order what they feel they should, just because a salesperson took them out to lunch today. The end result is the business doesn't have the right product to sell at the regular time, and/or at the correct price.

It's a funny thing, but have you ever gone into any of the nationally franchised fast-food chains and found them out of something? Sure, they might have an equipment breakdown and so might not be able to make that milk shake you ordered, but have they ever been out of hamburgers? Buns? French fries? Why not? Well, you think, *that's their business,* and you're right. But isn't the same true in your own line of work? Enough said.

## Inside Inventory

Business graphics are probably not the best way to examine the product quantities you should have on hand (there are mathematical formulas to tell you that), and perhaps not even a really helpful way to determine when one item or another should be ordered. Instead, graphics lend themselves to a detailed look at specific aspects of the inventory process, details that might escape a casual glance at the procedure.

As with sales, we're not going to chart the obvious—total inventory this year versus last is the one that most people automatically track. It's one you may want to follow, of course, on a monthly basis, as it gives you a feel for one year compared to the other. Since you know how you did financially last year, you'll get a feeling for how things are going this year.

Because everything in any business starts with sales, we'll begin at the same point with inventory. There's always a connection between the sales we produce and the inventory we control. This doesn't necessarily mean that more inventory will mean more sales (it might, though—will it for *your* business?).

Figure 9-1 is a simple line graph that plots the month-end sales for our fictitious business, along with month-end inventory totals, over a 12-month period. As we know, this type of graph can cover a calendar-year period or the latest 12 months, whichever the business owner finds most helpful at a particular time.

This is the picture you should get when you compare sales and inventory—as your sales increase, your inventory total will rise to support it . . . or is it vice versa? It seems to be a question of what comes first (like the chicken or the egg)—does more inventory produce more in sales, or does an increase in sales volume *force* a growth in the stock on hand? Although each business is different, it's obvious that you won't have *any* sales unless you have something to sell, so it stands to reason that inventory is the starting point for all that follows. The sales line will go up and down more sharply

FIGURE 9-1

INVENTORY AS A PERCENTAGE OF SALES

**FIGURE 9-2**

than the inventory line, as your sales data is plotted on a retail basis, while your inventory totals are recorded at their wholesale cost.

It's more of a help to take this same information and use a spreadsheet program to divide your inventory figures by your total monthly sales, to see what percentage your inventory is of your total sales. Figure 9-2 illustrates this.

Again, Figure 9-2 is the picture you'd expect to see, as your inventory as a percentage of your total sales remains pretty steady. There was a little blip early in the period where the dollars you had invested in inventory totaled more than half of your sales volume. That might be fine, of course, for some businesses, and not for others. In this particular example, since the rest of the data indicates the inventory amount is most often less than 50 percent of the sales figure, when it rose above that mark it should have warned the business owner that there could be a problem with inventory. As your inventory as a percentage of sales starts to increase, it's a sign that what you have in stock simply isn't moving. Since the percentage figure is directly tied to sales, an increase points a worrisome finger right at inventory as a problem area. There are only two reasons for inventory to increase as a percentage of your total sales: if your inventory value increases and/or sales decrease—both of which mean what you have on hand simply isn't selling. Period.

# Moving the Stock

Probably the most widely accepted method to examine inventory is to look at its turnover rate—how often you *turn*, or sell the stock you have on hand. This is most often expressed in the number of days it takes your inventory to be sold and taken out of stock. This figure is computed by taking the cost of goods sold for a particular period and dividing it by the average inventory during the same period. On a yearly basis, you'd calculate your average inventory by adding up the totals for each month-end inventory figure and dividing the result by 12.

If you spent $500,000 for merchandise during one year, and your inventory during this same time averaged out to $50,000, you can say that you *turned* your inventory ten times. You carried an average stock of $50,000 and sold (on a cost basis) $500,000 worth of merchandise—ten times the amount you had on hand, on the average.

If you spent that same $500,000 on merchandise (the *merchandise purchased* figure from your income statement) and maintained an average inventory of $100,000, then you only turned your stock five times.

Generally, the more often you can move your stock, the more profit the business will make, because the whole idea in any business is to *sell* things. In a moment we'll move to a method that ties your inventory directly to sales, but let's examine what a graphed turnover rate looks like.

Figure 9-3 shows how often, in days, our fictional business turned its inventory, on a historical basis. This figure is calculated by dividing 365 (days in a year) by the turnover rate (in the example above, the 10 or 5 times each year the inventory turned). If your inventory turned 10 times over the year, you divide 365 (days) by 10 for a result of 36.5—every 36½ days, you moved your entire stock of inventory. The second example, where the turnover rate was 5, yields 365/5, or 73—it took you 73 days to turn your stock.

It's obvious that the business that can move more products will be more successful, so the general rule of thumb is to work to lower your turnover rate. The spreadsheet program you use to track your financial information (before you send it to your graphic package) is ideal for doing these calculations for you.

Figure 9-3 plots the average days our fictitious business took to turn its inventory. It's an interesting look at things, because you can almost gauge the profitability of the business once you discover how successful it is at making sales, moving its inventory.

Year 1 was good (at least in the terms we're currently examining). From the first two quarters where the business moved things over about a 48-day period, the end of the year found it with only about a 33-day turnover period. Stock was simply moving much faster. Whatever the business was

THE DAYS IT TOOK TO "TURN" THE INVENTORY

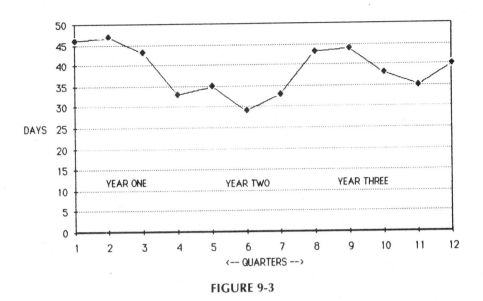

**FIGURE 9-3**

doing, it was doing it right; by the middle of year 2, the turnover rate was under 30 days.

Then things took a turn for the worse, and the rate at which this business moved its stock started to rise. By the end of year 3, after showing an improvement along with a few discouraging periods, the business found itself with a 40-day turnover period.

Why were there fluctuations? Since this information ties the cost of the goods you buy and put into stock directly to the sales you make (in terms of inventory cost as it leaves your store), it simply means there were periods when the stock on hand was not selling. *Why not?* is obviously the question you must answer—how would you do so if this were your business?

While general business conditions obviously influence how your sales are, even in bad times some businesses do well. Why? There's no complex answer—they simply sell what they have available for sale. As we know, this covers a lot of ground, and includes not just retail inventory, but merchandise that must be ordered and/or produced to order. What information would you collect and look at to find out why your turnover rate varied so widely?

One good way would be to go back through your past records and examine—closely—what you had on hand during the slow periods, as well as what you had in stock when things were moving rapidly. A comparison of the two lists (and it probably can be pretty general) will give you the answer you need. You most likely won't have to list 100 individual items, but can concentrate on *areas* of your work, general sections here and there that you had more (or less) inventory for.

Perhaps you'll discover that in the slow periods you had a lot of X items in stock, while in the better periods you carried only a few of those, but more of the products your Y department sold, and in the best periods you concentrated on Z items.

You might also want to examine and study the advertising you did, especially in relation to the items that did move well. Were there special promotions that worked particularly well? Sales for this or that? Did advertising in one media or another lower or raise your turnover rate?

# Days of Sales

Any examination of inventory should include a look at a different approach to the relationship between the stock you have on hand and the sales you make with it. For this examination to be accurate, the sales figure you divide your inventory into should be the sales you record that can be traced directly to that inventory stock. Labor and items that have to be ordered should not be totaled in your sales amount, as they did not come from your on-hand inventory.

Since inventory is most often recorded on a cost basis, and your sales are totaled at a retail level, to link the two accurately means you need to adjust one of the amounts; the easiest thing to do is to use inventory—for this purpose—on its retail basis, what you expect to sell it for. For instance, if you normally double the cost of your merchandise to arrive at its selling price, then simply *double* your inventory cost amount to make the comparisons for this example. If you mark things up by 40 percent, then divide your inventory cost figures by .60. This is, of course, an ideal task for your spreadsheet package.

For example, if during one month you made sales of $9,000 you can directly trace to your inventory, you can figure your average daily (from inventory) sale was $300—you just divide 30 days into the $9,000 sales figure. Every day, then, you used up $300 worth of inventory (on a retail basis).

If your inventory at the end of that particular month was $18,000 (again, at the retail price at which you expect to sell the merchandise), you can be said to have 60 days worth of inventory in stock. In other words, you had enough goods on hand to support two month's worth of sales. That's overly obvious with this example, of course, as you could simply divide the monthly sales of $9,000 into the retail inventory total of $18,000 and get the same result: two months. However, the process is exactly the same with odd figures, and again, this is an area where your spreadsheet program can help.

This figure—the days of sales in inventory—can be graphed, just like any other. For most of us, the faster you can turn your stock, the better. Obviously, there has to be a happy medium—if you sell all your inventory too quickly, you're essentially out of business until you can get more into stock. So the smart business owner looks at the days of sales they have available in their inventory from both directions—you don't want too little, or too much, sitting on your shelves.

Figure 9-4 plots the days of sales our fictional business had in its inventory over a 24-month period. Certainly the most significant thing this graph tells us is that this enterprise generally has 40 to 50 days worth of goods on hand at any one time. If the business made a profit during this 24-month period, we probably can assume this figure—40 or 50 days of sales stored in inventory—is about right. Since this graph was created like our others, we can give some significance to its scale markings; in this case, they were designed to highlight the 40–50 day area.

The break at month 21, then, where the days of sales in inventory rose through the 50-day level (and has remained up there) is a significant change in the way this business is doing its business. Very quickly, the business owner finds he or she is carrying much more inventory than he or she has been, and/or sales have slowed significantly. One of the two has to have happened—since this ratio plots the relationship between sales and inventory, one of the two has changed to create the rise in the plotted line.

The end result of all this means the inventory isn't moving—if it were,

DAYS OF SALES IN CURRENT INVENTORY

FIGURE 9-4

sales would be better. This can be the result of poor merchandise selection, incorrect pricing policies, bad service and selling practices, and so on; whatever the reason, the business has a problem with its inventory. For much of the period charted, this business kept around 40 days worth of sales in its on-hand inventory. Now it's got more than 50 days worth of sales stored there—a significant difference in the amount invested in that material. Why isn't it moving?

## A Closer Look

When you spot something like the break in what appeared to be a pretty normal operating level (40 to 50 days worth of sales on hand), it's a good idea to take a closer look at things.

Figure 9-5 plots the same days of sales in inventory figure we just examined. This time, though, we've added a trend line based on those 24 months worth of information. Of course, the trend line also indicates the general direction our days of sales have been going, which, unfortunately, is up; this is one line we'd like to head downward.

The business owner who looks at these last two graphs can see he or she has a problem, and knows where the problem is—in the goods in stock.

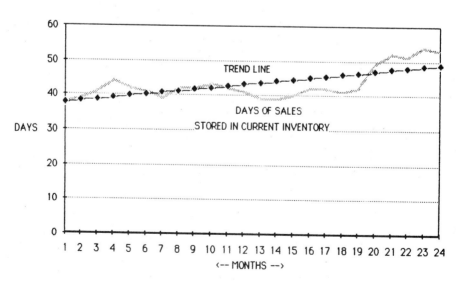

FIGURE 9-5

There *must* be a problem with the inventory, because it's simply not selling. If it were, sales would be up and so the inventory figure would decrease, and with it, the days of sales stored there.

In reality, Figure 9-5 should have been created before the break-through at month 21, as it may have indicated the problem before it became a serious difficulty. Now the business owner finds he or she has had four months of high inventory levels, a rising trend and—worst of all—a seemingly poor inventory selection to try to get rid of. It's a difficult thing to correct at this stage, because the stock on hand, if it was right for the market and priced properly, would be selling. Sadly, it isn't.

This particular graph is really useful to the retailer, whose success depends so much on the whims of fancy and fashion. With some historical data to go on, you should be able to see exactly what your days of sales in inventory should be, and if it deviates, you'll see it and know it as a danger signal. Along with the raw data, chart a trend line, as often sales rise and fall in such a way that without one it's difficult to determine which *direction* they're headed.

## You're Out of What?

The bane of having something in inventory is its opposite: you're out of what a customer happens to need. The goal of any inventory control system is to avoid this, of course, but it happens to the best of us. All we can do is try to minimize how often we goof, and so Figure 9-6 is a helpful chart to create monthly, just so we can see if our efforts along this line are working or not.

Figure 9-6 shows us a 24-month picture that's designed to disturb anyone who owns a business. This graph charts the percentage of items our fictional business happens to be out of at the end of each month. For nearly the first year and one-half of this illustration, we were at least able to keep this figure below the 5 percent level.

For some reason, for the last eight months our out of stock percentage has gone through the roof, and the obvious question is *why*? Aren't we ordering when we should? Has our inventory control system broken down? Aren't people telling us what they took out of stock? Have shipments from a major supplier been slow?

Figure 9-6 might be way out of line for your business—perhaps you work at only a 1 or 2 percent out of stock level. The only way you'll know what your own figure should be is, of course, to track it over a period of time. You'll quickly discover what's right for you, and so you'll spot any variations in the total. As noted, this figure must be examined in light of your own historical data, and not compared to what someone else figures it should be.

Whatever the cause, Figure 9-6 is reason for alarm. Even without a

PERCENT OF ITEMS OUT OF STOCK

<-- MONTHS -->

**FIGURE 9-6**

trend line, it's obvious our record on out of stock items is getting worse by the month, probably by the day, and more and more prospects walk out of our store empty-handed.

Since we have such an obvious problem, it might not seem necessary to make a trend line to show us how fast our record is getting worse, but it's actually a good thing to do for a couple of reasons. It'll show us where we can expect our data to be at the end of a few months, if we continue to do things as we have been. It also gives us a better feel for the *rise* in the information itself; the raw data, even though obviously heading up, still fluctuates. Finally, perhaps it will scare us enough to motivate us to action. After all, if we don't have it, we're not going to sell it. Without something to sell, our business won't be in business.

Figure 9-7 plots the 24 months of information we just examined, along with a trend line based on that data. The sad part is that the percentage of things we showed out of stock was only about 3 percent back at the start of this graph. The trend line ends up much higher, so in the space of two years, this business has gone from a decent out of stock level (for it) to one totally unacceptable.

The ideal rate at which you should be out of stock would be zero— you'd always have everything every customer asked for. In the real world, this is rarely achievable, but is certainly a goal worth working toward. By plotting it as we've done here, you get a look at not only where you've been,

PERCENT OF ITEMS OUT OF STOCK

FIGURE 9-7

where the general movement of your information has gone, but with the addition of a trend line can show you where you'll probably be in a few months. Is it where you want to be? If so, keep working the same way; if not, then it's an indication that something in your method of operation needs to be changed.

## Sales/Inventory Per Square Foot

Another way to gauge how a store or division performs is to examine the relationship between sales and inventory on a per square foot basis. If one of your locations has 2,000 square feet and keeps $20,000 worth of merchandise on hand, it has $10 worth of goods for every square foot of store space it uses. You calculate this by dividing the inventory ($20,000) by the square feet (2,000): 20,000/2,000 = 10. If that same location did $40,000 worth of business during a specific period, you can say it produced $20 of sales for every square foot it has available. You calculate this by dividing the total sales ($40,000) by the square feet in the store (2,000): 40,000/2,000 = 20.

Figure 9-8 plots this data for each of our stores, for the month of June. The column chart format is used because it lends itself to a dual comparison—the left (solid) column is the amount of inventory each store carried

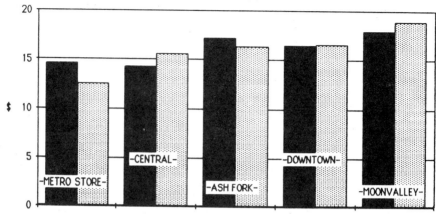

THE SOLID BAR (LEFT BAR) REPRESENTS INVENTORY AT WHOLESALE COST; THE LIGHTER
BAR (RIGHT BAR) REPRESENTS THE SALES FOR EACH OF OUR LOCATIONS

**FIGURE 9-8**

during the month, on a square foot basis. It's important to note the inventory figure is at *wholesale*—our cost, and not what we expect to sell the merchandise for. This is the manner in which we normally talk about inventory, and the way we'll find the figures inside our accounting system. The right column (dashed) represents the sales each location did for the same month, on a per square foot basis.

An examination of this data tells us that two locations—Metro and Ash Fork—both carried *more* inventory than they produced in sales volume. Our downtown store's inventory and sales were about the same. The other two locations created more sales than the total value in their inventory was.

While one month of data is insufficient on which to base any decisions, let's assume for a moment that what we've seen in Figure 9-8 holds true over a length of time. This means in effect, since the dollar totals are as close as they are for the amounts illustrated, that Figure 9-8 tells the business owner that he or she must keep in stock roughly the same dollar figure he or she expects to sell. Put another way, if one of your stores has wholesale value in inventory of $15,000, that's about what it can expect to sell during the next month. Certainly more study is needed, over a longer period of time, but the basic concept is accurate: once you determine the relationship between what you have on hand (on a wholesale basis) and your gross sales (on a retail level), you'll have a good feel for not only what dollar total you'll need on hand to produce the sales you want to, but also whether a selective increase in inventory will bring a like rise in sales. Isn't that the whole idea of inventory control and analysis?

Someone who has the stores we've been examining also has the chance to experiment a bit. Why not increase the inventory at one store by 20 percent and see if sales follow it? Since (based on our assumption that Figure 9-8's story holds true for a long period of time) our sales seem to approximate our inventory cost, on a per square foot basis, might not it follow that if we increase our inventory from $10 to $12 for each square foot of area we have in the store, that sales might not also go up by 20 percent? Would it be worth a try?

## Summing Up

At the bottom of every sale is inventory, but to sell your merchandise, you not only have to have it on hand (or quickly available), but you must price it right, handle the selling process properly, and so on. People who deal on the retail level have an advantage (from an inventory standpoint) over all other merchandisers, as they see the daily interaction between the items they have in stock and the people who consider buying them. But it's important to note that every business shares the same basic types of inventory difficulties. If you order most of what you sell, you still must know what's available, price it right, speak about it in an intelligent manner to your prospects, and so on. The wholesaler perhaps must be more price conscious than other businesspeople, and has inventory hardships imposed by the nature of this end of things—most notably, the large amounts of cash required to start and stay in wholesaling.

Since inventory control is so important, we must handle it as something vital. Surely, no businessperson would turn over control of his or her checkbook to someone he or she just hired yesterday, yet businesspeople do it all the time when it comes to inventory. *Stockpersons* are expected not only to do their jobs—put away the merchandise—but also to reorder when it's necessary, determine who to buy from, and so on. Sadly, the smallest business—which needs tight inventory control for every dollar it spends—gets the worst of things here, as it often doesn't have the cash to pay (or, at least believes it can't afford) someone to handle the inventory in the way it should be taken care of.

Since inventory must come before any sales are consummated, it's logical to plot monthly sales along with monthly inventory totals, to see how one compares to the other. Because everything depends on the inventory you have on hand (or can get), an increase in sales will often follow a rise in your inventory level. How much can you increase it before you reach the point of diminishing returns? Graphics can tell you.

As with most financial information, once you make a study of the raw data, it's helpful to see how things look on a percentage basis, to examine (in this case) what inventory is as a percentage of your total sales. Since your sales depend directly on your inventory, this figure should remain pretty stable. If it does not, it's a reflection of a problem with the stock on hand—it simply is not selling.

Associated with inventory control is how fast things are sold—the *turnover rate* your business has. This needs to be examined both as raw information as well as with a trend line, to see where it's headed. Generally, the faster you can move items from your shelves and out the door the better, as long as the rapidity of this movement doesn't cause out of stock conditions that are unacceptable. The most common way to look at your turnover rate is in terms of the number of days it takes you to move your stock.

It's also useful to convert the dollar total of your inventory from a cost figure to a retail level and compare it to sales; this tells you how many days of sales you'd have left, if you stopped buying right now. It's another indication of how well what you have in stock is moving. Again, a trend line is helpful to give you an idea of how your business will look down the road a month or two.

All of the comparisons with sales and inventory tell the business owner how good his or her merchandise selection is (or, conversely, how poor the product line is). If you have a rapid product turnover, a normal level in terms of the days of sales you have available in inventory, you have a good product mix. If the trend lines of these comparisons are rising, it means products are starting to sit in your stock longer than they should, and you have a problem.

With any inventory comes its Achilles' Heel: you're bound to be out of this item or that, at one time or another. Every business has its own percentage that's right; too low a percentage might mean you have things in stock that no one will ever ask for, while too high a rate means too many prospects leave your business without making a purchase. While industry averages are fine as a general guide, it's more important to extract and study this data for your business over a period of time, to find out what's right for you.

Finally, it's helpful to break sales and inventory down on a square foot basis, and plot them as a column chart. This gives the business owner a feel for the level of sales a certain amount of inventory will produce. If you have more than one location or department, plot them the same way. In general, does a larger inventory mean more sales? For only certain areas of your business, or for them all? Would it be wise to raise your inventory investment here or there to see what happens? *Which* store or division would you increase inventory for? *Why?*

## Other Ideas

Inside your own inventory, you probably can find all sorts of examinations it might be helpful to plot. For example, would you like to see visually how many items you're selling per month? While it's not as accurate in terms of financial data as dollar amounts, it's a useful thing to do once in a while, just to get some feel for the number of individual items you and your people handle. Doing this on a historical basis gives you an idea of whether your inventory base is growing or shrinking; you may discover that your sales are up dollar-wise, but you're only handling 40 percent of the number of items you did at the same time last year. Or that last year your business sold 750 different things, and this year it's working with only 400—is your market shrinking because of what you handle, rather than for competitive and/or economic reasons?

This is a special danger when times are good—we concentrate only on the most profitable areas of our business and (subconsciously, perhaps) start to eliminate those things that don't make as much money, or have a low per-unit volume, or just aren't as interesting as some other things we do. We don't ignore them on purpose, but since the other areas of our work are more important (in our mind), they kind of get pushed to one side. Parts don't get ordered. Jobs don't get scheduled. Work tickets are lost. When the business cycle changes, and it always does, we find ourselves with a constricted base of operations. Where once our business performed, say, 20 distinct services, it now might only handle 12. If business slows down, will those be enough to support the level of sales we need?

It's also a good idea to break our inventory down to a low level and chart its course on a per salesperson basis, or per hour of operation basis—anything to get a feel for the way things are headed. You can tie in a trend line, of course, with all of these comparisons, to forecast where you'll be down the road a bit.

A pie chart examination of the different areas inside your inventory—by product group or category—is helpful, because it displays where your dollars are invested. If you can break sales and profits down in the same manner, you might be surprised that a large and costly stock of one product or another simply doesn't pull its own weight, sales and/or profit-wise. Another, seemingly insignificant area of your business might produce profits far in excess of the investment you have there—wouldn't this be a likely candidate for an increased inventory total?

# Internal Measurements

# 10

Whatever type of business you're in, perhaps the hardest area to understand and change (if it's required) is the one that concerns the internal workings of your company.

When you sell something, you have obvious costs: X amount of materials were used, Y dollars of labor were spent to complete the sale. When you add in an overhead percentage, you'll have a pretty good idea of how well you did on each particular sale. Everything is there in black and white—your materials and payroll and fringe benefits and insurance—everything you spent last month.

Inside any business, though, it's more difficult to understand what's going on. Just as we looked at sales in relationship to its associated cost totals, we need to examine some parts of our business that we often don't consider very much.

## Sales and Hours

Although an obvious and easy comparison is to look at sales compared to total payroll or to direct labor, it's often more useful to graph sales compared to the number of hours your people work. You can turn this around—as we'll do in a moment—to determine the *sales value* for each hour worked, but let's start with Figure 10-1, which charts the sales and hours worked for our fictitious business. Since the hourly total is much lower in terms of raw numbers than our sales information, we need to multiply the hours-worked figure by 10 (for this example) so we can plot them both on the same scale.

**FIGURE 10-1**

In this particular case, Figure 10-1 shows us just about what we'd expect. Labor hours and sales rose and fell at roughly the same time. The *trend* of both appears to be increasing at about the same rate of climb—which is as it should.

While this general overview of things is helpful to some degree, it's much more valuable to break these raw totals down a bit and to convert all those hours into a figure everyone can understand and chart.

## Inside Finances

Most large corporations publish a financial statement, which puts all their associated data on public display. The average small business, though, often prefers to keep this information confidential. Many small- and medium-size businesses don't even release their financial statements to business information services (like Dun & Bradstreet) but consider it to be only for their own use. One thing not done often enough is to communicate the financial condition of the business to its employees. While they certainly have a stake in how the business is doing—and each business's condition is directly dependent on its people—it's difficult to come up with a method to handle this properly. It's naive to think we can let our people know that we made a $32,000 profit last year without some expectation that they might ask for part of it back in the way of wages and/or profit sharing. Likewise, it's difficult to tell our people we *lost* $15,000 last year; they may not even believe us.

Would it be helpful to your business to have some method to let your employees know exactly how your company is doing financially and how they, as a group, are performing, but without disclosing any precise profit and loss data? You can do it with your Macintosh.

The starting point is to divide your monthly sales totals by the number of hours your employees worked during that month. If your sales were $50,000 and your people put in 1,000 hours, they produced $50 in sales for every hour they worked. If your employees spent 2,000 hours on the job, they're producing at the rate of $25 per hour.

If you collect your sales and hours-worked figures for a year or so, you'll have a good idea of what the average dollars-per-hour figure is for your business. If you spend a little more time and list the figures for two or three years, you'll know about what figure you need in order to make money. You'll find that your people will produce a specific figure in sales for each hour they work during those periods when your business is profitable, and a *lower* figure when you're in the red. Each business is different, of course. We've found in our own business that we need $31 dollars of gross sales per hour worked in order to show a profit.

## Walt's Secret Formula

Walt Webb is an astute businessperson who makes exquisite glass cases for things like Hummel figurines and Indian kachina dolls. He's a typical small business owner, and he takes this concept a step further. Although it's helpful to let your employees know what the dollars per hour figure should be, too often, if you post it or put it in a letter, it somehow seems to go over their heads. Business managers are used to working with figures, but employees are more often concerned with the installation or delivery or the service for what we sell. They're often not comfortable with *our* financial data. So Walt *plots* the dollars per hour figure every month and puts the graphs out for all to see.

Figure 10-2 is a look at this data for our fictional business over a nine-month period. In this particular chart, we have two lines—one for this year's monthly figure and another for the same months from last year.

For the first seven months of both years, the monthly figure for this business ran in the low twenties; each hour its employees worked, they produced $21 or $22 in sales. Although it doesn't tell us if the business was profitable during these periods, it does give the owner a basis of comparison. During the first few months of this year, the employees weren't quite as effective as they were the prior year. The period from month 3 through month

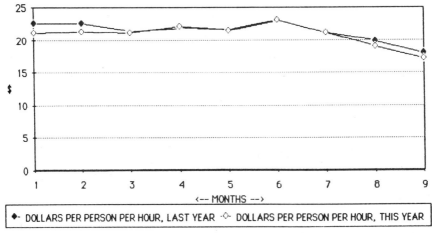

FIGURE 10-2

7 showed the lines on an almost identical basis, perhaps as the result of some corrections the owner made in his or her operation.

The three-month period from month 7 to month 9 showed a sharp drop in the figure for both years. If the business made a profit last year, the owner wouldn't be too concerned about the drop. Perhaps it's due to a seasonal fluctuation in the product mix the business sold during this period.

It's important to consider the factor of *seasonal change,* because what you sell can distort your dollars-per-hour figure. For example, you might charge out one of your employees at $35 per hour. If he or she works for eight hours and sells nothing but labor, your total gross for this employee would be eight hours × $35, or $280. It's obvious this person created $35 in sales for each hour worked.

However, if this same employee installed a major appliance on that particular day, you'd have to add its value to the sales total. Perhaps a water-softening unit was sold and connected, for a price (including labor) of $480. If we divide this amount by the eight hours worked, the employee comes out with a $60 sales figure, on a per-hour basis.

This tells us two things. First, we often cannot study this data over a short period like a day or even a week, because the fluctuations will be too great. Even on a monthly basis, you'll show a lot of ups and downs. In the case of Figure 10-2, though, since you're comparing the same months for two consecutive years, you will probably get a valid picture. What you sold last July will most likely be close to what you'll sell this July, in terms of how it will add to your dollars-per-person-per-hour figure. Second, the important thing about Figure 10-2 is that it's a *comparison* of two similar periods, and as such, seasonal variations are taken into consideration. This business seems to have an obvious problem, though, with its huge drop in *both years* from June to September. That doesn't mean it can't be profitable, but that the owner needs to be aware of what happens inside the business from a seasonal standpoint.

## Individual Totals

In a case where you want to examine just your service technicians who, let's assume, sell *nothing* but their labor, you can make a direct comparison from person to person. Since labor is the only thing involved, different periods of the year should produce about the same results. If you can isolate the sales for each individual service technician, you can divide their sales by the hours they worked and arrive at a sales figure per person, per hour.

Figure 10-3 is a bar chart (a column chart would be equally as effective) for the month of January for our fictitious business. Sales produced per hour by each of the four service technicians are displayed, running from the worst to the best. Obviously, one month's look at this shouldn't make you want to let Ray go, or to give Tony a raise. That decision depends on a lot more information. This examination, though, is helpful as it gives you an in-

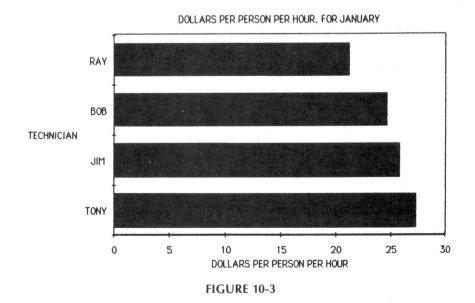

FIGURE 10-3

stant picture of how your people did for this specific month. Why is one better than another? Did he or she work harder? Smarter?

Certainly another consideration is the *job mix* each employee happened to get during the month under study. For any sort of service work, you'll get a wide variety of work. A service call that should take a half-hour drags out into a half-day. A repair job that could have eaten up six hours goes smoothly and is done in two. One month's worth of information isn't enough to make a proper determination and should only be used as a general guide to give you something of an impression of how your people are doing. Of course, if Ray shows up at the bottom of your graph *every* month, you know you have a problem with him.

It's almost always worthwhile to compare each employee, using, for example, a line graph over a period of time. However, one of the limitations of a line chart is that once you get over three lines on it—especially if those lines are close to each other—it becomes impossible to read the thing, much less understand its information. In this particular case, our fictional business employs four people in its service department—too many to chart effectively over time.

## Breakdown Dollars

A much more helpful graph to plot is your people as a group over a period of time, with what you determine is your breakeven point shown on the chart. Once you do some study in the area of dollars per person per hour, you'll know about what each employee (as part of the employee group) needs to produce if you're to make a profit.

This lets you take the concept to your people and post the graph, or even give each one a copy along with their paycheck. Since no one individual or department is singled out, your people will be comfortable receiving this information. But *as a whole* they will be able to see exactly how they're performing and when "their" business is profitable.

Figure 10-4 shows a nine-month picture of our fictitious business, charting the dollar-per-hour figure produced by all employees. Let's assume that this business needs $20 of sales per person, for every hour worked, to break even. It should be obvious to employees that when the graph shows they produced more than $20 per hour, the business was profitable. When they did not, the business lost money. Thus, we have a visual picture that lets people see how both they *and* the business are doing, without disclosing any exact sales or profit (loss) figure.

Anyone who looks at this graph who has the knowledge that the business needs $20 per hour to break even can see this company has a significant problem. What's worse is that the *trend* of the data shows a steep drop

DOLLARS PER PERSON PER HOUR, THIS YEAR

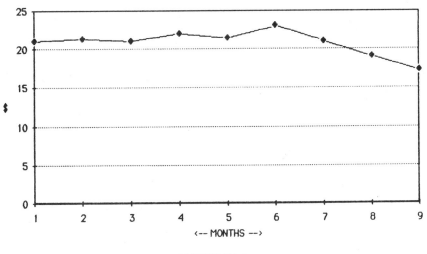

FIGURE 10-4

that dates back to June. Even the fact that we found in Figure 10-2 that the drop this year parallels last year's decrease over these same months doesn't make it any more acceptable and in fact simply means the manager isn't doing a proper job.

## Debt and Equity

The investment the owners of a business have in that enterprise is called *equity*. If you're the sole owner of your business, you've made all the investment into the enterprise. Large corporations have stockholders who collectively invest cash into the business. Equity also comes from any *retained earnings* the owner(s) leaves in the business.

In many small companies, the owner(s) doesn't have enough cash invested to cover the required purchases of major equipment and/or buildings, things necessary (in the eyes of management) for the business to properly do its business. So the business owner finds himself or herself with some long-term debt—long-range financing to cover these major purchases.

Although it seems obvious that there should be some relationship between the *equity* the owner(s) of a business have invested in the company to the *long-term debt* that business determines it can service without a cash flow problem, we often don't consider the connection between the two when a possibly profitable venture comes along. Perhaps we'd like to expand to another area of the city or county and have the opportunity to buy a building there. A used piece of major equipment might become available. Often these opportunities seem to arrive when our cash position is at its worst, so while we make a good investment, we add to our long-term debt at the same time.

Figure 10-5 charts the amount the owner(s) has invested in the business along with the long-term debt the business has, for the first six months of the year. The owner's equity has remained fairly stable (which it would, barring the infusion of more capital and/or some large profits that can add to the retained earnings figure), but the long-term debt total grew rapidly in the March to April period. The business took on a major obligation during this time; let's say that it bought a major new piece of equipment. The graph shows us visually that with this particular purchase, the business suddenly finds itself in a position where outside creditors essentially have nearly as much invested in the company as do its owners.

This isn't necessarily a bad thing, of course, and some businesspeople strive for just this sort of leverage. *Leverage* in this context allows the business owner to expand his or her own financial base with the investments and/or loans of others. But it's important to note that there are certain dangers associated with this position, not the least of which is the fact that almost certainly there's another (possibly large) monthly payment to be made in order to service the new debt.

From a working capital standpoint, the company now will find itself with less cash to use for business operations. Naturally, it would expect the

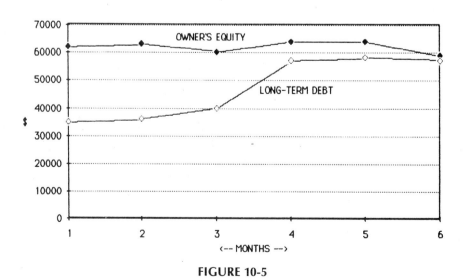

**FIGURE 10-5**

new equipment to start to pay its own way (and thus end up as a good investment), but in real life this often takes time. What do you suppose might happen to this business if it experienced a sudden, sharp drop in sales revenues? Those monthly payments for its long-term obligations would still be there, but perhaps the *cash* to make the payments would not. This is one major danger that confronts you if your business invests more than it should through long-range financing.

Figure 10-5 should also disturb the business owner during the early months of the year. Generally, unless a major investment in plant or machinery is made, the total dollar value of a business's long-term debt should decline, even if only slightly, every month. Most things are handled these days on a monthly payment basis, and so the debt total should have decreased (at least a bit) during the time before the major equipment purchase was made. Instead, it rose slightly, which might indicate that for some reason this company wasn't making its payments on time. If that's the case, the intelligent manager should be aware of it, and this fact might even be a good reason to *postpone* the purchase of the major obligation this business took on during the March to April period.

Figure 10-6 shows us the same basic information we just looked at, but with the long-term debt translated into its percentage of owner's equity. Unfortunately, we can see the percentage rising during the first quarter of the year, just as the dollar total increased. Even *after* the business made the investment in new equipment, its long-term debt as a percentage of equity continued to increase—a possibly hazardous condition. This is especially

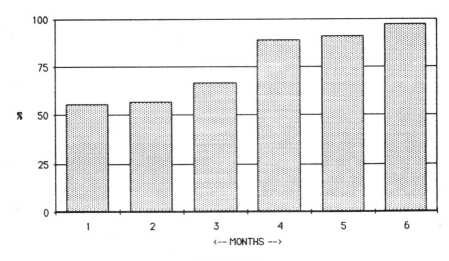

LONG-TERM DEBT AS A PERCENT OF EQUITY

<-- MONTHS -->

**FIGURE 10-6**

true as the percentage of long-term debt to owner's equity gets close to that 100 percent mark, as in effect that means others own more of your business than you do. This severely restricts your ability to borrow money, cash that might be needed to get through one of those short-term sales slumps we all have.

## Investment and Depreciation

Associated with any examination of long-term debt and its relationship to cash outflow is a connection between the total amount invested in equipment and/or physical plant (including buildings and major equipment) with the depreciation we can take on this investment. Because the gross value of our physical plant and equipment is so much larger than the depreciation amount(s), it's difficult to create a graph that shows both items so we can understand their relationship. The easiest way to look at this is with a line graph that displays our depreciation as a percentage of the total value we have for our operating plant and associated equipment.

Since depreciation can often be a major expense in terms of what we see on our balance sheet (and will eventually require some cash or financing to replace the depreciated items), a good way to examine it is as a percentage of the total value of our plant and equipment, as shown in Figure 10-7. In truth, depreciation does affect our year-end cash position,

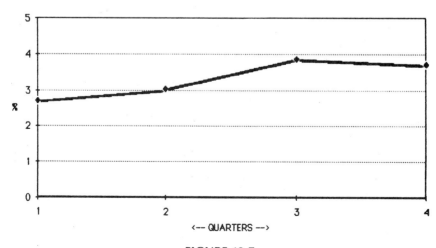

DEPRECIATION AS A PERCENT OF PLANT AND
EQUIPMENT

FIGURE 10-7

because with less depreciation we'll have more income taxes to pay—*in cash.*

Figure 10-7 shows the percentage that current depreciation amounted to, compared to the total value of physical plant and equipment. The business owner who looks at Figure 10-7 can visually see the percentage jump for the third quarter because of the equipment purchase he or she made. A machine will be depreciated over a shorter period than a building would be, and thus a purchase like the one our fictitious business made could cause this rise in depreciation as a percentage of the value of equipment and physical plant.

## The Bottom Line

To tie this all together, we also need to examine an entire year's graph that tracks long-term debt as a percentage of the equity invested in the business. The drop we just saw in depreciation as a percentage of plant/equipment won't always be matched in terms of the rate of fall with a drop in debt as a percentage of equity; that will depend on exactly what the business owner does to reverse the trend. Let's look again at the long-term debt as a percentage of equity for our fictional business.

Figure 10-8 stretches out the same debt we looked at earlier in Figure 10-6 and displays what a graph *should* look like, assuming the owner(s)

LONG TERM DEBT AS A PERCENT OF EQUITY

FIGURE 10-8

took the correct steps to change the situation. We can see the rise in long-term debt as a percentage of owner's equity during the first half of the year, when (perhaps) both late payments and a major investment caused a sharp jump. From July on, the owner(s) of this business turned the situation around—they found a dangerous condition back in the early summer and took steps to reverse it. Perhaps more cash was invested into the business. Maybe a location with a negative effect on this ratio was sold. Perhaps the company restructured its payment schedule for its long-term debts. The important thing is, *something* was done to reverse the situation to lower the ratio of the owner's equity to long-term debt. This business gained some breathing room and has protected itself against a sudden drop in sales.

## Working Capital as a Form of Control

As another way to examine how things are inside our business, a look at working capital is often helpful. *Working capital* is defined as the excess of current assets over current liabilities and in effect is the amount of cash your business has available to do business with.

A line graph like Figure 10-9 charts the first six months of the year for both the sales and the working capital for our fictitious business. As always, any aberration in the figures is a sign to look at things a bit closer. In this case, while working capital remained stable for the first quarter of the

**FIGURE 10-9**

WORKING CAPITAL AS A PERCENTAGE OF SALES

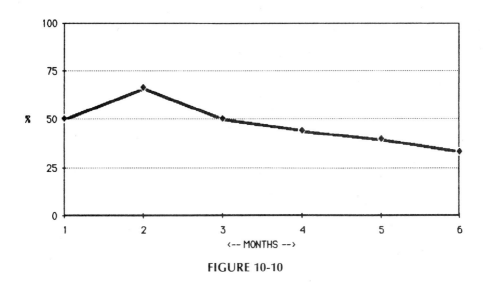

**FIGURE 10-10**

year, its total dropped during the second quarterly period. Sales, meanwhile, rose.

This may not indicate anything significant—perhaps the sales we made during the last three months were those which required we put out a lot of capital to finance them. If that's the case, this cash will be returned to us in the form of revenue. It's equally possible, though, that we've lost money during this period, and the cash that's disappeared from our graph is really gone. The alert manager will spend some more time to find out why working capital is decreasing. Is it because of the rise in sales or because there are problems with the type of sales we're making?

Figure 10-10 paints the picture as even more of a problem than what Figure 10-9 intimated. Here we see our working capital as a percentage of sales. This gives us a good feeling for the *trend* of our working capital, whether the sales revenue we're creating adds to or subtracts from it; here, it's been heading lower since February.

It's important to note that working capital isn't an end-all; we might be making all sorts of profits and putting that cash into another area of our business. Perhaps we used it to reduce some of those long-term debts. The purpose of Figure 10-10 is to tell the business owner that working capital is *shrinking*. A sharp decrease in working capital may mean the business could have a future problem doing business.

As always, the *amount* and *percentage of sales* of working capital vary by business. If the majority of your work creates cash-only transactions, you don't require as much working capital as the business that lets its customers charge everything they buy and then allows liberal payment terms. This latter type of business might gain something in the finance charges it tacks onto late bills, but in the meantime it needs more cash just to operate.

Figure 10-10 shows our fictional business going from a high percentage of working capital in relationship to sales back in month 2 (about 60 percent) to a low in month 6 of around 33 percent. No business should have this much variance, and that's the real point of this example. Your business does things a certain way. You handle your customers in a specific manner. Unless you change the way you do business, your working capital as a percentage of sales should remain pretty stable. If you find something inside your business that causes a fluctuation like we've seen here—a 27 percent change in working capital as a percentage of sales within a four-month period—you need to find out *why*.

Another way to examine this same thing is to plot working capital on a basis of its *percentage* increase or decrease, month to month or every quarter. It really brings home whether your cash position is getting better or worse, and by how much.

# Old Bills

In almost every business, certain items are charged and carried in the form of an obligation as accounts payable. While we all make comparisons between accounts payable this year versus last, and receivables compared to payables, and even sales compared to accounts payable, there's another helpful relationship that involves payables that we often don't consider.

Assume that we purchased $9,000 worth of materials in January. If we divide this by 30 days (to keep things simple, we'll assume each month contains 30 days), this means we averaged $300 worth of material purchases per day. If we have $3,000 in accounts payable as of January 31st, we can say that *we have ten days worth of purchases* in our accounts payable total. We calculate this by dividing our accounts payable ($3,000 in this example) by our average daily material purchases ($300): $3000/300 = 10$. This means we have ten days worth of purchases in our accounts payable total. Likewise, if we owe $6,000 worth of payables at the end of January, we could say that we have 20 days worth of purchases in that payables total.

The significance of this figure is simply that it gives us an exact indication of how well we're paying our bills (or how poorly we're doing so). Whereas we'll age our accounts receivable totals, we often don't do the same with what we owe (we'd much rather concentrate on the monies owed us, rather than vice versa). It serves as a good method of internal control because it tells us precisely how we stand; if we chart it, we can see how our bill-paying habits look.

DAYS OF PURCHASES IN ACCOUNTS PAYABLE

**FIGURE 10-11**

Figure 10-11 graphs the number of *days worth of purchases* we have in accounts payable for the first six months of the year. For this particular example, the total rose from about 60 days worth of purchases back in January to almost 100 days worth for each month during the April–June period. For one reason or another, our payables total is getting progressively worse. The business owner should have noticed the trend during the first three months, and once he or she spotted the large jump in the March–April period, should have taken immediate steps to correct it.

This is the sort of condition that is only remedied one way: we have to somehow come up with some cash to cover our accounts payable. Figure 10-11 shows we have more than 90 days worth of purchases in our accounts payable total—a time frame that starts to cause phone calls and demands for payment from anxious suppliers.

To help put things into their proper perspective, Figure 10-12 charts the same data we've been examining, but over a whole year. Steps were taken after those terrible first six months to reduce our accounts payable, and at least at the end of the year their total wasn't much more than it had been at the start of the year. However, even Figure 10-12 doesn't present a promising picture, in that we still show more than 60 days worth of purchases in our accounts payable total. This can create credit problems, raise the possibility that someone will close our open account, and might start to put black marks into our credit file. A good goal would be to reduce the total purchases in our accounts payable down to less than a 30-day level (or whatever is normal for your business).

FIGURE 10-12

## Summing Up

Any study of internal measurements—some way to see exactly what's happening inside our business—must start with sales, and a good way to examine it is in relationship to the hours worked by our people. The more hours they work, the more our sales should be. If these two lines don't move in line with one another, we might have a problem.

This same approach should be carried further to determine the sales volume each employee produces for every hour worked. Unless you have a specific group of people who don't sell parts or supplies or equipment, you almost have to examine this figure for all of your people as a group. However, if you have a class of employees you can look at on an individual basis, it's worthwhile to do so.

Once you determine how your people perform in relationship to your sales volume, you have an exact figure you can graph and present to them as an indication of how well they're doing their job. You can compare their dollars per-person-per-hour this year to last year. Another way to show the same information is to put a breakeven line on the graph; employees can instantly *see* if their work is making money for the business or not.

Another helpful relationship to watch is that between the owner's equity (what the owner(s) has invested in his business) and the long-term debt (what others have invested on a long-range basis). As the two figures move closer together—and especially if their *trend* shows them starting to meet—the business can face future difficulties if sales happen to decrease.

Depreciation is an expense that doesn't consume cash at the time it's recorded. In any business with a major investment in plant and/or equipment, it's necessary to watch depreciation both in terms of raw data and on a percentage basis. What's a healthy depreciation percentage for your business? Is the *trend* of your depreciation rising or falling? *Why?*

As sales increase, working capital is often used up (at least over the short term) to make the purchases to support the sales. However, sales should eventually *add* to the total working capital, as profit is produced and accumulated. Working capital as a percentage of sales is a comparison we need to make monthly, with an eye to its trend, its movement.

Finally, accounts payable form a significant part of the debt of many businesses, and one way to gauge our payables position is to examine it in view of the number of days of purchases we have *stored up* in our accounts payable total.

## Other Ideas

Since the investment a business has varies widely with the nature of the business itself, your company might have a major interest in property, buildings, and equipment while another may not. As a general rule, the *net value* of your plant and equipment should exceed your long-term debt. As long as its figure is higher than the dollars you owe and must pay back over a long period of time, this ratio is acceptable. When the ratio exceeds 1:1, however, it's an indication that you're using long-term money to finance immediate cash flow problems, that you're borrowing on a long-range basis to come up with payroll money. That's a danger sign, as a working business must be able to generate its own operating cash as it does business.

Another helpful idea for many business owners is to examine their assets and liabilities in the form of a pie chart, perhaps on a quarterly basis. This gives them a feel for the condition of things as they relate to one another, an idea of how each specific asset or liability category grows and/or shrinks, as represented by the slices of the pie. It's a useful visual picture of the information.

# How "Mac" Can Help You Sell

# 11

You may not think about it, but you probably already use graphs as a sales tool. A lot of consumer literature includes charts to make a point, to compare one brand against another, to promote the product through the use of graphed data.

Obviously, any use of graphs as something to help you sell more effectively depends on what your business happens to handle. It takes some creative thinking to come up with an idea or two that make sense and will present your product and/or service to your prospects in a manner that encourages them to want to buy from you.

One of the best things about using graphs to help your sales is that they complement each other: both selling and graphics are essentially a form of communication. When you make your sales presentation to a potential customer, you want to tell your story, to make the prospect understand that you're the right person to buy from, that you'll have the best service and warranty, that the customer will want to buy from you over and over. To do an effective job, you must capture the prospect's time and interest.

Because business graphs lend themselves to the basic process of communication, they can help in a number of ways. It's because of the sales presentation that salespeople have a reputation for talking fast: they want to get as much of their presentation said before the prospect says "No." Pictures can help hold a prospect's interest during an extended presentation. Graphs drive home a point. They can illustrate some things better than pages of facts and figures. With your Macintosh, you can personalize your graphs, to make them seem like they're specifically designed for each prospect, an advantage your competition may not be able to duplicate. You wouldn't present a quotation to a major prospect that didn't have the prospect's name filled in on it, would you? Instead of handing the person you're talking to a piece of factory literature, why not give him or her a personalized graph?

# Where to Start

The place to begin your search on how business graphs can help your sales is to look at what you sell, in relation to the selling process itself. You need to list how things happen for your business and then go over your list to see where graphs might be able to help. Once you have a prospect (either because they contacted you or vice versa), what happens? Do you go to their home or do they come to see you at your place of business? What sort of sales presentation do you make? Is there a chance to sit down with your prospect and show him or her a graph or two, to explain why he or she should buy from you? Almost anytime you have a situation where literature is involved—where you give your prospect something to look at and examine— you can find a way to use a graph to help get your message across. ·

You also must focus on your own products or services and ask yourself why a prospect should buy from you. What makes you better than the store down the street? Better prices? Do you have higher quality products for sale? Why are your products better than anyone elses? Do you sell more than one *grade* of equipment? Why is one better than another? And the bottom line: how can you demonstrate this to your prospect, so he or she will be convinced that you're the one to buy from?

You want to examine your entire selling process, with an eye to finding out when and where graphs might be of value to you.

Most (if not all) products are purchased to solve a problem. This extends all the way from the basics (food, shelter, transportation) to the extras we all want. What problems do you solve for your prospects? A heating and air conditioning business helps with indoor comfort problems; a clothing store helps people not only look good but succeed in their work; a hardware store lets its customers fix things without expensive service labor. Make a list of the problems your business solves for people, constantly searching as to how graphics can make you more effective in explaining how you'll do it.

Get out the consumer literature you have available and examine it. What's on there that could be converted into graphs for a specific customer? A comparison of operating costs? One brand of equipment against another? Often, you can re-create graphs from pieces of sales literature and personalize them with your micro, to make them a more effective sales tool.

It's not an easy task, and you won't be able to translate every idea you come up with into a way to use a graph. The important thing, though, is to have just one or two charts you can call on for each sales presentation. It's interesting that (perhaps) these can be the same basic graph, with only the names changed. After all, what you tell one prospect is probably true for the next person you speak to, so why not use the same picture for each one?

# Savings

These days, much of what's talked about during the selling process involves energy costs. Most things you buy today—from a copy machine to a dishwasher to the car you drive—use some form of energy to operate. Given a choice of two (or more) seemingly equal items, it makes sense to choose the one that's going to cost the least to operate over its expected lifespan. As energy bills continue to rise, the operating cost of a product becomes even more important, at least in the minds of your prospects.

There's a danger here, though, when you get into the area of comparing one product to another in terms of its operating costs. The tendency is to list or graph the expected expenses over time, to let your prospect know that one brand will cost, say, $2400 to run for five years, while another might only cost $1300 to operate during the same period. The problem is that the focus is on *costs*, rather than on *savings*. The natural tendency for a prospect to say is something like, "You mean, it'll cost me *that much* to run this thing?" Once that happens, you might have lost the sale. The focus instead should be on the cost *savings* your proposal will give the prospect, as shown in Figure 11-1.

Figure 11-1 is an area chart that is but one variation that you might use when you speak about any energy savings that [whatever you sell] provides your customers. The focus is on the savings aspect—brand A will save more than brand B will. While the graph doesn't spell it out, the comparisons are obviously made to the customer's current brand of equipment. The chart is also personalized with a particular prospect's name, which indicates it was prepared especially for the person you happen to be making your sales presentation to. It's impressive. The area chart format is used because you're working with cumulative data here, the accumulated savings over the three-year period shown. An area chart is ideal to show how the savings dollars grow with each passing year.

One warning on this type of example: it's easy when you talk about cost savings to show the maximum, and sometimes you might want to extend a graph over a long period of time. It's difficult for people to see much further than three or four years down the road, so an illustration like Figure 11-1 is probably more helpful than a graph that plots potential utility savings over a

FIGURE 11-1

ten-year period. That's simply too long a time to relate to. If you find it necessary to look over that long a time frame, use it in combination with a graph like Figure 11-1, so your prospects can see what they'll save over the near term, as well as over a long period of years.

You'll note that there are no yearly dates listed on this example, which means it can be used at any time during the year, for any prospect who's considering these two brands of equipment. All you have to do is change the prospect's name and reprint the graph to personalize it. You don't need to redo all the data and redraw the graph before you print it for your current prospect. And your Macintosh lets you put the graph right in the body of your specification sheet/quotation/estimate, etc.

# A Trend Line

It's often worthwhile, once you're talking to your prospect about potential energy savings, to have your plotting program create trend lines for your data and plot just them.

The process to accomplish this requires you to enter the initial information, use the statistical part of your graphing program to create cumulative totals, and then ask the analysis part of the package to create trend lines based on the cumulative information. This example shows your prospect the projected *trends* of the two brands under consideration in terms of their cost savings. In some ways, it's a better way to look at things than Figure 11-1 was. This is because it tells the prospect a long-range story, what his or her savings will amount to over a long period of time, but since the trend lines climb so rapidly even during the early years, a prospect can still relate to the information.

You'll notice that Figure 11-2 is based on completely different data than Figure 11-1 was, and because of the large dollar amounts involved could be used for a commercial application. This sort of look can cover anything from a new cooling system for a large hotel to a computerized energy management program for a hospital. It makes it easy for your prospects to see what cost picture they'll look at over the next few years.

These graphs—a study of the cost savings someone might expect if they buy what you suggest—are also valuable for another reason. In selling, there's something called *buyer's remorse,* and we've all run into it. It's when, after a prospect has signed a contract, he or she begins to have second thoughts. The problem most often comes along when the prospect gets home. His or her spouse or neighbor is often more than willing to volunteer that, "You didn't buy one of those, did you? Mary Jones down at work had one once and it gave her nothing but trouble. She finally had to sue the dealer. . . ."

The prospect starts to wonder if he or she made a good decision or bought a lemon, if a better deal could have been made elsewhere, and so on. Once armed with your personalized graphs that show how many dollars will

TREND LINES FOR OPERATING COST SAVINGS

FIGURE 11-2

be saved over the next few years, the prospect can whip them out and show them to the kind soul who has all the words of wisdom to impart. Graphs like these help eliminate buyer's remorse.

## Startup Problems

Every so often, a brand new unit, fresh out of the box, simply won't run. The factory is supposed to check everything, of course, but something happens in shipment that knocks the unit out of whack, and products come through that just won't work. It happens not just to air conditioning units and furnaces, but also to televisions and stereos and automobiles, and, yes, even microcomputers.

For any major purchase, a potential customer is concerned about how well something is made. They'll more often than not ask about the warranty a product has but usually don't even consider that something might not operate the first time it's used. After all, it's brand new.

In our business, we try to check every unit before it goes to a customer's home, to make sure it works properly, runs quietly, and so on. If we don't, every now and then we'll get a unit that we install and then find won't operate. The problem is that the customer doesn't really want the defective unit repaired; he or she demands a *new* unit. After all, they don't want to buy a lemon, something that's going to give them a problem in a year or two, they want a new, perfect system right out of the box. And they're right—that's what they bought and paid for. Often, equipment manufacturers don't see things the same way, and while they're glad to repair the unit, they refuse to replace it with a new one. So, you have people problems right off the bat when you don't check the equipment you sell before you deliver and/or install it.

This is a helpful selling tool, though—tell your prospects that you check out each unit before you deliver it, just to make sure it's not freight-damaged, that it runs correctly, and so on. Once you explain this to them, they won't object if you unpack the product and will appreciate the extra care. Of course, you want to tell them this *before* they make the purchase, as another reason to buy from you.

Figure 11-3 tells your prospect that things sometimes do happen to new units, that every so often they won't work after they're unpacked and plugged in or installed. Many of us have an aversion to knocking the competition (it's bad selling, anyway), but you don't have to even name the brands your competition sells to make this comparison. Just the fact that you'd produce such a graph, give it to your prospects and explain it to them raises your stature in the eyes of the people you talk to.

Wouldn't you be impressed with, say, a television salesperson who

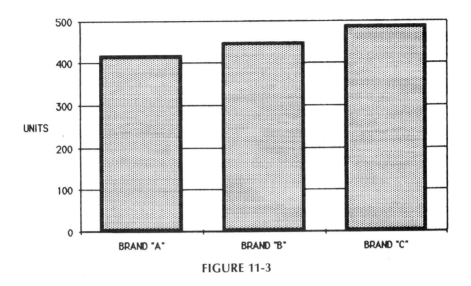

STARTUP PROBLEMS, PER 10,000 UNITS SOLD

**FIGURE 11-3**

handed this graph to you? "Now, it doesn't happen very often," he or she will tell you, "but once in a while one of the sets doesn't work after it's unpacked. To make sure none of our customers have a problem, we unpack and check every set before it goes out here on the display floor. And here's the record for these three brands in terms of initial startup problems. It helps explain why this one costs more than that one. . . ."

There's not a lot of difference in the plotted data, but it's the point that counts: you took the time and trouble to explain to your prospect how equipment sometimes doesn't work right. He or she will appreciate you for it. If you can't get this data from industry sources, dig it out of your own service records. It doesn't have to be startup problems, of course, but can be things like *first-year warranty claims* or *expected lifespan.*

## How Noisy Is That?

In our business, some air conditioning units and furnace systems are quieter than others. Noise level might not apply to your business, but there may be something involved with the *use* of your product that a prospect may be concerned with. It might be the size or speed at which a tree will grow (for someone in the nursery business), the paper quality and longevity (for a book bindery), how fast images will fade (for a custom photo store). Since our business is involved with the operating sound levels of indoor comfort equipment, we'll look at an example of how to talk about it in a selling situation.

Most equipment manufacturers supply more than one grade of equipment. They'll have a basic model, which is the least expensive but also the noisiest, has the fewest self-test and safety features, the greatest number of warranty repair calls, and so on. Many also supply a medium grade of equipment, a cut above the cheapest model, as well as their top-of-the-line equipment. This best item might include things the other grades haven't even thought of in terms of extra safety controls, higher-quality components, lower sound levels, etc. Naturally, your prospect will get what he or she pays for, and it's your job to illustrate why one grade of equipment might in reality be a better buy than another, less expensive one.

Figure 11-4 illustrates the sound levels of three grades of air conditioning units. All are from the same brand, and as you'd expect, the unit with the highest cost makes the least amount of noise. The helpful thing about this example is that it illustrates visually to your prospect that there is a choice, and exactly what one difference is between the available grades of equipment within a given brand. You could carry this out a bit and compare different brands, and even different approaches to the same problem. In our line, that might mean we'd recommend a unit on your roof as the quietest (but most expensive), a second choice as a system in your garage (you might hear it a little, but it costs less than the rooftop unit), and so on. If our prospect wants the quietest system available, he or she will have to spend

SOUND RATINGS IN DECIBELS, BRAND "A" UNITS

FIGURE 11-4

the extra cash to get it. Something like noise level is difficult to really understand, too, and a graph like this one helps bring the concept home.

## More on Costs

While the general focus should be on the potential savings a prospect can realize if he or she buys what you suggest, there are situations where you can use the projected cost figures to your benefit.

Figure 11-5 illustrates the operating costs for [whatever the customer is using], over a five-year period, based on two different levels of insulation a prospect may put into his or her home. You'll note that you want to stay away from cumulative costs here, as they grow so rapidly that you might get a bad reaction from the prospect. A line graph that shows two cost levels, like Figure 11-5 does, brings home to your prospect the difference in cost if he or she puts either 4″ or 8″ of insulation into his or her attic.

While this chart is obviously designed for someone selling insulation, the basic concept can be used in many other cases and is particularly suited to those *options* you have available for sale.

For example, in our own business, we sell clock thermostats, units that automatically lower the temperature inside your home or office at night, when you don't want it as warm. Then, they'll bring the temperature back up to a comfortable level before you get up in the morning. If you—through

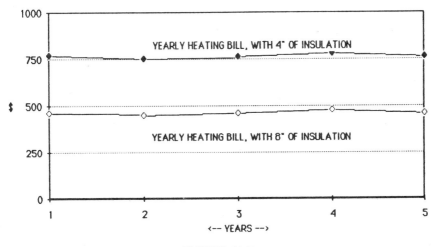

OPERATING COSTS BASED ON THE INSULATION
LEVEL IN YOUR ATTIC

**FIGURE 11-5**

ENERGY SAVINGS, COMPARING A FIVE AND A TEN
DEGREE NIGHT SETBACK

FIGURE 11-6

the use of one of these thermostats—lower the nighttime temperature, you can save on your overall operating costs. A graph like Figure 11-5 is ideal to explain the concept, because a prospect can quickly see (if the chart was designed to show operating costs with and without one of these clock thermostats) the exact cost to operate the furnace if the extra cash is spent to buy one, and the costs if a standard thermostat is used. The same application works for those things you sell that don't give a prospect a lot of savings, where a cumulative chart would show a large accumulated savings. Instead, show the difference in costs through the use of a line chart.

You can take things a step further, too, with a picture like the column chart of Figure 11-6.

On most clock thermostats, there are various *setback* periods. The more you set back the temperature, the more you can save on operating costs. To help get this across to your customers, Figure 11-6 illustrates the savings they can expect for two different setback temperatures—five degrees and ten degrees. This example makes the information easy to understand and *see*. The data is available in the literature from Honeywell.

# Payback

In many things, there's a *payback period* that can be calculated to let prospects know that if they spend a certain amount of money today, they'll save it back (in the form of operating costs or maintenance expenses) over a specific period of time. It gets complex to try to create a computer-generated

WARRANTY PERIOD FOR THE MAIN UNIT

**FIGURE 11-7**

graph to plot this information, and in reality it's often more effective to use a table of figures from your spreadsheet to illustrate the point. The idea is a valuable tool, however, and one you should use if the products you sell lend themselves to it.

Another way to illustrate the strength of your product is to explain thoroughly its warranty to your prospect. Unfortunately, a lot of this sort of detail seems to go over people's heads, but you can get around this problem with a graph like Figure 11-7.

If you create a graph like Figure 11-7 and leave it with your prospect, it gives him or her something that really drives home the differences between the warranty periods for the three brands under consideration. Often, when someone hears "this has a 20-year warranty," it doesn't mean much. When he or she sees it in this form, though, it's easy to see and relate to the differences among brands.

## More on Efficiency

Operating efficiency has more to it than just operating costs. Different things you sell might work better than others, may do a more effective job for a prospect. Or, they might operate better under certain conditions, engineering ideas that are often difficult to explain.

Figure 11-8 illustrates the efficiency rating for an electronic air cleaner,

EFFICIENCY RATING CHART FOR AN AIR CLEANER
(PREPARED FOR MR. AND MRS. FLOYD COLLINS)

**FIGURE 11-8**

over different air volume levels. An air cleaner is something that takes dust and pollen out of the air and in effect does just what it says: it *cleans* the air. While it might seem obvious that the more air you move over one of these units, the less efficient it will be, it's sometimes hard to explain this to a prospect.

You'd use this example to show a potential customer that it's best to operate this particular unit at between 1,000 and 1,100 cubic feet of air per minute (CFM). Once, as shown by the graph, you start to exceed those air volume levels, the efficiency of the unit drops off rapidly. The graph should also be personalized, as this one is, and given to the prospect; it's a good sales tool.

If you're wondering where you might find information like this, examine some of the literature and specification sheets you get from your suppliers. This particular data can be found in literature from Honeywell, which makes the electronic air cleaners we sell. However, while the same chart is available in Honeywell's literature, it's more effective to create a personalized graph for a prospect.

# Where the Dollars Go

In any business, one objection we all run into is, "It costs too much." In many cases, this is a valid complaint, but just because this objection is voiced doesn't mean you won't make the sale. On the contrary, it's altogether different than, "We can't afford it," which, sadly, is sometimes the case. But a price objection means simply that the prospect isn't convinced that your product is worth what you're asking for it, that you haven't done an effective selling job.

With most things, it's a question of priorities as to where people put the cash they do have. They obviously need food and shelter, transportation, clothing, and so on—income most likely will be first spent for the necessities of life, or, in reality, for what the prospect *perceives* as something he or she must have. There are all kinds of ways to counter a price objection. One of the easiest is to use a graph to show how the cost of what you want to sell fits in with a larger picture. When we present a proposal for a heating and cooling system for a new home, we sometimes hear that our price is too high, and when we do, the graph shown in Figure 11-9 is useful.

Figure 11-9 shows a prospect a visual representation of the total he or she will spend for their new home, based on six types of subcontractor work. Our end of things, heating, is printed as the darkest area, to highlight it. Once a prospect examines this illustration, he or she often concludes that our price is really not as expensive as originally thought.

If your own line of work doesn't show up as the least expensive based on the other trades you work with, how does it look compared to the whole project? How about on a per square foot or per unit basis? If you weren't competitive within your industry, you wouldn't still be in business, so there's something to your work that will put you in a favorable light when it

CONSTRUCTION COSTS BY SUBCONTRACTOR

**FIGURE 11-9**

comes to price. Perhaps it's a price/performance ratio for what you sell compared to what others handle.

A pie chart is very useful for this examination, as it effectively shows comparisons on a percentage basis, without dealing with the dollar figures (which, as you know, is where the objection came from to start with).

## Summing Up

Business graphs can be used in a variety of ways to illustrate what you want and need to tell a prospect; you may be using them now as illustrations on customer literature you hand out. If any of these can be personalized with information about a specific prospect, it makes your potential customer feel that since you spent the time and effort to create the graph, you'll probably do a conscientious job for them. So, the first place to start is with your own sales process and the items you sell. Not everything lends itself to a graph that helps sell it; on the contrary, it takes some hard thinking to come up with a few ideas that apply to any business. Think about *why* someone might want to purchase from you; outline the problems your business solves for its customers.

Since many products require energy to operate, a logical place to start is with any savings a customer will enjoy if he or she buys what you propose. A good way to show potential customers the savings they might expect if they buy from you is with an area graph, because it illustrates the cumulative dollars (or kilowatt-hours of electricity used, or therms of gas consumed, and so on) the savings will amount to.

One other advantage of giving a graph (and for that matter, anything that supports a purchase from you) to your prospect is that it will help with the problem of buyer's remorse. Almost everyone experiences this (both from the viewpoint of a buyer and a seller), and anything we can do to support a customer's purchase, the better our chances are that we'll have a satisfied buyer.

You might not want to talk about the unit that won't work fresh out of the box, but every business gets them now and again. You might as well greet the problem at your front door and do something constructive about it. As for graphics, it's useful to talk to your prospect about the ways your company looks after him or her both before and after the sale, and even to use a chart to illustrate why one grade of equipment and/or brand might be the best way to go. If you deal with things that *run*, you may have some units that are quieter than others. Why not create a simple graph to explain this to your prospect?

You can also focus on the add-on items your business handles (again, with the energy-savings approach) and use graphs to illustrate any potential savings customers will enjoy, if only they spend a little more to start with. Or, does something (as an example from our business, we looked at electronic air cleaners) operate more efficiently under specific conditions?

Finally, if you get price objections, try putting what you sell into perspective in relation to a larger dollar total. A pie chart can help you do this; it's up to you to find and select and graph the proper things that will put your product in its best light. In our business, for example, we can create an interesting comparison when we compare the cost—as a percentage of the total cost—for air conditioning for your home, as compared to what you spend to put it into your car. In a $100,000 home, a $3,000 refrigeration system represents only 3 percent of the total. A car air conditioning unit might run $600, which for a new auto that retails for, say, $8,000, comes to 7.5 percent. When you break your price down like this, it seems more reasonable to your prospect.

## Other Ideas

Since each business is so different in terms of what it sells and the way it does its selling, perhaps the best suggestion for other ideas is to ask you to concentrate on two things: First, think about what you want to get across to your prospect. What do you want and need to say to tell your sales story? What's the most important thing about what you sell? What would you say to this prospect if you only could have one minute of his or her time? This thinking forces you to concentrate on the most important areas of your sales presentation, and perhaps you'll list them, which will give you ideas for graphs that can help. Always try to personalize things, too, for each prospect.

Second, try to put yourself in your prospect's shoes and consider what questions he or she would like answers to. What's important to this prospect? Why? You can often learn the answers to those questions by listening for a few minutes to what the prospect has to say. Once you have some idea of what problem(s) this potential customer wants and needs to solve, then you can figure out the best solution for it. If you think about things from his or her point of view, you'll also come up with some ideas on how graphs can help; if you were this prospect, what sort of chart would convince you to buy from *you*?

# A Tutorial:
# Multiplan to Chart

# 12

Microsoft's Multiplan and Chart give you the powerful combination of an electronic spreadsheet with a multitude of functions (Multiplan) that can interface with an outstanding graphics/statistical package (Chart). As with all products that run in the Macintosh environment, data you create and work with on one program can be *communicated* to the other. This lets you store and manipulate your financial information with Multiplan and then send it along to Chart to create an understandable picture of it. As the Macintosh system continues to develop and grow, other spreadsheets and graphics packages will join the ranks of these two, and while the exact instructions will vary somewhat if you use different programs to handle your data, the basic thrust will be the same.

The purpose of this chapter is to present a tutorial for creating a graph, starting with entering data onto a Multiplan worksheet, to use this program to perform mathematical calculations on the information, to show you how to transmit the data to Chart, and finally, to use the latter program to create a graph.

Our function here is *not* to teach you how to operate either of these systems; the program manuals do an effective job. As we did in Chapter 1—where we went through the on-screen pictures of a graph—we'll take you step-by-step through the process. Here, we'll go all the way from initial worksheet creation and data entry within Multiplan to the transfer to Chart, where we'll create a column graph.

You're expected to have enough familiarity with each package to boot

the program and generally operate it. Thanks to the Macintosh user interface—what you see on your screen—the way each program operates mimics
the other; once you're familiar with one, you can quickly use another.

## The Main Process

Our main approach here will be to track our sales information on a monthly
basis, along with our labor costs for the same period, let Multiplan compute
our labor dollars as a percentage of our sales, send this data to Chart, and
graph it. If you're working along with us, let's boot Multiplan and start with
its blank screen.

Figure 12-1 illustrates the Multiplan worksheeet area after you've
started the program: it's blank and ready to use. Our first step will be to
enter Months as a title in the cell at column 1, row 1, and then abbreviations
for the 12 following months under this name. To make data entry a little faster, select the first 13 cells in column 1 by positioning the cursor (shaped
like a hollow plus sign) over cell R1C1 (it's already highlighted). Press the
button on the mouse and hold it down while you move the cursor down to
cell R13C1. Then, release the button.

Figure 12-2 shows the effect this has—the cells you selected are high-

FIGURE 12-1

**FIGURE 12-2**

lighted. By selecting the cells you want to work with in advance, as you've done here, you can enter your information by typing it in followed by a press of the Enter key—that will automatically move you to the next highlighted cell. Now, enter Months in cell R1C1 and the abbreviations for the months of the year in the cells immediately underneath. Then, move the cursor to cell R1C2 and click the mouse button; your picture should look like Figure 12-3.

Figure 12-3 shows our first main heading—Months—and the monthly abbreviations. Let's now enter Sales in cell R1C2, Labor cost in cell R1C3, and Percent in cell R1C4. First, select the cell you want to use by clicking on it, and then enter the headings. When you're done, click on cell R1C5. Your screen should look like Figure 12-4.

Figure 12-4 shows your worksheet with all the major column headings in place, along with the months of the year running up and down the left side of your screen, in column 1. For this example, we have not changed the column widths from their standard default setting, although in actual practice you might want to, so you could have titles like Total labor cost and Labor percent.

Now let's enter the dollar amounts for our monthly sales for the first seven months of the year in cells R2C2 through R8C2, and the totals for our monthly labor costs in cells R2C3 through R8C3. Your worksheet should look like Figure 12-5.

| | 1 | 2 | 3 | 4 | 5 | 6 |
|---|---|---|---|---|---|---|
| 1 | Months | | | | | |
| 2 | Jan | | | | | |
| 3 | Feb | | | | | |
| 4 | Mar | | | | | |
| 5 | Apr | | | | | |
| 6 | May | | | | | |
| 7 | Jun | | | | | |
| 8 | Jul | | | | | |
| 9 | Aug | | | | | |
| 10 | Sep | | | | | |
| 11 | Oct | | | | | |
| 12 | Nov | | | | | |
| 13 | Dec | | | | | |
| 14 | | | | | | |
| 15 | | | | | | |

FIGURE 12-3

| | 1 | 2 | 3 | 4 | 5 | 6 |
|---|---|---|---|---|---|---|
| 1 | Months | Sales | Labor cost | Percent | | |
| 2 | Jan | | | | | |
| 3 | Feb | | | | | |
| 4 | Mar | | | | | |
| 5 | Apr | | | | | |
| 6 | May | | | | | |
| 7 | Jun | | | | | |
| 8 | Jul | | | | | |
| 9 | Aug | | | | | |
| 10 | Sep | | | | | |
| 11 | Oct | | | | | |
| 12 | Nov | | | | | |
| 13 | Dec | | | | | |
| 14 | | | | | | |
| 15 | | | | | | |

FIGURE 12-4

FIGURE 12-5

Figure 12-5 shows data for the first seven months of the year, for both sales and labor costs. To arrive at labor as a percentage of sales, the next step might seem to be to insert a formula into cell R2C4 that divides the figure in cell R2C3 by the number in cell R2C2. However, when you copy this formula cell into the cells below it, when Multiplan encounters 0 in a cell it tries to divide into another (which it will when it hits cell R9C2), you'll get an error that tells you the system was trying to divide by zero. The error message reads #DIV/0!.

There's a way around this, using Multiplan's built-in IF () function. This is explained in both the tutorial and in the reference section of your Multiplan manual, although neither does a terrific job. The logic is similar to what you'd find in an IF-THEN BASIC programming statement:

IF [data A] is EQUAL TO [data B], THEN [put C into the cell]
BUT
IF [data A] IS NOT EQUAL TO [data B], THEN [put D there]

You write the formula like this:

IF ($A=B,C,D$)

In essence, this says if *A* is equal to *B*, then put *C* into the cell you're working on. If *A* is not equal to *B*, then put *D* into it. The actual *argument* is the part with the equal sign (*A*=*B*), while the displayed results will be one of the two things after the first comma—either *C* or *D*. This argument can be phrased other ways, of course. If you want to check if *A* is less than *B*, you'd write the first part as IF ( *A* < *B*). "Greater than" is indicated by > and "not equal to" is < >.

In the world of mathematics and computers, these letters are known as variables, so once you have the basic logic down, you can substitute real numbers or formulas for the *A*, *B*, *C*, or *D* figures in the expression.

Our purpose here is to eliminate those #DIV/0! comments you'd get in column 4, when the program doesn't have any data in column 2 or 3 to work with. So essentially what you want to tell Multiplan is that if there's no figure in the cells in column 2, then print zeros in the calculated cells in column 4.

In our example, if there *is* data in cell R2C2, you can expect there'll be information in the labor cost column, too (cell R2C3), so you can go ahead with the formula you started with—divide the number in cell R2C3 by that in cell R2C2 (in this example, divide 18,000 by 30,000).

To start this process, position the cursor over cell R2C4 and select it by clicking on it; Multiplan will highlight this cell. Then go to the Edit selection from the menu and select Paste Function. . . . Using the scroll bar or arrow, search down through the selections (they're in alphabetical order) until you see the IF() function listed.

Figure 12-6 shows the Paste Function screen. If you move the cursor over the IF() function and click the button to select it, the function will be highlighted, as shown in Figure 12-6. Then, click the OK box and Multiplan's IF() function will be "pasted" into the active cell. Both the cell and the formula bar will reflect this when you do it—they both read =IF(), and

**FIGURE 12-6**

there's a flashing entry point shown between the two parentheses in the formula bar. Once you start to enter your formula, it will automatically go *inside* the IF () function's parentheses.

What we want to tell Multiplan now is that if there is something in cell R2C2, go ahead and do the division we want; if there is not, then display zero. However, we want to make sure that we're working with relative data, and not just to use cell R2C2. We need to refer to the cell "2 cells to the left" of the cell we're in. The first part of our expression should say, "if there's a figure in the cell two cells to our left, then proceed with the formula." So, move the cursor to cell R2C2 (it shows 30000) and select it by clicking on it; Multiplan (in its own strange way of cell reference) will refer to this cell as the current location *less* 2 cells to its left: RC [−2].

Just as Multiplan interprets = to mean *equal to*, it will understand that <> means *not equal to*. So now type <>0, which tells the program that if what it finds in cell R2C2 is not 0, then continue with the formula. The comma following the 0 (IF ( RC [−2] <> 0,) tells Multiplan that the first stage of this three-step process is complete.

The second stage is to enter the calculation, and the easiest way to do this is to simply point at the figures you want to work with and click the button to select them. In this case, move your cursor over the 18000 in cell R2C3 and click the mouse button. The formula bar will reflect your formula so far (so will your active cell, but it's not wide enough to see all the math). Now you need to let Multiplan know what you want to do with this number. Since you want to divide it by your sales total for the same month, enter a slash (/) to tell the program you want to divide. Finally, move the cursor over the 30000 sales figure in cell R2C2 and click the mouse button.

You now need to complete the expression. You've told Multiplan where to check if there's anything other than zero (IF (RC [−2] <>0,), and the formula to use if it does find a number there (RC [−1] / RC [−2] ). To tell the program that this calculation ends the second part of this process, enter a comma.

The last part of this procedure tells Multiplan what to enter into the active cell if it *doesn't* find anything in cell R2C2. Since we want it to display a zero, enter 0 and press the Enter key, to tell the program you're done.

The expression in the highlighted cell (R2C4) will immediately evaluate and show as 0.6, while the formula bar will express your complete formula. Figure 12-7 further details each part of the structure of Multiplan's IF () function.

In effect, Figure 12-7 says that if the first part of this formula is true, then *do* the calculation in the second part. If it's not true, then *do* what follows (in this case, we simply put a zero into the cell; you could have a formula here, too).

Let's now copy this entire formula into the cells for the rest of the year. To do this, select the active cell (R2C4, which now reads 0.6) and press and

```
                .................        ..................                  .......
                :              :        :               :        :      :
  =IF  (        :  RC[-2] <> 0 :  ,     :  RC[-1] / RC[-2] :  ,   :  O  :  )
                :..............:        :...............:                  :.....:
                      ^                        ^                     ^
                      ^                        ^                     ^
                      ^                        ^                     ^
  IF THIS IS TRUE--^                           ^                     ^
                                               ^                     ^
  THEN PUT THE RESULTS OF                      ^                     ^
  THIS FORMULA INTO THE CELL------------^                           ^
                                                                    ^
  IF IT ISN'T TRUE, THEN PUT THIS IN THE CELL-------------^
```

**FIGURE 12-7**

hold down the mouse button as you move down to cell R13C4, opposite December, the end of your yearly data space, and release the button.

Now move to the Edit menu and select Fill Down. The cells from R3C4 down to R13C4 will fill with numbers—calculated answers if there is data to evaluate, zeroes if there is not. Let's move the cursor to a blank cell (say, R5C1) and click, to remove the highlighting from our cells, and your picture should look like Figure 12-8.

As Figure 12-8 shows, where the worksheet did not have data to evaluate, it displays 0 in the cell—quite an improvement from #DIV/0!.

The next step is to transfer this computed data to our graphics program and see what it looks like as a column chart. Since all we really want to plot is

| | 1 | 2 | 3 | 4 | 5 | 6 |
|---|---|---|---|---|---|---|
| 1 | Months | Sales | Labor cost | Percent | | |
| 2 | Jan | 30000 | 18000 | 0.6 | | |
| 3 | Feb | 35000 | 21000 | 0.6 | | |
| 4 | Mar | 38000 | 23000 | 0.6052632 | | |
| 5 | Apr | 42000 | 25000 | 0.5952381 | | |
| 6 | May | 42000 | 27000 | 0.6428571 | | |
| 7 | Jun | 39000 | 21000 | 0.5384615 | | |
| 8 | Jul | 52000 | 29000 | 0.5576923 | | |
| 9 | Aug | | | 0 | | |
| 10 | Sep | | | 0 | | |
| 11 | Oct | | | 0 | | |
| 12 | Nov | | | 0 | | |
| 13 | Dec | | | 0 | | |
| 14 | | | | | | |
| 15 | | | | | | |

**FIGURE 12-8**

our labor cost as a percentage of sales, and we have seven calculated figures, it would seem that we'd just select that section of data—from cell R2C4 to R8C4.

However, when Multiplan transfers its information to Chart, it does it with full decimal precision—the numbers you see in Figure 12-8's worksheet will transfer just as they're shown. These figures are correct, of course, from a mathematical viewpoint, but they're not in the format people expect them to be. When we hear "60 percent" (the amount represented in cell R2C4), we expect to see 60%, not 0.6.

The obvious solution is to use Multiplan's Format menu to select the function that will convert these numbers into a percentage form. While that's easy to do, what's not so obvious is that when you make the transfer to Chart, the numbers will revert back to the form you see them in now—as decimals.

You're left with two ways to handle this. One is to simply transfer the data as is; Chart will properly scale the pictures you create from it. However, with data like these, the scale markings will look odd to people, because they're not in the percentage format they expect. A better solution is to ask Multiplan to create another column with the data in column 4 multiplied by 100, to change it into a form people are used to.

The procedure is simple: you click on cell R2C5 to select it, and press the = key to tell Multiplan that you want to enter a formula. Then, you select cell R2C4 (that shows 0.6) by clicking on it. Finally, type * 100 and press the Enter key to complete the formula. The highlighted cell (cell R2C5) will display 60 (0.60 times 100). Then, to copy this formula into the cells immediately below, use the same method you did before: select the entire range by positioning the cursor on cell R2C5 and pressing the mouse button. Hold the button down as you move down to the last cell for data, R13C5. When you release the mouse button, all these cells will be highlighted. You then go to the Edit menu and select Fill Down to put the new, adjusted numbers into the cells. Click on cell R14C5 to remove the highlighting.

Figure 12-9 reflects all this, and now you have a column—column 5—that you can transfer to Chart with its numbers in a form that people expect to see.

To make the data transfer, select the cells with the information you want to plot—in this case, just the (adjusted) percentage amounts in cells R2C5 through R8C5. Once you select these cells (by positioning the cursor over the first one, pressing the mouse button and holding it while you move to the last cell), they will be highlighted. Now Copy them to the clipboard (by selecting Copy from the Edit menu) and quit Multiplan by going to the File menu and selecting Quit. A dialogue box will ask if you want to save your worksheet before you exit the program, which you can do if you wish. Eject the Multiplan disk and start the Chart program.

You can, if you wish, create a permanent link between your Multiplan worksheets and the Chart program, so that whenever you update the data,

| | 1 | 2 | 3 | 4 | 5 | 6 |
|---|---|---|---|---|---|---|
| 1 | Months | Sales | Advertising | Percent | | |
| 2 | Jan | 30000 | 18000 | 0.6 | 60 | |
| 3 | Feb | 35000 | 21000 | 0.6 | 60 | |
| 4 | Mar | 38000 | 23000 | 0.6052632 | 60.526316 | |
| 5 | Apr | 42000 | 25000 | 0.5952381 | 59.52381 | |
| 6 | May | 42000 | 27000 | 0.6428571 | 64.285714 | |
| 7 | Jun | 39000 | 21000 | 0.5384615 | 53.846154 | |
| 8 | Jul | 52000 | 29000 | 0.5576923 | 55.769231 | |
| 9 | Aug | | | 0 | 0 | |
| 10 | Sep | | | 0 | 0 | |
| 11 | Oct | | | 0 | 0 | |
| 12 | Nov | | | 0 | 0 | |
| 13 | Dec | | | 0 | 0 | |
| 14 | | | | | | |
| 15 | | | | | | |

(Window title: Untitled)

**FIGURE 12-9**

the charts you create from it will automatically be based on the new information.

When you first boot Chart, it creates a new series box, as shown in Figure 12-10. Before you can transfer your information from the clipboard, you need to name this data series, so move the cursor to the Data selection and press the mouse button. You'll see a choice of types of data you can work with; since ours is a simple series of numbers, select Sequence. A box will appear asking for the series name and other information. Let's call our series DIRECT LABOR AS A PERCENTAGE OF SALES. For our category name, which represents, in this case, the monthly periods, let's enter ← MONTHS →. To do this, click in the Category box to the *right* of the X and then use the delete key to eliminate the X. Then you can enter ← MONTHS →. Use the same procedure for the Value name (click to the right of the Y and delete it) and enter %, since we're working with percentage data. Once you've done this, click the OK box to tell Chart you're done entering information here.

It's almost always a good idea to enter descriptive data here, as Chart takes the Series Name from the first series it plots and makes it the graph title; the identification for the X and Y axes are also plotted, then, automatically.

Now, select Edit from the menu and Paste the data from the clipboard into your data series.

Figure 12-11 is what your Data Series box will look like now, with all of

**FIGURE 12-10**

your calculated data filled in. You'll note that all of the numbers are repro-
duced as they were after we adjusted them by multiplying the original data
by 100. Since Chart's default image is a column chart, select the Plot Series
box and click the mouse button. The graph will automatically be created and
when you click on the chart window, you'll see your graph.

**FIGURE 12-11**

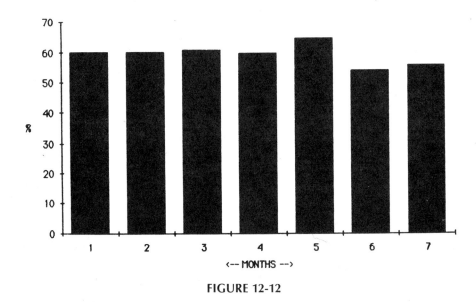

FIGURE 12-12

Figure 12-12 is the first graph that Chart creates for you, based on the data you calculated within Multiplan and sent to the graphics program in a column chart format.

Congratulations! You've used a complex and powerful spreadsheet (Multiplan) to store and manipulate your business figures and transferred that data to a graphics program (Chart) and used it to create a picture of your information.

You could stop here, but this chart could use a bit of improvement. Let's add a border around the plotted area by pressing on the Chart menu selection, and picking Select Plot Area from it. You'll see a series of black dots around the plotted part of your picture. Then, press on Format, and select Patterns. . . .

Figure 12-13 is Graph's pattern area, where you can add a background pattern or put a border around whatever part of your picture you marked a moment ago. Just to keep things simple, let's click on the leftmost border pattern (plain black); the dot in the circle next to Invisible will disappear as Chart accepts your command. You could change the line weight for the border from its default size, but let's leave that the same and click on the OK box.

We also should add horizontal grid lines to our picture, to make it easier to read. If you press on the Chart selection, one of its selections is Axes. . . .

**Patterns**

**Background Pattern**      ⊙ Invisible

■ ■ ■ ▦ □ ☰ Ⅲ ▨ ▨ ⊞ ⊠ ▨ ▨ ◩ ◪

**Border Pattern**      ⊙ Invisible

■ ■ ■ ▦ □ ☰ Ⅲ ▨ ▨ ⊞ ⊠ ▨ ▨ ◩ ◪

**Border Weight**      [⬭]   [▭]   [▬]

[  OK  ]   [ Cancel ]

**FIGURE 12-13**

Select it. In this case, since we want horizontal lines (that will mark the values we've plotted), click on the box marked Major Grid Lines under the For Values Show heading, as we've done in Figure 12-14.

Figure 12-14 shows Chart's Axes. . . . selection area, with the proper boxes checked to produce the lines you want. Once you click on the OK box, you'll be back at the chart area, this time with the grid lines shown as you requested. Figure 12-15 is your final result.

There are any number of other things you could do to the picture you see in Figure 12-15 to make it say what you want it to. You might want to widen the scale, from 0 to 100. Perhaps a lighter shade of bar would be more

**Axes**

**For Categories Show**      **For Values Show**

☒ Axis                ☒ Axis

☒ Tick Mark Labels    ☒ Tick Mark Labels

☐ Major Grid Lines    ☒ Major Grid Lines

☐ Minor Grid Lines    ☐ Minor Grid Lines

[  OK  ]   [ Cancel ]

**FIGURE 12-14**

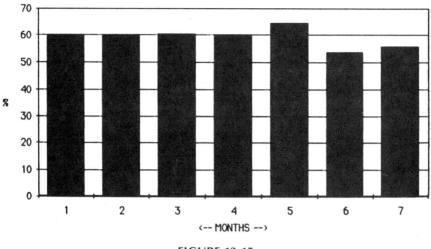

DIRECT LABOR AS A PERCENTAGE OF SALES

**FIGURE 12-15**

effective, or grid lines that only appear every 20 data points. Once you have your information in the system, spend a bit of time to explore all the things Chart can do for you. You'll be amazed at the results you get, and what you'll learn about your business!

# Magazine Bibliography

A

The articles listed below focus on the current literature on *Macintosh,* general business where it concerns itself with graphic images, and business graphics in particular. While some magazines, like *Desktop Computing,* are no longer published, their information is still listed for reference purposes.

Following the article citations are the names and addresses of the most popular computer-oriented magazines, where you can order back issues.

Alker, Pauline Lo. "Accent on the Visual: Business Computer Graphics," *Desktop Computing,* 8/83, pp. 32–37.

"Apple Unveils Macintosh," *Micro-Times,* 2/84, pp. 1–2.

Barney, Clifford. "Not a toy, but the real thing," *Whole Earth Software Review,* Spring 1984, pp. 33–37.

Bartimo, Jim. "Mac / PCjr Face-off Unlikely," *InfoWorld,* 2/27/84, pp. 71–73.

Bartimo, Jim. " 'Smalltalk' with Alan Kay," *InfoWorld,* 6/11/84, pp. 58–62.

Bayle, Elisabeth. "Picture This—and do it yourself," *Personal Computing,* 8/82, pp. 50–54, 58–64, 150.

Benson, Terry. "Graphics Capabilities for the Small Business," *Interface Age,* 2/83, pp. 66–69, 138–141.

Bonner, Paul. "Communicating with Presentation Graphics," *Personal Computing,* 7/83, pp. 110–119, 174.

Bonner, Paul. "Punching up your Presentation with Powerful Pictures," *Personal Computing*, 9/83, pp. 86–92, 209.

Bonoma, Thomas. "Thumbing Through Disk Magazines," *Microcomputing*, 1/84, pp. 28–36.

Bryan, Shawn. "Straight Talk on the Mac," *Microcomputing*, 9/84, pp. 100–105.

Bunnell, David (an interview with Bill Gates of Microsoft). "Polishing the Mac," *Macworld*, Volume 1, Number 1 (4/15/84), pp. 43–45.

Bunnell, David. "The Next Wave," *Macworld*, May/June 1984, p. 11.

Busch, David D. "A Decision for Business Graphics," *Microcomputing*, 1/84, pp. 58–60.

Caffrey, Morgan P. "Macintosh and the Apple 32-bit family," *Apple Orchard*, 2/84, pp. 42–54.

Caffrey, Morgan P. "MacTerminal," *Apple Orchard*, 2/84, p. 50.

Canon, Maggie and Steve Rosenthal. "Mighty Mac," *A+ Magazine*, 3/84, p. 26.

Cates, Annie. "MacPaint (review)," *InfoWorld*, 7/9/84, pp. 67–71.

Cates, Annie. "MacWrite (review)," *InfoWorld*, 7/9/84, pp. 71–74.

Chin, Kathy. "Apple to release Fat Mac," *InfoWorld*, 10/1/84, p. 11.

Chin, Kathy. "Business Graphics: Integrated vs. Stand-Alone," *InfoWorld*, Volume 5, # 45 (10/83), pp. 52–54.

Chin, Kathy. "The Macintosh Factory," *InfoWorld*, 3/19/84, pp. 82–84.

Clapp, Doug. "The History Begins," *ST.MAC*, 2/84, pp. 18–19, 21.

Clapp, Doug. "Graphics Wizardry: The Art of Bill Atkinson," *ST.MAC*, 2/84, pp. 38–43.

Clapp, Doug. "Make Mine Macintosh," *InfoWorld*, 2/13/84, pp. 26–34.

"Creating a 'Macgritte' Masterpiece," *Popular Computing*, 3/84, pp. 92–94.

Derfler, Frank. "Graphics Software Comes of Age," *Microcomputing*, 4/84, pp. 32–34.

Diocco, John. "In the Third Dimension," *Business Computing*, 12/83, pp. 54–57.

Douglas, Matthew. "Inside the Mac," *Macworld*, Volume 1, Number 1 (4/15/84), pp. 34–41.

Farber, Daniel. "Desktop Accessories," *Macworld*, Volume 1, Number 1 (4/15/84), pp. 20–21.

Farber, Daniel. "A Mouse in the Hand," *Macworld*, Volume 1, Number 1 (4/15/84), pp. 28–30.

Farber, Daniel. "Clean Up Your Electronic Desktop," *Macworld*, May/June, 1984, pp. 38–44.

Farber, Daniel. "Redefining User-Friendly," *Macworld*, May/June, 1984, pp. 66–71.

Farber, Daniel and Adrian Mello. "The Imagewriter and beyond," *Macworld*, September/October 1984, pp. 76–83.

Fluegelman, Andrew. "A New World," *Macworld*, Volume I, Number 1 (4/15/84), pp. 10–11.

Fluegelman, Andrew. "Word Processing's New Look," *Macworld*, Volume 1, Number 1 (4/15/84), pp. 62–71.

Fluegelman, Andrew. "Tips for MacWriters," *Macworld*, Volume 1, Number 1 (4/15/84), pp. 104–109.

Fluegelman, Andrew. "The Making of the MacIntosh," *Macworld*, Volume 1, Number 1 (4/15/84), pp. 126–135.

Fluegelman, Andrew. "The Macintosh Magazine," *Macworld*, May/June 1984, pp. 8–9.

Fluegelman, Andrew. "Exploring Microsoft Chart," *Macworld*, May/June, 1984, pp. 72–84.

Fluegelman, Andrew. "Creating a Custom Chart Format," *Macworld*, May/June, 1984, pp. 104–108.

Free, John. "The Creativity Explosion in Computer Graphics," *Popular Science*, 6/82, pp. 80–83.

Fritson, Richard. "The Good, the CAD and the Apple," *Microcomputing*, 1/84, pp. 88–98, and 2/84, pp. 88–96.

Glau, Gregory R. "Graphs Make the Point," *inCider*, 2/83, pp. 136–141.

Glau, Gregory R. "Pick the Perfect Picture," *Desktop Computing*, 8/83, pp. 20–22.

Glau, Gregory R. "A Slice of Time," *inCider*, 8/83, pp. 40–45.

Glau, Gregory R. "Cash Flow Woes," *inCider*, 1/84, pp. 152–154.

Glau, Gregory R. "Selling Savings," *inCider*, 3/84, pp. 126–128.

Glau, Gregory R. "Taxing Times," *inCider*, 4/84, pp. 116–117.

Goodman, Danny. "The Electronic Drafting Set," *Macworld*, September/October 1984, pp. 76–83.

Heid, Jim. "Mac, Meet Macintosh," *Microcomputing*, 4/84, pp. 38–42.

Heid, Jim. "Magabytes for Macintosh," *Microcomputing*, 10/84, pp. 74–78.

Hogan, Thom. "Using MacPaint on the Macintosh," *A+ Magazine*, 4/84, pp. 101–108.

Keogh, Jim. "Power Presentations," *Personal Computing*, 10/83, pp. 56–68.

Kleiner, Art et al. "First look at Macintosh software (brief reviews including Multiplan)," *The Whole Earth Software Review*, Fall, 1984, pp. 106–110.

Kolata, Gina. "Computer Graphics comes to Statistics," *Science*, 9/82, pp. 919–20.

Lambert, Steve. "Making a case with Multiplan and Chart," *Macworld*, September/October 1984, pp. 89–96.

Lambert, Steve. "Presentation Graphics Primer," *Macworld*, May/June, 1984, pp. 96–102.

Latamore, Bert. "A Graphic Display," *Desktop Computing*, 12/82, pp. 8–15.

Lincoln, John. "Make Mine Mac," *Micro-Times*, 3/84, pp. 1–3.

Mace, Scott. "Apple Bets on the Macintosh," *InfoWorld*, 2/13/84, pp. 16–20.

Mace, Scott. "Taking Measure of the Mac," *InfoWorld*, 2/13/84, pp. 20–22.

Mace, Scott. "Drexel U. meets the Macintosh," *InfoWorld*, 6/4/84, pp. 24–28.

Machrone, Bill. "Synthesis, Anyone?," *PC Magazine*, 4/17/84, pp. 69–71.

McCandless, Janet. "Macintosh," *ST.MAC*, 2/84, pp. 4–15.

"Macware News," *Macworld*, Volume 1, Number 1 (4/15/84), pp. 86–92.

Martellaro, John. "Finger in the Socket: Macintosh," *Peelings II*, Volume 5, #2, p. 10.

McClain, Larry. "A Guided Tour of Business Graphics," *Popular Computing*, 11/83, pp. 86–96, 156–157.

McLamb, Ken. "Persuasion made easy with Powerful Presentations," *Personal Computing*, 2/82, pp. 34–39.

McMillan, Tom. "The mind behind MacPaint," *Popular Computing*, 3/84, p. 95.

Meinel, C. "Computer graphics on every desk," *Technology Review*, 10/82, pp. 74–75.

Miller, Michael J. "Introducing Lisa-like technology in a personal package," *Popular Computing*, 3/84, pp. 82–91, 98–100.

Mimms, Forrest M. "Quick on the draw: inexpensive plotters," *Computers & Electronics*, 3/84, pp. 50–53, 104–105.

Myers, E. "Computer Graphics: Boom in Business Graphics," *Datamation*, 4/81, pp. 92–99.

Neudecker, Thomas. "Review: Multiplan for the Macintosh," *InfoWorld*, 4/9/84, pp. 41–42.

Neudecker, Thomas. "Macintosh (review)," *InfoWorld*, 3/26/84, pp. 82–90.

"New Apple Factory Produces Macintosh," *Micro-Times*, 4/84, pp. 1, 23.

Nichols, John R. "In Praise of the Mac," *InfoWorld*, 4/16/84, pp. 7.

"No MS-DOS Tartan for Macintosh," *PC Magazine*, 3/6/84, p. 57.

"Peeking Under Mac's Skin," *ST.MAC*, 2/84, pp. 12–13.

"Peripherally Speaking," *ST.MAC*, 2/84, p. 14.

Poole, Lon. "A Tour of the Mac Desktop," *Macworld*, Volume 1, Number 1 (4/15/84), pp. 6–19, 22–26.

Poole, Lon. "Apple's Imagewriter Printer," *Macworld*, Volume 1, Number 1 (4/15/84), pp. 81–85.

Poole, Lon. "Get Info," *Macworld*, May/June, 1984, pp. 48–51.

Poole, Lon. "The Lisa Connection," *Macworld*, May/June, 1984, pp. 52–63.

Powell, David. "Buyer's Guide to Low-Cost Plotters," *Popular Computing*, 11/83, pp. 120–122.

Reitmann, Kearny. "Smoothing the Critical Path," *Macworld*, July/August 1984, pp. 52–63.

Richards, Evelyn. " 'Brave Pirates' Build Macintosh," *Micro-Times*, 2/84, p. 3.

Rubin, Charles. "Macintosh: Apple's powerful new computer," *Personal Computing*, 2/84, pp. 56–61, 65–69, 72–75, 79–81, 85, 199.

Ryan, Bob. "Macintosh: The Gloves come off at Apple," *inCider*, 3/84, pp. 42–50.

Ryan, Bob. "In the Wake of Macintosh," *inCider*, 4/84, p. 8.

Schmidt, Allan H. "What a CAD," *Microcomputing*, 1/84, pp. 65–69.

Schnatmeir, Vanessa. "Macintosh: Big step, small footprint," *Computers & Electronics*, 3/84, pp. 43–48.

Schnatmeir, Vanessa. "Breeding a new variety of Apples," *Computers & Electronics*, 3/84, pp. 48–49.

Shea, Tom. "Personal Computer Graphics: Pushing Technology to the Limit," *InfoWorld*, Volume 5, #51, 1983, pp. 34–36.

Shotwell, R. "Computer Graphics: new picture possibilities for publishers," *Publisher's Weekly*, 6/4/82, p. 32.

Solomont, David and Donna Stein. "Computer Graphics: Productivity Picture," *Business Computer Systems*, 12/82, pp. 41–44.

Spezzano, Charles. "An IBM PC Lover Meets the Mac," *Macworld*, May/June 1984, pp. 12–14.

Spezzano, Charles. "Breaking the chains that bind," *Whole Earth Software Review*, Spring 1984, pp. 31–32.

Stahr, Lisa B. "Presentation Graphics," *Personal Computing*, 9/84, pp. 117–124.

Stryker, Timothy. "What you didn't know about NEC Spinwriter," *Microcomputing*, 10/82, pp. 32–37.

Thompson, Keith. "A Mac Duet: Chart and Plan by Microsoft," *Microcomputing*, 9/84, pp. 92–97.

Thompson, Keith. "Macintosh: Apple's Saucy New Micro," *Microcomputing*, 3/84, pp. 66–73.

Tommervik, Al. "Will Apple Torpedo the Macintosh?," *ST.MAC*, 2/84, p. 16.

Waese, Jerry R. and Jim Heid. "Teledin," *Microcomputing*, 1/84, pp. 62–64.

Weiglin, Peter C. "Marketing Mac and Relatives," *Apple Orchard*, 2/84, p. 45.

Whitmore, Sam. "Should Mac snub MS-DOS?," *inCider*, 3/84, p. 8.

Williams, Andrew T. "Multiplan meets the Mac," *Macworld*, Volume 1, Number 1 (4/15/84), pp. 72–79.

Williams, Andrew T. "Investing with Multiplan," *Macworld*, Volume 1, Number 1 (4/15/84), pp. 95–102.

Williams, Gregg. "A Graphics Primer," *Byte*, 11/82, pp. 448–470.

Wilson, Gene. "Macintosh Goals," *Apple Orchard*, 2/84, p. 44.

Wilson, Gene. "Mac's Organizer," *Apple Orchard*, 2/84, pp. 51–52.

Woodard, Alden. "Using MAC," *ST.MAC*, 2/84, pp. 23–34.

Young, Jeffrey S. "Zooming through the Macintosh Window," *Macworld*, Volume 1, Number 1 (4/15/84), p. 14–15.

Young, Jeffrey S. "MacPaint: the Electronic Easel," *Macworld*, Volume 1, Number 1 (4/15/84): pp. 50–61.

Young, Jeffrey S. "Macworld Gallery," *Macworld*, Volume 1, Number 1 (4/15/84), pp. 136–140.

# Magazine Addresses

*A+ Magazine*
Ziff-Davis Publishing
11 Davis Drive
Belmont, CA 94002
(415) 594-2290

*Apple Orchard*
910 A George Street
Santa Clara, CA 95050
(408) 727-7652

*Business Computer Systems*
Cahners Publishing
221 Columbus Avenue
Boston, MA 02116
(617) 536-7780

*Business Computing*
119 Russell Street
Littleton, MA 01460
(617) 486-9501

*Byte*
P.O. Box 372
Hancock, NH 03449
(603) 924-9281

*CAP*
Computers and Peripherals
2900 Bristol Street, #A107
Costa Mesa, CA 92626
(714) 751-2533

*Compute!*
Small Systems Services, Inc.
625 Fulton Street
P.O. Box 5406
Greensboro, NC 27403
(919) 275-9809

*Computer Buyer's Guide and Hand-
book*
Computer Information and Publishing,
    Inc.
Box 1563
FDR Station
New York, NY 10020

*Computers and Electronics*
Ziff-Davis Publishing Company
One Park Avenue
New York, NY 10016
(212) 725-3500

*Computer Shopper*
P.O. Box F
Titusville, FL 32780
(305) 269-3211

*Creative Computing*
Ziff-Davis Publishing
One Park Avenue
New York, NY 10016
(212) 725-3500

*Desktop Computing*
CW Communications/Peterborough
Peterborough, NH 03458
(603) 924-9471

*inCider*
CW Communications/Peterborough
Peterborough, NH 03458
(603) 924-9471

*InfoWorld*
530 Lytton Avenue
Palo Alto, CA 94301
(415) 328-4602

*Interface Age*
16704 Marquardt Avenue
P.O. Box 1234
Cerritos, CA 90701
(213) 926-9544

*Macworld*
555 DeHaro Street
San Francisco, CA 94107
(415) 861-3861

*Microcomputing*
CW Communications/Peterborough
Peterborough, NH 03458
(603) 924-9471

*Micro Co-op Newsletter*
610 East Brook Drive
Arlington Heights, IL 60005
(312) 228-5115

*Micro Discovery*
5152 Katella, # 102
Los Alamitos, CA 90720
(213) 493-4441

*Micro Times*
P.O. Box 87
Moline, IL 61265
(309) 762-0194

*PC Magazine*
Ziff-Davis Publishing
One Park Avenue
New York, NY 10016
(212) 725-4694

*PC World*
555 DeHaro Street
San Francisco, CA 94107
(415) 861-3861

*Peelings II*
P.O. Box 699
Las Cruces, NM 88004
(505) 526-8364

*Personal Computing*
Hayden Publishing Company
50 Essex Street
Rochelle Park, NJ 07662
(201) 843-0550

*Popular Computing*
P.O. Box 372
Hancock, NH 03449
(603) 924-9281

*ST.MAC*
Softalk Publishing
7250 Laurel Canyon Blvd.
North Hollywood, CA 91605
(818) 980-5074

*Small Business Computers Magazine*
Ziff-Davis Publishing
One Park Avenue
New York, NY 10016
(212) 725-3500

*Softside*
Softside Publications
6 South Street
Milford, NH 03055
(603) 673-0585

*Softalk*
Softalk Publishing Company
11160 McCormick Street
Box 60
North Hollywood, CA 91603
(213) 980-5074

*Software*
Fast Access
2803 Ocean Park Blvd., Suite K
Santa Monica, CA 90405

*Whole Earth Software Review*
POINT Inc.
150 Gate Five Road
Sausalito, CA 94965
(415) 332-4335

# Book Bibliography

**B**

Alves, Jeffrey R., Dennis P. Curtin, and Anne K. Briggs. "Planning and Budgeting for Higher Profits." New York: Van Nostrand Reinhold, 1983, 170 pp, $15.50. This good-sized book focuses on the use of VisiCalc (Apple edition, although other computers can use the information) to create templates designed to help with what the title says.

Anderson, Anker V. "Graphing Financial Information: How Accountants Can Use Graphs to Communicate." The National Association of Accountants, 919 Third Avenue, New York, NY 10022, 1983, 51 pp. A helpful guide to the benefits and pitfalls of business graphics, from an accounting viewpoint. This booklet is well written, with good illustrations.

Bernstein, Leopold. "The Analysis of Financial Statements." Homewood, IL: Dow Jones-Irwin, 1978, 311 pp. An excellent accounting book with the focus on what its title says.

Caggiano, Joseph. "The Easy Guide to your Macintosh." Berkeley: Sybex Computer Books, 1984, 280 pp., $12.95.

Carey, Omer, and Dean Olson. "Financial Tools for Small Business." Reston, VA: Reston Publishing, 1983, 269 pp., $12.95. A useful book filled with case examples focused on financial statement data.

Clapp, Doug. "Macintosh! Complete," Hollywood, CA: Softalk Books, 1984, 329 pp., $19.95. Doug's an intelligent and interesting writer and has produced an excellent book on the Macintosh.

Connoly, Edward S. and Phillip Lieberman. "Introducing the Apple Macintosh." Indianapolis: Howard W. Sams & Co., 1984, 188 pp., $12.95. Seemingly rushed into print, you don't get much information here.

Curtin, Dennis P., Jeffrey R. Alves, and Anne K. Briggs. "Controlling Financial Performance for Higher Profits." New York: Van Nostrand Reinhold, 1983, 170 pp., $15.50. This excellent book uses VisiCalc templates to help with what the title says. Even though it's focused on the Apple (and there's an IBM PC version), anyone who works with a spreadsheet can easily adapt the techniques here to other computers, like the Macintosh.

Dayton, Rick. "Understanding the Macintosh." Reston, VA: Reston Pubishing, 1984, 204 pp., $18.95. This book is too brief to justify its price, but does an effective introductory job.

Dixon, Robert L. "The Executive's Accounting Primer." New York: McGraw-Hill, 1971, 328 pp. This volume is a nuts-and-bolts look at accounting, with helpful real-world examples.

Edwards, James Don, et al. "How Accounting Works—A Guide for the Perplexed." Homewood, Illinois: Dow Jones-Irwin, 1983, 374 pp., $19.95. An excellent book that not only explains the ins and outs of accounting, but often why things need to be done a certain way. There's also good information on the analysis of financial data.

Green, Kenneth C. and Rica van Dam. "The Macintosh Apple: A Comprehensive Reference Guide." Beaverton, OR: dilithium Press, 256 pp., $14.95.

Greenburg, Donald, Aaron Marcus, Allan H. Schmidt, and Vernon Gortner. "The Computer Image: Applications of Computer Graphics." Reading, MA: Addison-Wesley, 1982, 128 pp., $27.95. A general discussion of the hardware end of computer images, with the central focus on scientific uses, with the emphasis on minicomputer applications. There's an excellent chapter on business graphics.

"Harvard Business Review on Management." New York: Harper & Row, 1975, 751 pp. A collection of the best reviews over the preceding 25 years that appeared in the *Harvard Business Review.*

Jarrett, Irwin M. "Computer Graphics & Reporting Financial Data." New York: Ronald Press (distributed by John Wiley & Sons), 1983, 250 pp., $49.95.

Lambert, Steve. "Presentation Graphics on the Apple Macintosh." Bellevue, WA: Microsoft Press, 1984, $18.95. A guide to Microsoft's program *Chart* and a good introduction to the use of effective graphics.

Lefferts, Robert. "How to Prepare Charts and Graphs for Effective Reports." New York: Harper & Row, 1981. ("Elements of Graphics" was its hardcover title.) This book is focused on the design of charts, starting with grid paper to the size ratio between the height and width of your images.

Lowry, Albert. "How to Become Financially Successful by Owning Your Own Business." New York: Simon and Schuster, 1981, 407 pp., $14.95. This book (constantly updated) contains a great deal of useful information on the examination of financial data.

Lu, Cary. "*Mac:* The Apple Macintosh Book," Bellevue, WA: Microsoft Press, 1984, 383 pp., $19.95. A most useful book about Macintosh, including a lot that you probably don't need (but you can skip the technical parts).

MacGregor, A. J. "Graphics Simplified: How to plan and prepare effective charts, graphs, illustrations and other visual aids." Toronto: University of Toronto Press, 1979, 282 pp., paperback. This book helps with what its title implies—how to hand-create graphs.

Miller, Merl K. and Mary A. Myers. "Presenting the Macintosh." Beaverton, OR: dilithium Press, 1984, 119 pp., $5.95. Rushed into print to ride the Macintosh wave, there's little useful advice here.

Oystein, Ore. "Graphs & Their Use." New Math Library, 1975, $7.50. This book is filled with algorithms and mathematical formulas.

Peters, Thomas J. and Robert H. Waterman, Jr. "In Search of Excellence." New York: Harper & Row, 1982. An outstanding collection of thoughts on why "excellent" companies are just that.

Poole, Lon. "MacWork/MacPlay." Bellevue, WA: Microsoft Press, 1984, 352 pp., $18.95.

Ramsay, Carol and Laselle, Joan. "Mac Multiplan." Hasbrouck Heights, NJ: Hayden Book Company, 1984, 224 pp., $19.95.

Runyon, Richard P. "How Numbers Lie." The Lewis Publishing Company, 1981, 182 pp., $7.95. The use and mis-use of statistics.

Sanders, William B. "The Apple Macintosh Primer." Chatsworth, CA: Datamost, 1984, 117 pp., $9.95. Not available when our manuscript was completed, but everything we've read by Bill Sanders has been excellent; we suspect this book will be, too.

Schmid, Calvin F. "Statistical Graphics: Design Principles and Practices." New York: Wiley Interscience, 1983, 224 pp., $24.95. This wide-ranging and excellent book has a lot of good examples of poor charts.

Tracy, John. "How to Read a Financial Report." New York: John Wiley & Sons, 1980, 156 pp. This book has more information in it than its short length would seem to allow. A good book for basic accounting concepts.

Uris, Auren. "The Executive Deskbook (second edition)." New York: Van Nostrand Reinhold, 1976, 330 pp., $10.25. Good advice on a wide range of ideas, from people-problems to how to delegate authority and effective communication.

Winston, Stephanie. "The Organized Executive." New York: W. W. Norton & Co., 1983. Good information on management, particularly on organization and time control.

# Index